HOUSTON, YOU HAVE A PROBLEM

A FoxTrot Collection by Bill Amend

**Andrews McMeel
Publishing, LLC**

Kansas City

FoxTrot is distributed internationally by Universal Press Syndicate.

Houston, You Have a Problem copyright © 2007 by Bill Amend. All rights reserved. Printed in the United States of America. No part of this book may be used or reproduced in any manner whatsoever without written permission except in the case of reprints in the context of reviews. For information, write Andrews McMeel Publishing, LLC, an Andrews McMeel Universal company, 4520 Main Street, Kansas City, Missouri 64111.

07 08 09 10 11 BBG 10 9 8 7 6 5 4 3 2 1

ISBN-13: 978-0-7407-6352-6
ISBN-10: 0-7407-6352-0

Library of Congress Control Number: 2006936981

www.andrewsmcmeel.com

———— **ATTENTION: SCHOOLS AND BUSINESSES** ————

Andrews McMeel books are available at quantity discounts with bulk purchase for educational, business, or sales promotional use. For information, please write to: Special Sales Department, Andrews McMeel Publishing, LLC, 4520 Main Street, Kansas City, Missouri 64111.

HOUSTON, YOU HAVE A PROBLEM

Other FoxTrot Books by Bill Amend

FoxTrot • Pass the Loot • Black Bart Says Draw • Eight Yards, Down and Out
Bury My Heart at Fun-Fun Mountain • Say Hello to Cactus Flats • May the Force Be with Us, Please
Take Us to Your Mall • The Return of the Lone Iguana • At Least This Place Sells T-Shirts
Come Closer, Roger, There's a Mosquito on Your Nose • Welcome to Jasorassic Park
I'm Flying, Jack . . . I Mean, Roger • Think iFruity • Death by Field Trip
Encyclopedias Brown and White • His Code Name Was The Fox
Your Momma Thinks Square Roots Are Vegetables • Who's Up for Some Bonding?
Am I a Mutant or What! • Orlando Bloom Has Ruined Everything
My Hot Dog Went Out, Can I Have Another? • How Come I'm Always Luigi?

Anthologies

FoxTrot: The Works • FoxTrot *en masse* • Enormously FoxTrot • Wildly FoxTrot
FoxTrot Beyond a Doubt • Camp FoxTrot • Assorted FoxTrot • FoxTrot: Assembled with Care
FoxTrotius Maximus • Jam-Packed FoxTrot

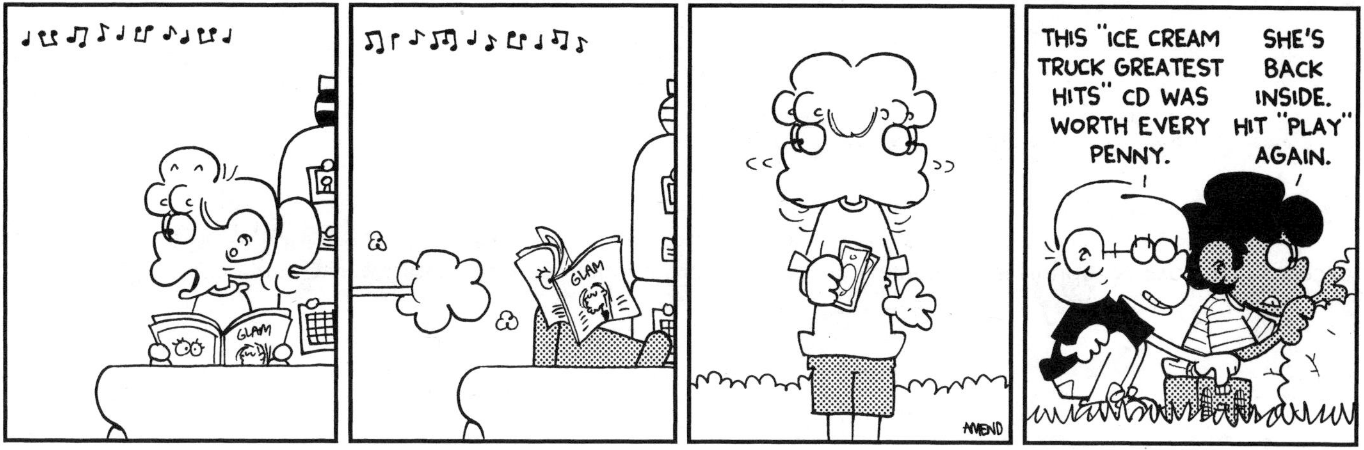
GLAM
GLAM
THIS "ICE CREAM TRUCK GREATEST HITS" CD WAS WORTH EVERY PENNY.
SHE'S BACK INSIDE. HIT "PLAY" AGAIN.
AMEND

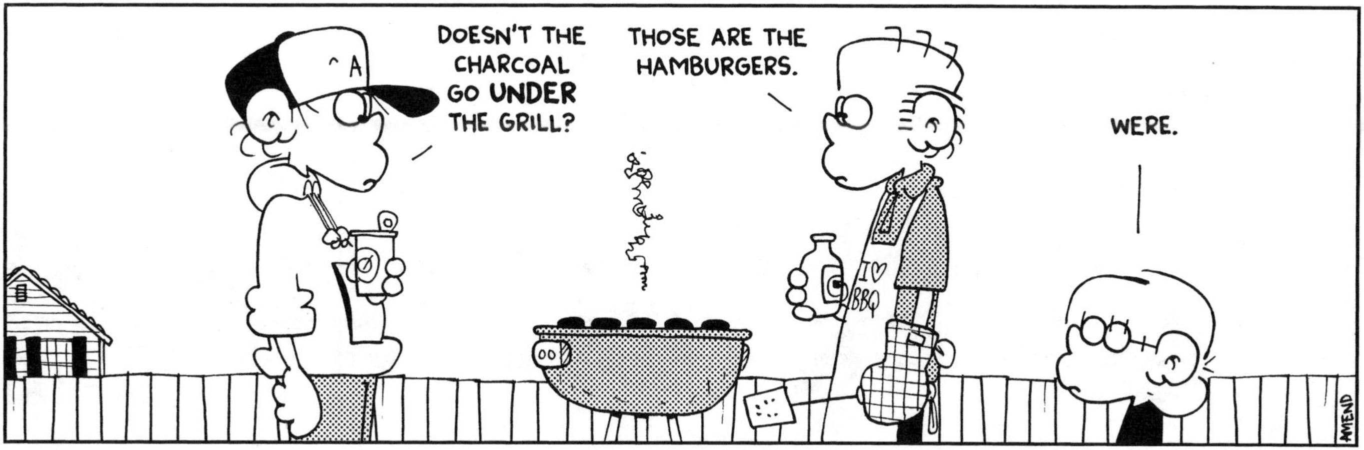
DOESN'T THE CHARCOAL GO **UNDER** THE GRILL?
THOSE ARE THE HAMBURGERS.
WERE.
I ♡ BBQ
AMEND

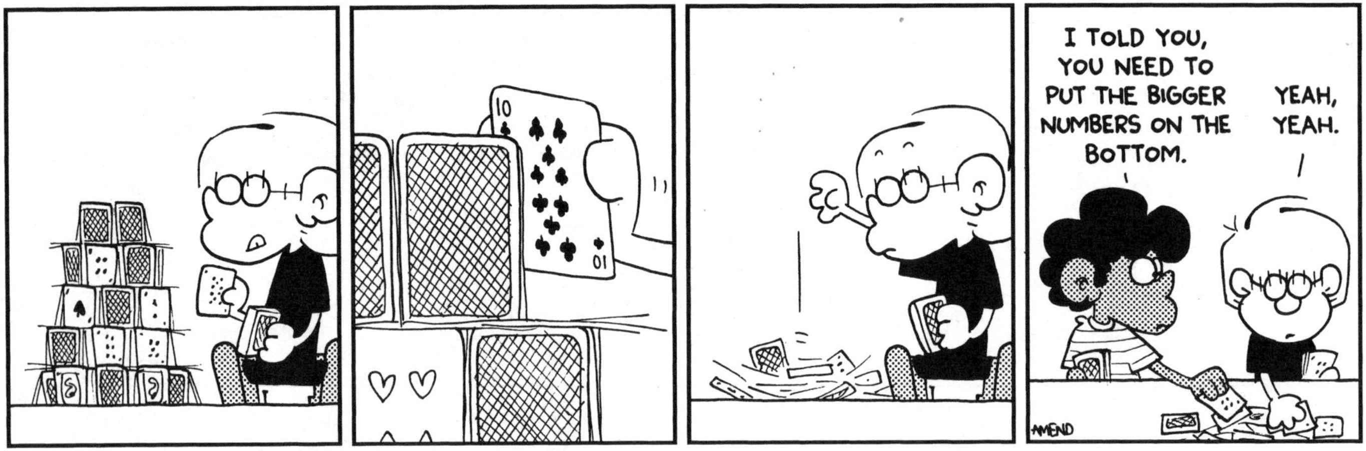
I TOLD YOU, YOU NEED TO PUT THE BIGGER NUMBERS ON THE BOTTOM.
YEAH, YEAH.
AMEND

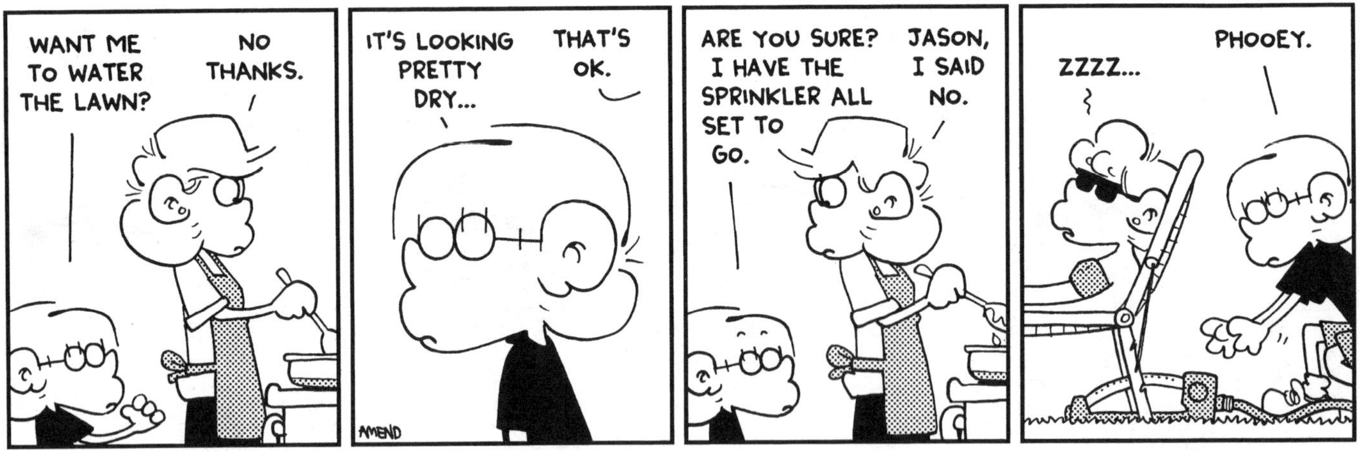
WANT ME TO WATER THE LAWN?
NO THANKS.
IT'S LOOKING PRETTY DRY...
THAT'S OK.
AMEND
ARE YOU SURE? I HAVE THE SPRINKLER ALL SET TO GO.
JASON, I SAID NO.
ZZZZ...
PHOOEY.

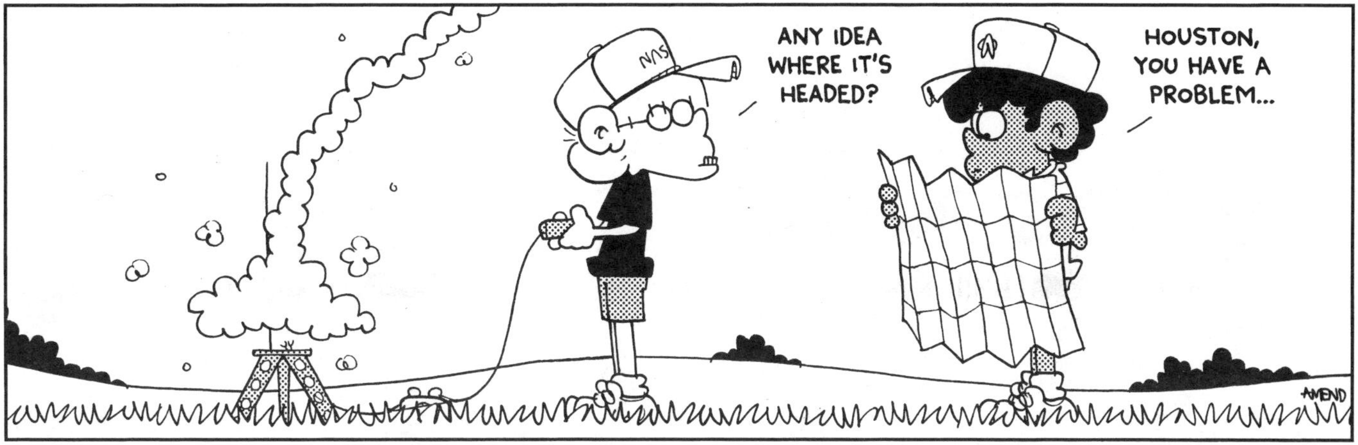
ANY IDEA WHERE IT'S HEADED?
HOUSTON, YOU HAVE A PROBLEM...
AMEND

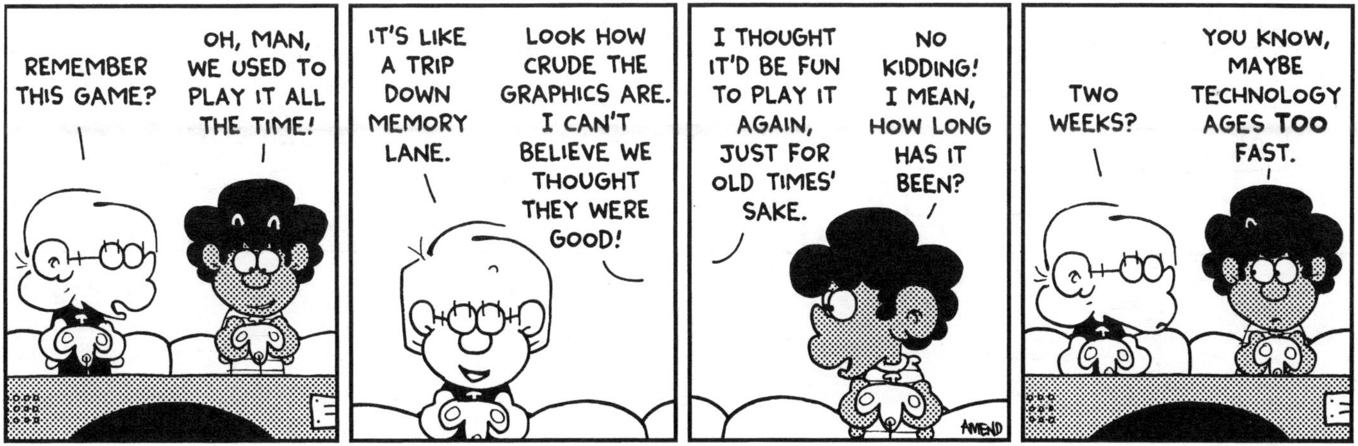
REMEMBER THIS GAME?
OH, MAN, WE USED TO PLAY IT ALL THE TIME!
IT'S LIKE A TRIP DOWN MEMORY LANE.
LOOK HOW CRUDE THE GRAPHICS ARE. I CAN'T BELIEVE WE THOUGHT THEY WERE GOOD!
I THOUGHT IT'D BE FUN TO PLAY IT AGAIN, JUST FOR OLD TIMES' SAKE.
NO KIDDING! I MEAN, HOW LONG HAS IT BEEN?
AMEND
TWO WEEKS?
YOU KNOW, MAYBE TECHNOLOGY AGES **TOO** FAST.

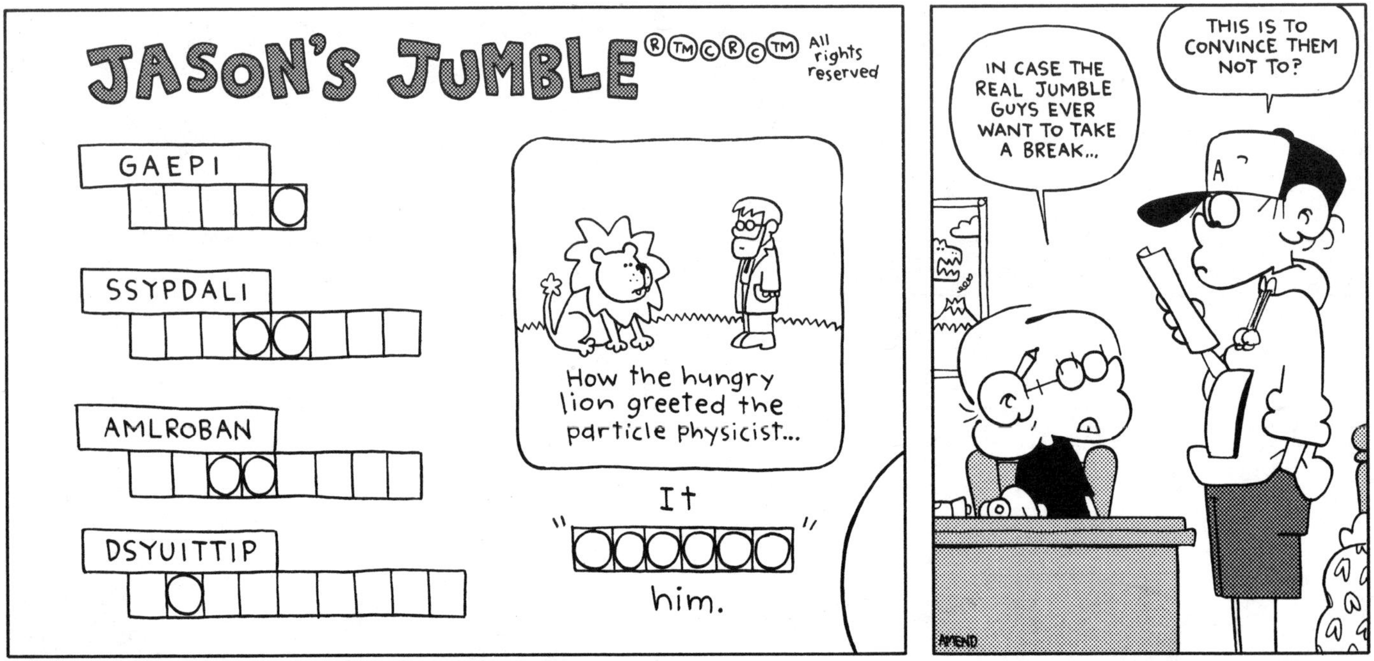
JASON'S JUMBLE®™©®©™ All rights reserved
GAEPI
SSYPDALI
AMLROBAN
DSYUITTIP
How the hungry lion greeted the particle physicist...
It " " him.
IN CASE THE REAL JUMBLE GUYS EVER WANT TO TAKE A BREAK...
THIS IS TO CONVINCE THEM NOT TO?
AMEND

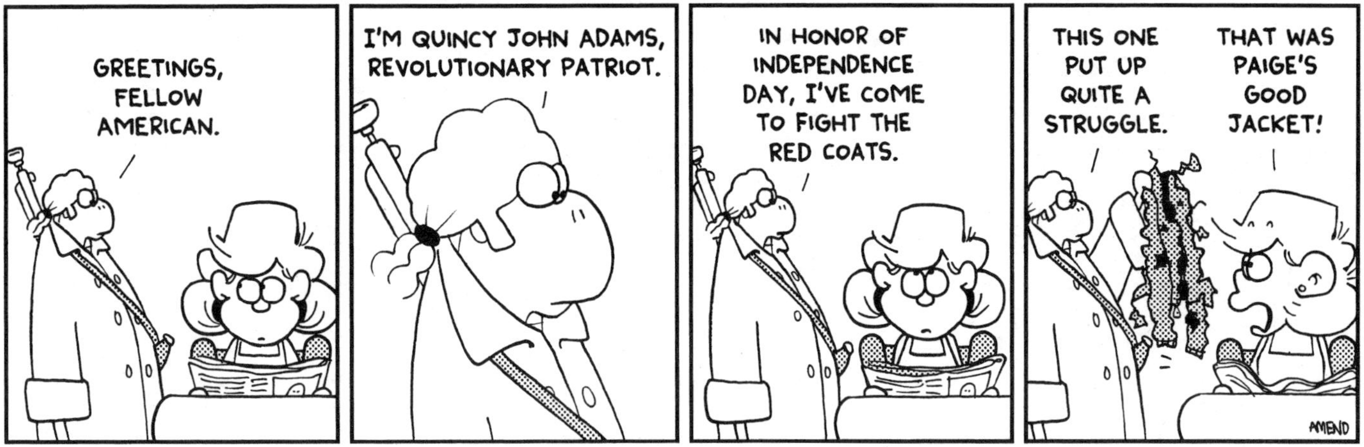
GREETINGS, FELLOW AMERICAN.
I'M QUINCY JOHN ADAMS, REVOLUTIONARY PATRIOT.
IN HONOR OF INDEPENDENCE DAY, I'VE COME TO FIGHT THE RED COATS.
THIS ONE PUT UP QUITE A STRUGGLE.
THAT WAS PAIGE'S GOOD JACKET!
AMEND

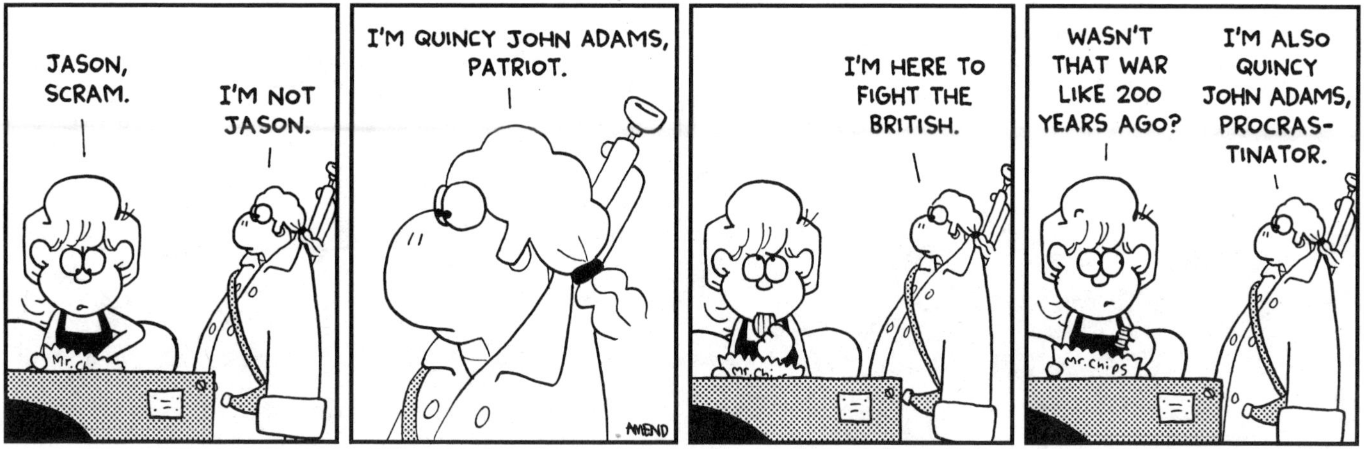
JASON, SCRAM.
I'M NOT JASON.
Mr. Chi
I'M QUINCY JOHN ADAMS, PATRIOT.
AMEND
I'M HERE TO FIGHT THE BRITISH.
WASN'T THAT WAR LIKE 200 YEARS AGO?
I'M ALSO QUINCY JOHN ADAMS, PROCRASTINATOR.
Mr. Chips

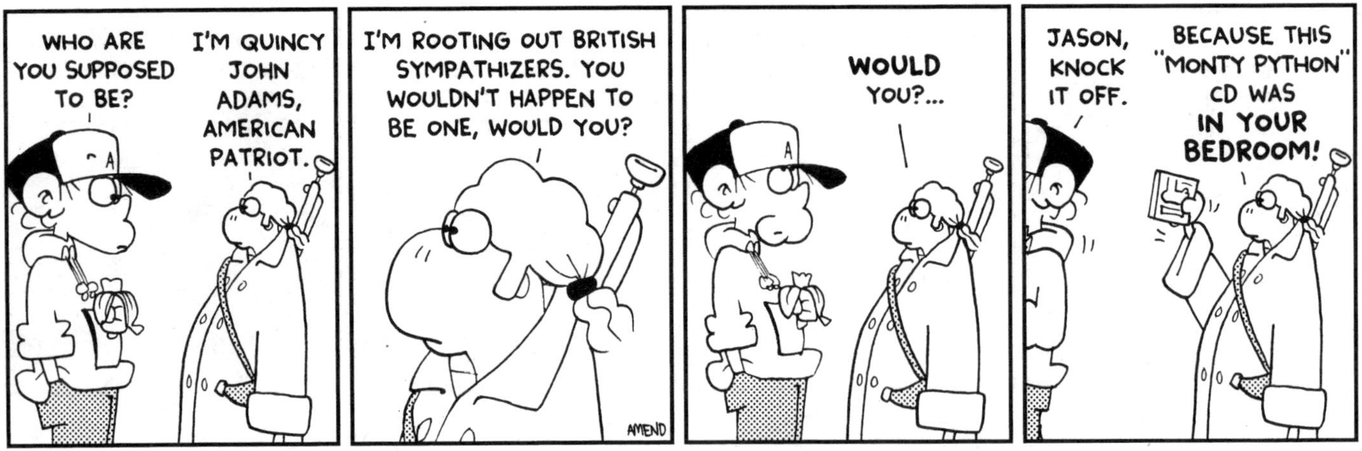
WHO ARE YOU SUPPOSED TO BE?
I'M QUINCY JOHN ADAMS, AMERICAN PATRIOT.
I'M ROOTING OUT BRITISH SYMPATHIZERS. YOU WOULDN'T HAPPEN TO BE ONE, WOULD YOU?
AMEND
WOULD YOU?...
JASON, KNOCK IT OFF.
BECAUSE THIS "MONTY PYTHON" CD WAS **IN YOUR BEDROOM!**

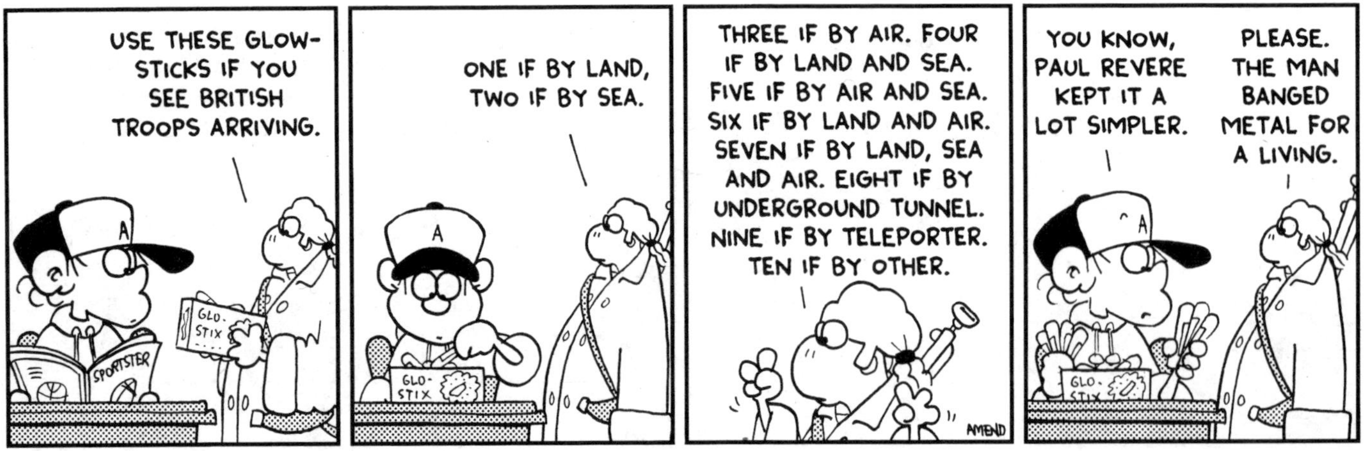
USE THESE GLOW-STICKS IF YOU SEE BRITISH TROOPS ARRIVING.
SPORTSTER
GLO-STIX
ONE IF BY LAND, TWO IF BY SEA.
GLO-STIX
THREE IF BY AIR. FOUR IF BY LAND AND SEA. FIVE IF BY AIR AND SEA. SIX IF BY LAND AND AIR. SEVEN IF BY LAND, SEA AND AIR. EIGHT IF BY UNDERGROUND TUNNEL. NINE IF BY TELEPORTER. TEN IF BY OTHER.
AMEND
YOU KNOW, PAUL REVERE KEPT IT A LOT SIMPLER.
PLEASE. THE MAN BANGED METAL FOR A LIVING.

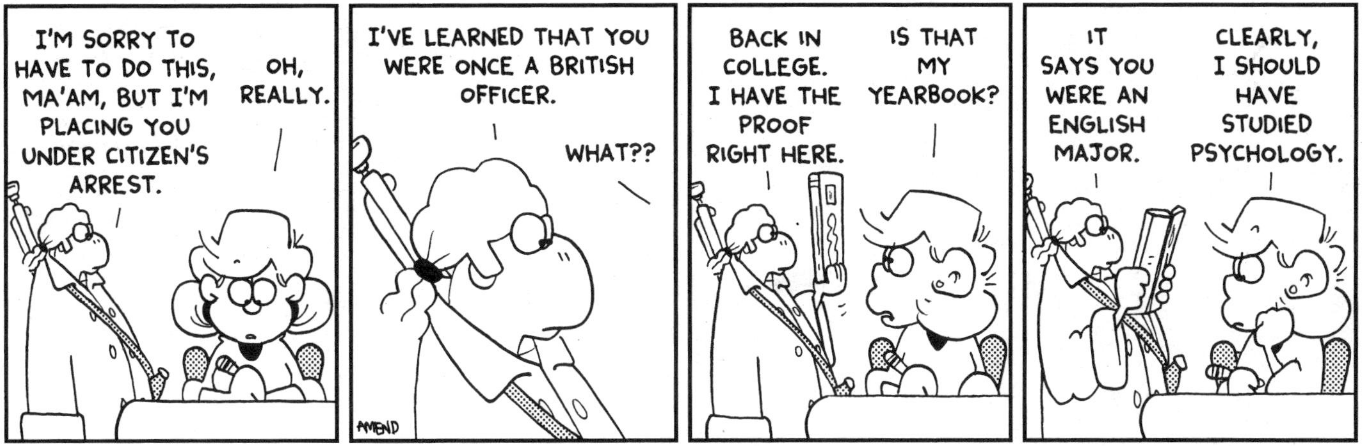
I'M SORRY TO HAVE TO DO THIS, MA'AM, BUT I'M PLACING YOU UNDER CITIZEN'S ARREST.
OH, REALLY.
I'VE LEARNED THAT YOU WERE ONCE A BRITISH OFFICER.
WHAT??
BACK IN COLLEGE. I HAVE THE PROOF RIGHT HERE.
IS THAT MY YEARBOOK?
IT SAYS YOU WERE AN ENGLISH MAJOR.
CLEARLY, I SHOULD HAVE STUDIED PSYCHOLOGY.
AMEND

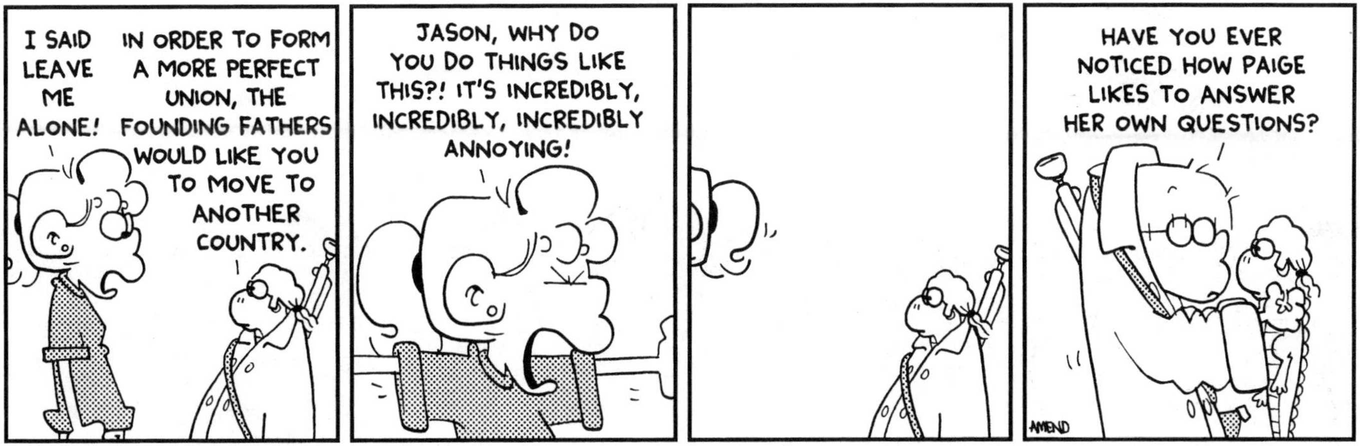
I SAID LEAVE ME ALONE!
IN ORDER TO FORM A MORE PERFECT UNION, THE FOUNDING FATHERS WOULD LIKE YOU TO MOVE TO ANOTHER COUNTRY.
JASON, WHY DO YOU DO THINGS LIKE THIS?! IT'S INCREDIBLY, INCREDIBLY, INCREDIBLY ANNOYING!
HAVE YOU EVER NOTICED HOW PAIGE LIKES TO ANSWER HER OWN QUESTIONS?
AMEND

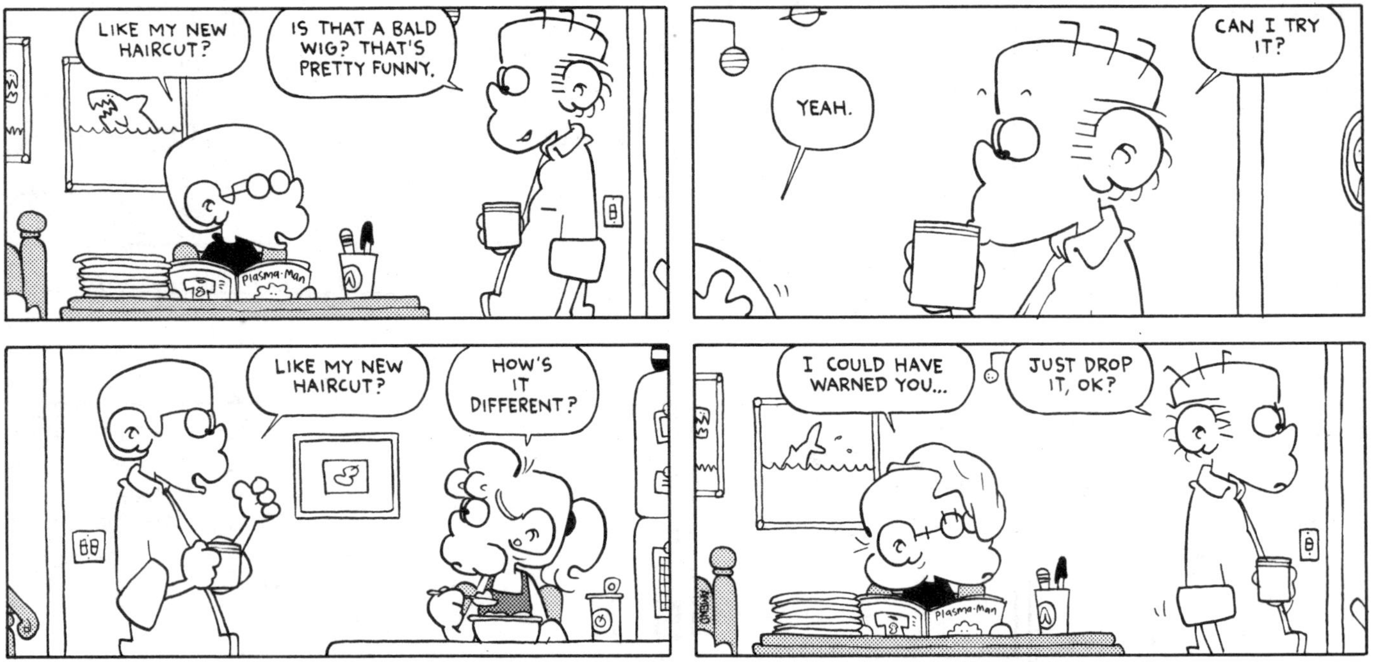
LIKE MY NEW HAIRCUT?
IS THAT A BALD WIG? THAT'S PRETTY FUNNY.
YEAH.
CAN I TRY IT?
LIKE MY NEW HAIRCUT?
HOW'S IT DIFFERENT?
I COULD HAVE WARNED YOU...
JUST DROP IT, OK?

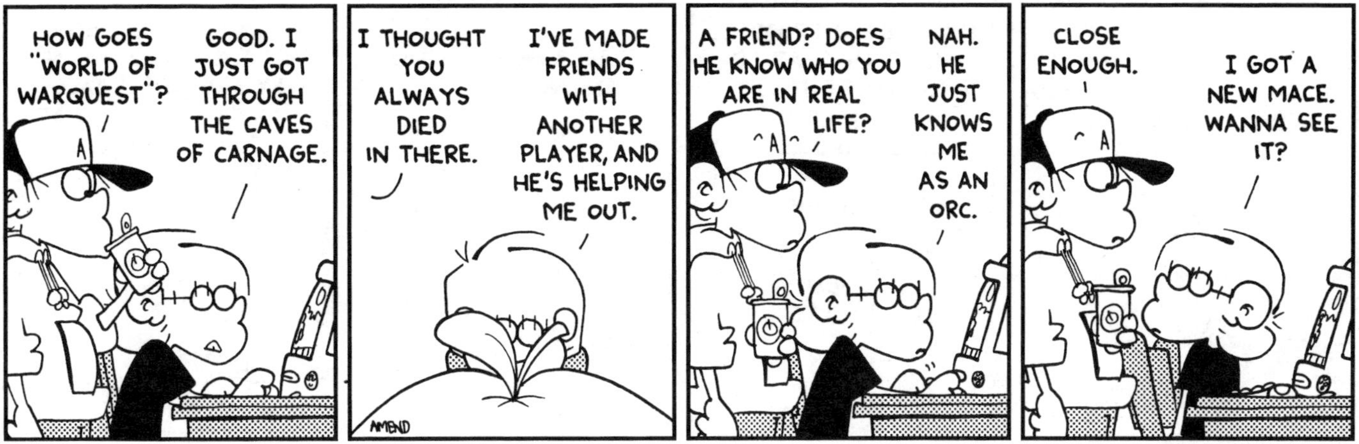
HOW GOES "WORLD OF WARQUEST"?
GOOD. I JUST GOT THROUGH THE CAVES OF CARNAGE.
I THOUGHT YOU ALWAYS DIED IN THERE.
I'VE MADE FRIENDS WITH ANOTHER PLAYER, AND HE'S HELPING ME OUT.
AMEND
A FRIEND? DOES HE KNOW WHO YOU ARE IN REAL LIFE?
NAH. HE JUST KNOWS ME AS AN ORC.
CLOSE ENOUGH.
I GOT A NEW MACE. WANNA SEE IT?

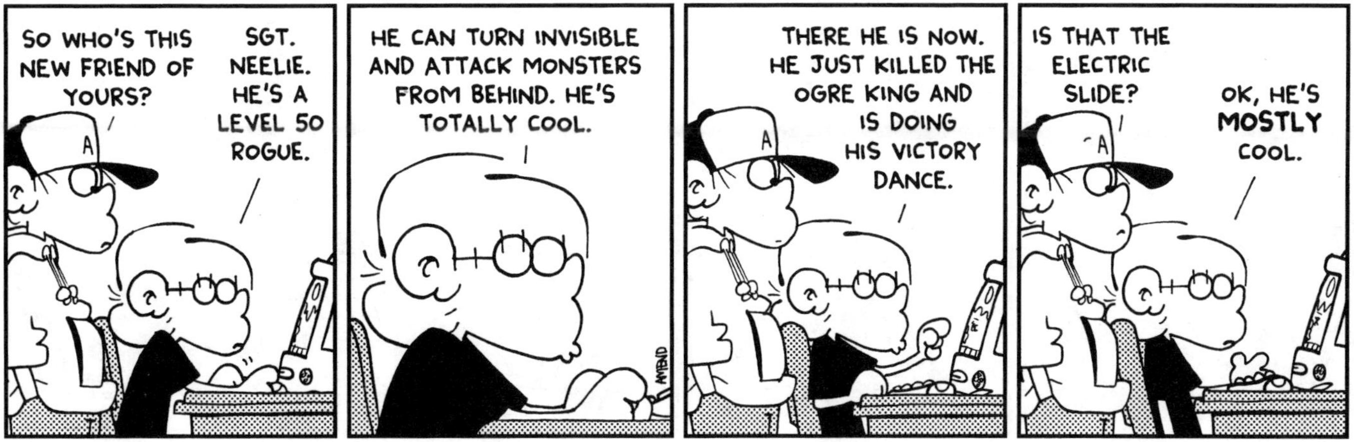
SO WHO'S THIS NEW FRIEND OF YOURS?
SGT. NEELIE. HE'S A LEVEL 50 ROGUE.
HE CAN TURN INVISIBLE AND ATTACK MONSTERS FROM BEHIND. HE'S TOTALLY COOL.
AMEND
THERE HE IS NOW. HE JUST KILLED THE OGRE KING AND IS DOING HIS VICTORY DANCE.
IS THAT THE ELECTRIC SLIDE?
OK, HE'S **MOSTLY** COOL.

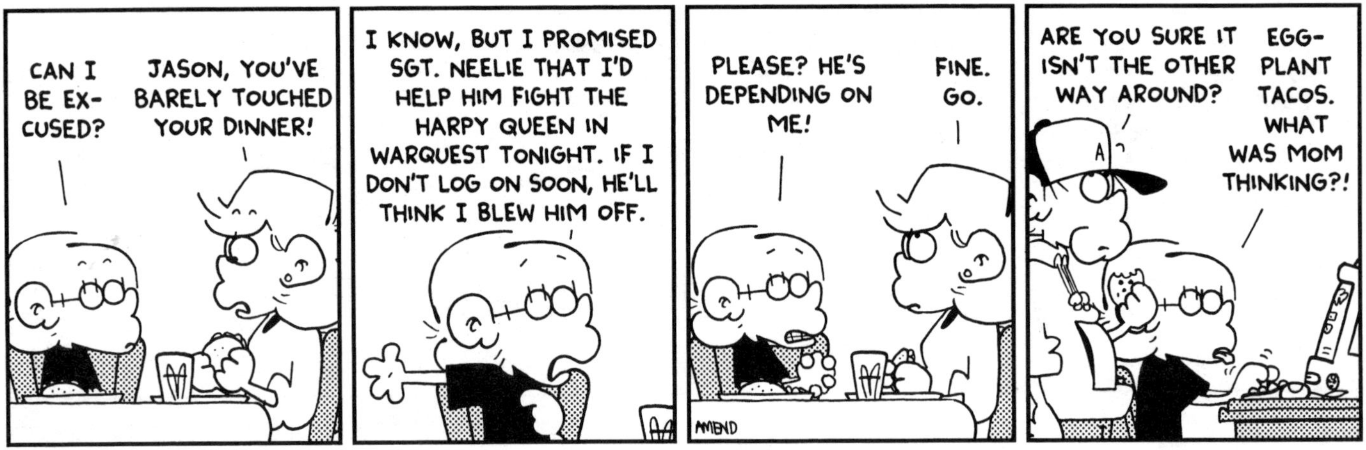
CAN I BE EX-CUSED?
JASON, YOU'VE BARELY TOUCHED YOUR DINNER!
I KNOW, BUT I PROMISED SGT. NEELIE THAT I'D HELP HIM FIGHT THE HARPY QUEEN IN WARQUEST TONIGHT. IF I DON'T LOG ON SOON, HE'LL THINK I BLEW HIM OFF.
PLEASE? HE'S DEPENDING ON ME!
FINE. GO.
AMEND
ARE YOU SURE IT ISN'T THE OTHER WAY AROUND?
EGG-PLANT TACOS. WHAT WAS MOM THINKING?!
A

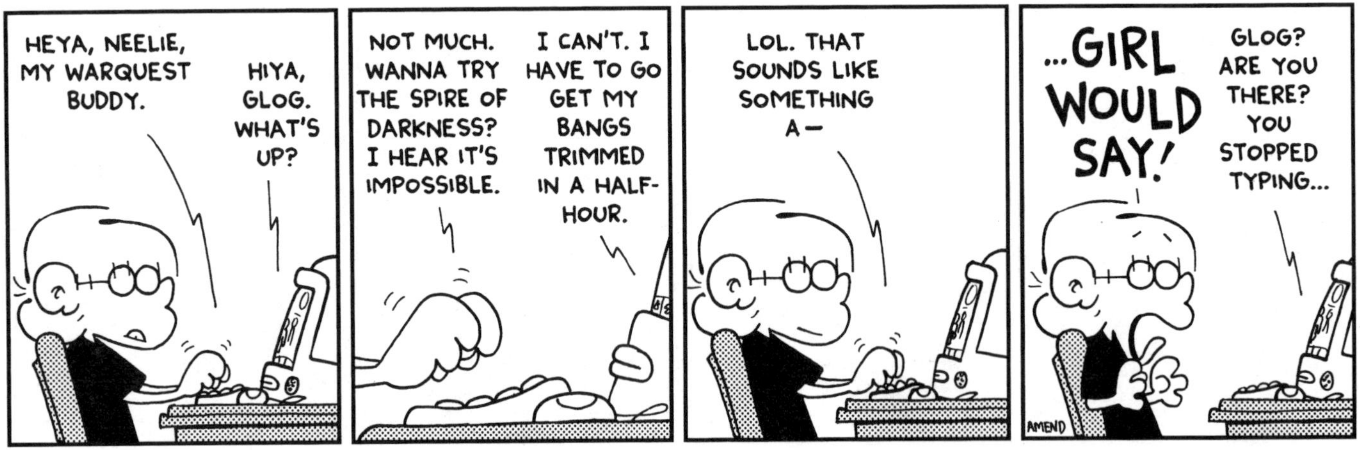
HEYA, NEELIE, MY WARQUEST BUDDY.
HIYA, GLOG. WHAT'S UP?
NOT MUCH. WANNA TRY THE SPIRE OF DARKNESS? I HEAR IT'S IMPOSSIBLE.
I CAN'T. I HAVE TO GO GET MY BANGS TRIMMED IN A HALF-HOUR.
LOL. THAT SOUNDS LIKE SOMETHING A—
...GIRL WOULD SAY!
GLOG? ARE YOU THERE? YOU STOPPED TYPING...
AMEND

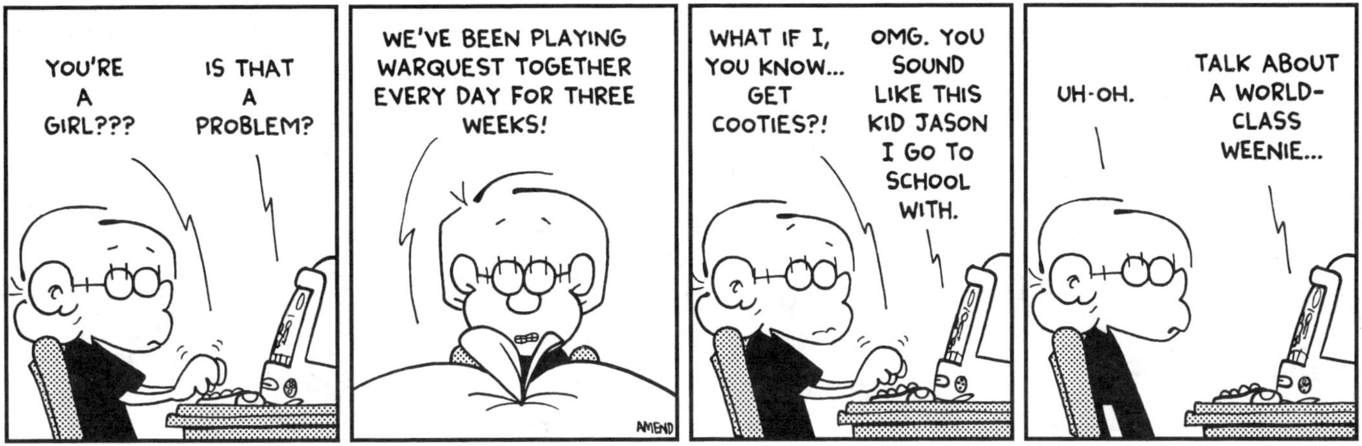
YOU'RE A GIRL???
IS THAT A PROBLEM?
WE'VE BEEN PLAYING WARQUEST TOGETHER EVERY DAY FOR THREE WEEKS!
WHAT IF I, YOU KNOW... GET COOTIES?!
OMG. YOU SOUND LIKE THIS KID JASON I GO TO SCHOOL WITH.
UH-OH.
TALK ABOUT A WORLD-CLASS WEENIE...
AMEND

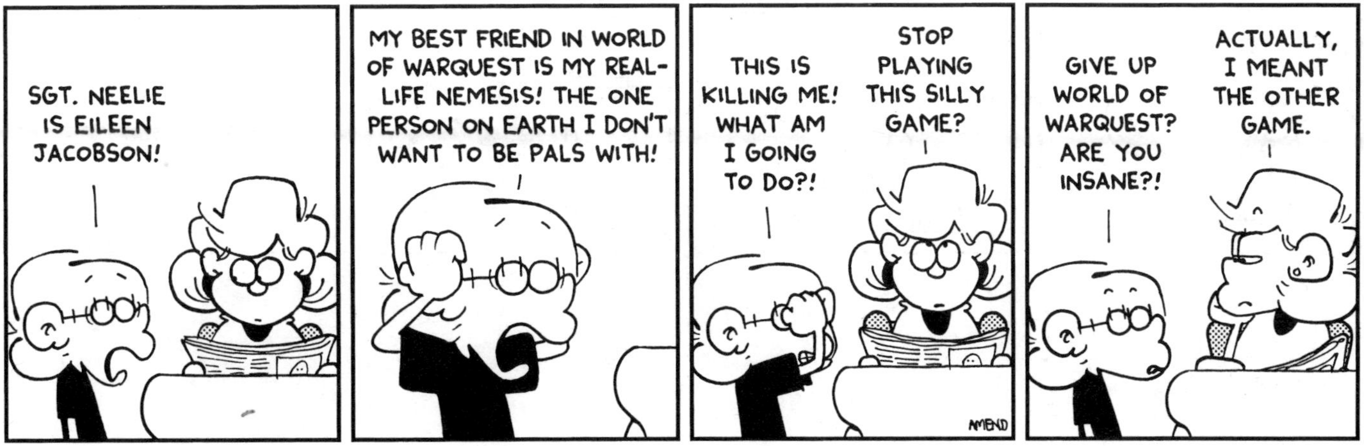
SGT. NEELIE IS EILEEN JACOBSON!
MY BEST FRIEND IN WORLD OF WARQUEST IS MY REAL-LIFE NEMESIS! THE ONE PERSON ON EARTH I DON'T WANT TO BE PALS WITH!
THIS IS KILLING ME! WHAT AM I GOING TO DO?!
STOP PLAYING THIS SILLY GAME?
GIVE UP WORLD OF WARQUEST? ARE YOU INSANE?!
ACTUALLY, I MEANT THE OTHER GAME.
AMEND

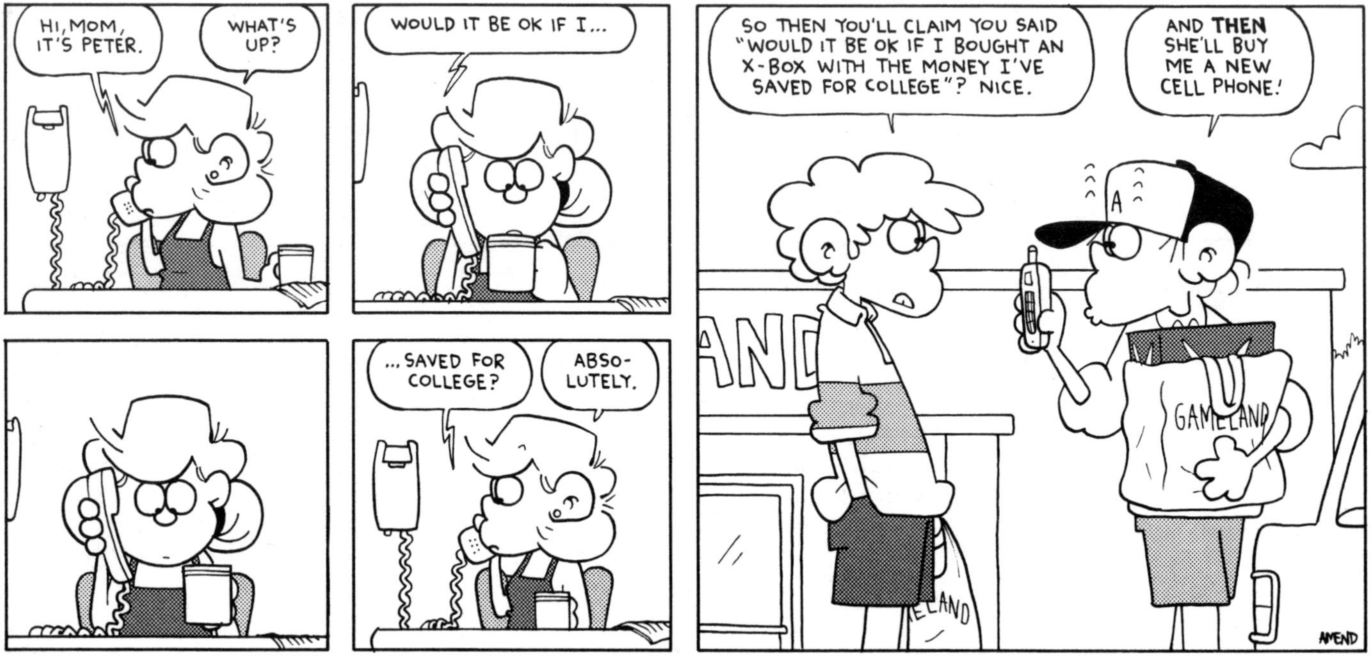
HI, MOM, IT'S PETER.
WHAT'S UP?
WOULD IT BE OK IF I...
...SAVED FOR COLLEGE?
ABSO-LUTELY.
SO THEN YOU'LL CLAIM YOU SAID "WOULD IT BE OK IF I BOUGHT AN X-BOX WITH THE MONEY I'VE SAVED FOR COLLEGE"? NICE.
AND **THEN** SHE'LL BUY ME A NEW CELL PHONE!
AND
A
GAMELAND
ELAND
AMEND

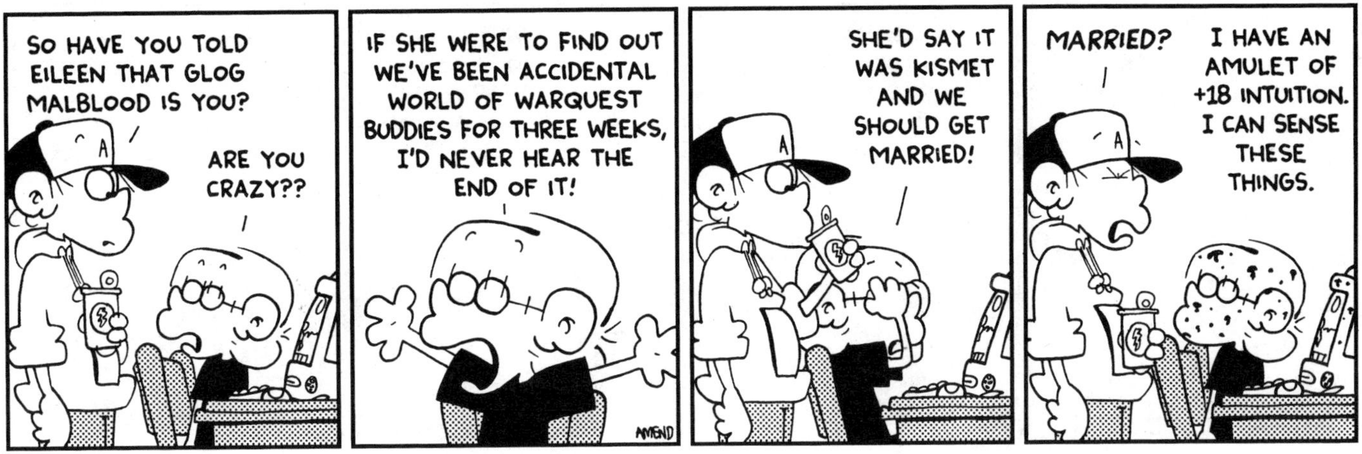
SO HAVE YOU TOLD EILEEN THAT GLOG MALBLOOD IS YOU?
ARE YOU CRAZY??
IF SHE WERE TO FIND OUT WE'VE BEEN ACCIDENTAL WORLD OF WARQUEST BUDDIES FOR THREE WEEKS, I'D NEVER HEAR THE END OF IT!
SHE'D SAY IT WAS KISMET AND WE SHOULD GET MARRIED!
MARRIED?
I HAVE AN AMULET OF +18 INTUITION. I CAN SENSE THESE THINGS.

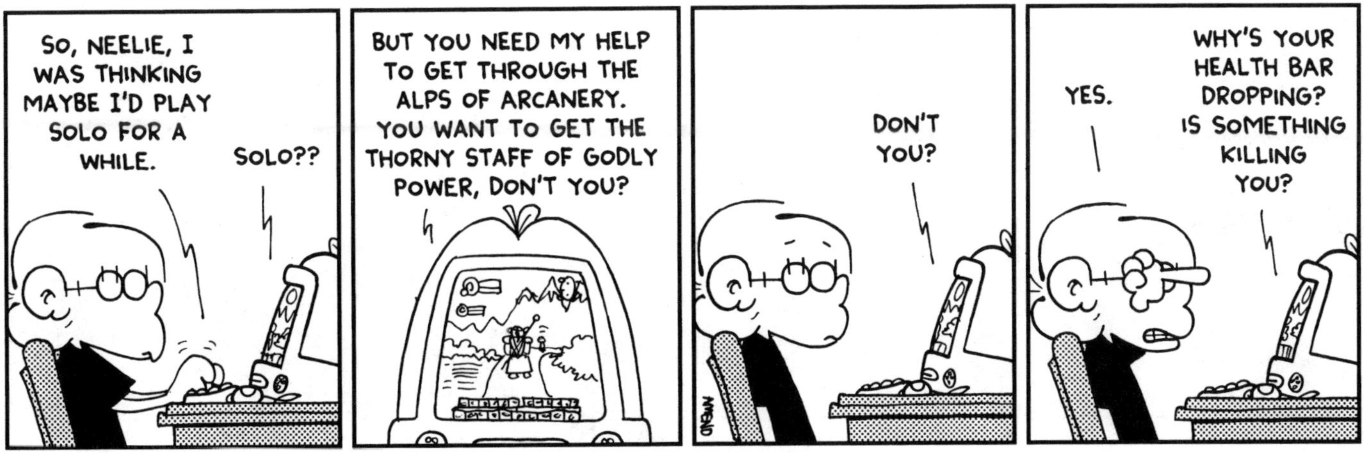
SO, NEELIE, I WAS THINKING MAYBE I'D PLAY SOLO FOR A WHILE.
SOLO??
BUT YOU NEED MY HELP TO GET THROUGH THE ALPS OF ARCANERY. YOU WANT TO GET THE THORNY STAFF OF GODLY POWER, DON'T YOU?
DON'T YOU?
YES.
WHY'S YOUR HEALTH BAR DROPPING? IS SOMETHING KILLING YOU?

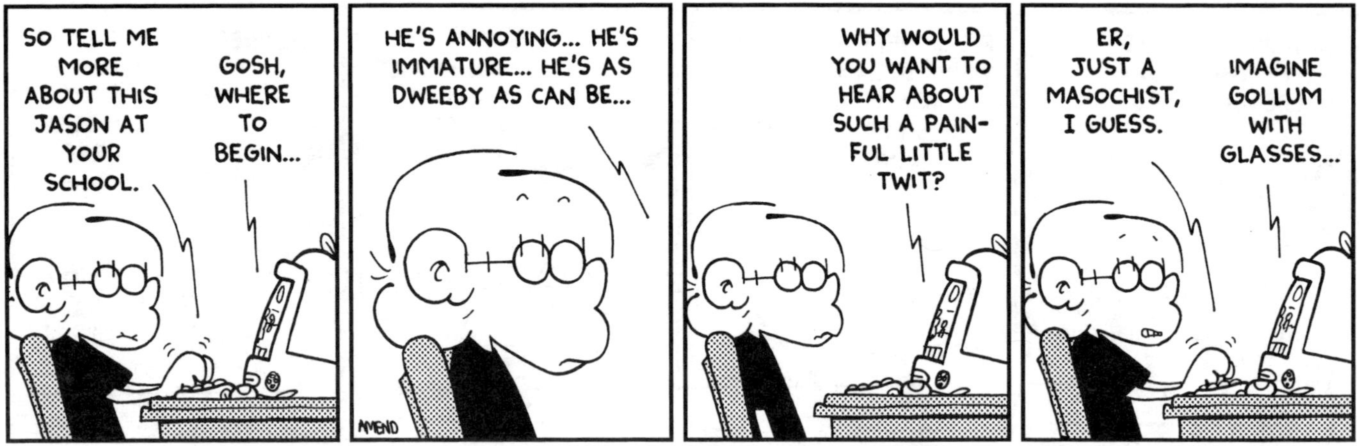
SO TELL ME MORE ABOUT THIS JASON AT YOUR SCHOOL.
GOSH, WHERE TO BEGIN...
HE'S ANNOYING... HE'S IMMATURE... HE'S AS DWEEBY AS CAN BE...
AMEND
WHY WOULD YOU WANT TO HEAR ABOUT SUCH A PAIN-FUL LITTLE TWIT?
ER, JUST A MASOCHIST, I GUESS.
IMAGINE GOLLUM WITH GLASSES...

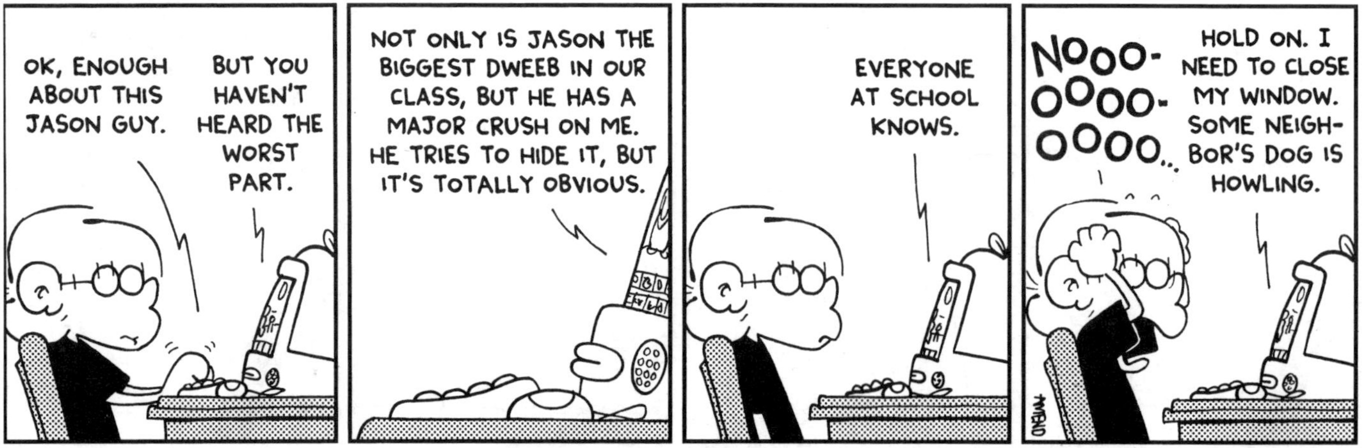
OK, ENOUGH ABOUT THIS JASON GUY.
BUT YOU HAVEN'T HEARD THE WORST PART.
NOT ONLY IS JASON THE BIGGEST DWEEB IN OUR CLASS, BUT HE HAS A MAJOR CRUSH ON ME. HE TRIES TO HIDE IT, BUT IT'S TOTALLY OBVIOUS.
EVERYONE AT SCHOOL KNOWS.
NOOO-OOOO-OOOO...
HOLD ON. I NEED TO CLOSE MY WINDOW. SOME NEIGH-BOR'S DOG IS HOWLING.
AMEND

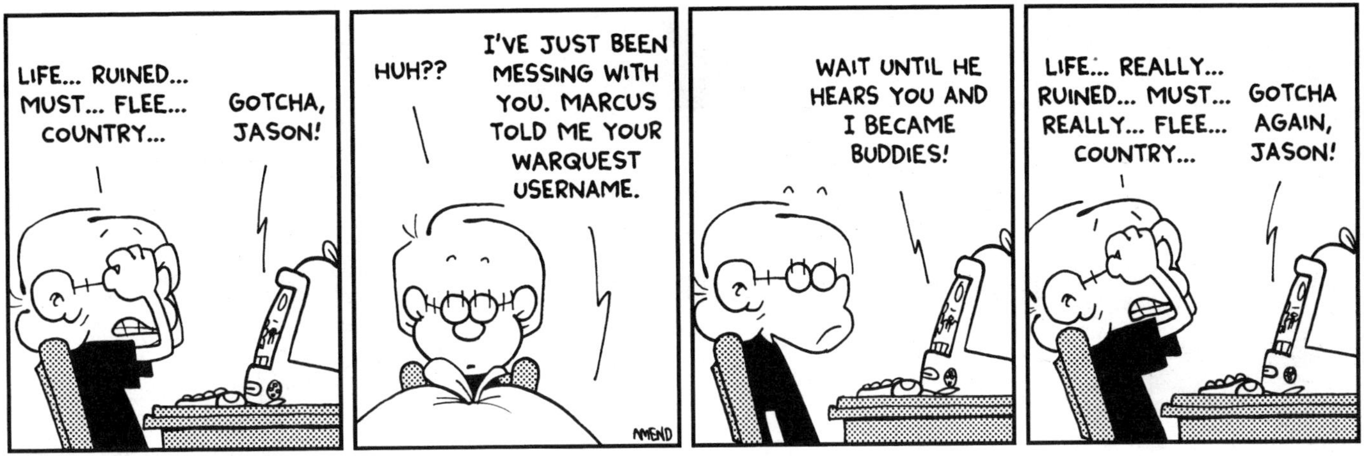
LIFE... RUINED... MUST... FLEE... COUNTRY...
GOTCHA, JASON!
HUH??
I'VE JUST BEEN MESSING WITH YOU. MARCUS TOLD ME YOUR WARQUEST USERNAME.
AMEND
WAIT UNTIL HE HEARS YOU AND I BECAME BUDDIES!
LIFE... REALLY... RUINED... MUST... REALLY... FLEE... COUNTRY...
GOTCHA AGAIN, JASON!

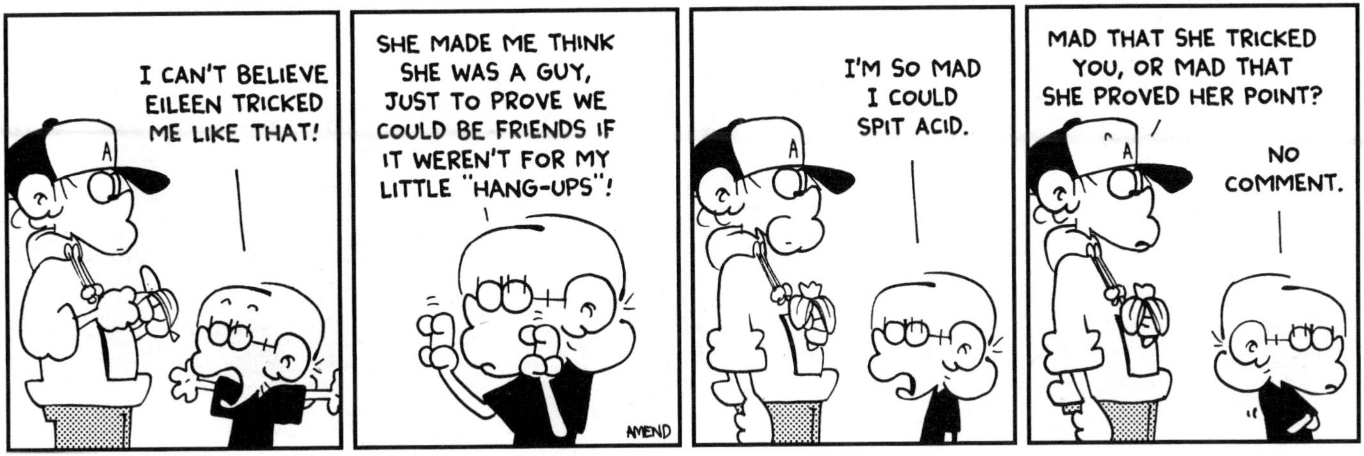
I CAN'T BELIEVE EILEEN TRICKED ME LIKE THAT!
SHE MADE ME THINK SHE WAS A GUY, JUST TO PROVE WE COULD BE FRIENDS IF IT WEREN'T FOR MY LITTLE "HANG-UPS"!
AMEND
I'M SO MAD I COULD SPIT ACID.
MAD THAT SHE TRICKED YOU, OR MAD THAT SHE PROVED HER POINT?
NO COMMENT.

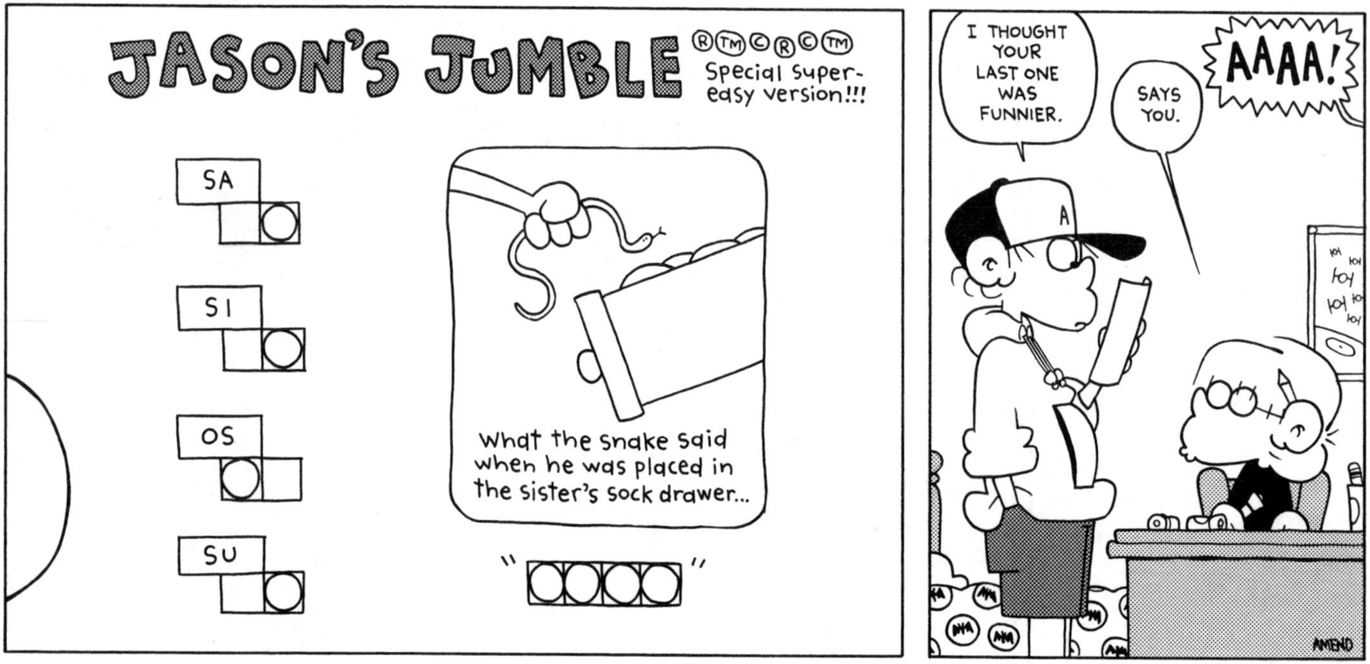

JASON'S JUMBLE ®™©®©™
Special super-easy version!!!
SA
SI
OS
SU
What the snake said when he was placed in the sister's sock drawer...
" "
I THOUGHT YOUR LAST ONE WAS FUNNIER.
SAYS YOU.
AAAA!
AMEND

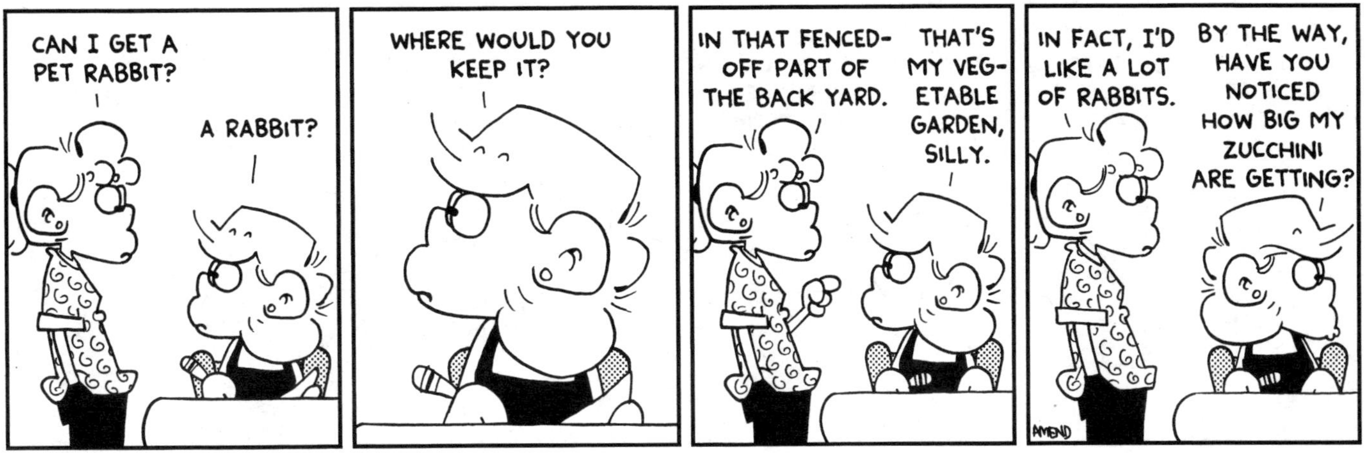
CAN I GET A PET RABBIT?
A RABBIT?
WHERE WOULD YOU KEEP IT?
IN THAT FENCED-OFF PART OF THE BACK YARD.
THAT'S MY VEGETABLE GARDEN, SILLY.
IN FACT, I'D LIKE A LOT OF RABBITS.
BY THE WAY, HAVE YOU NOTICED HOW BIG MY ZUCCHINI ARE GETTING?
AMEND

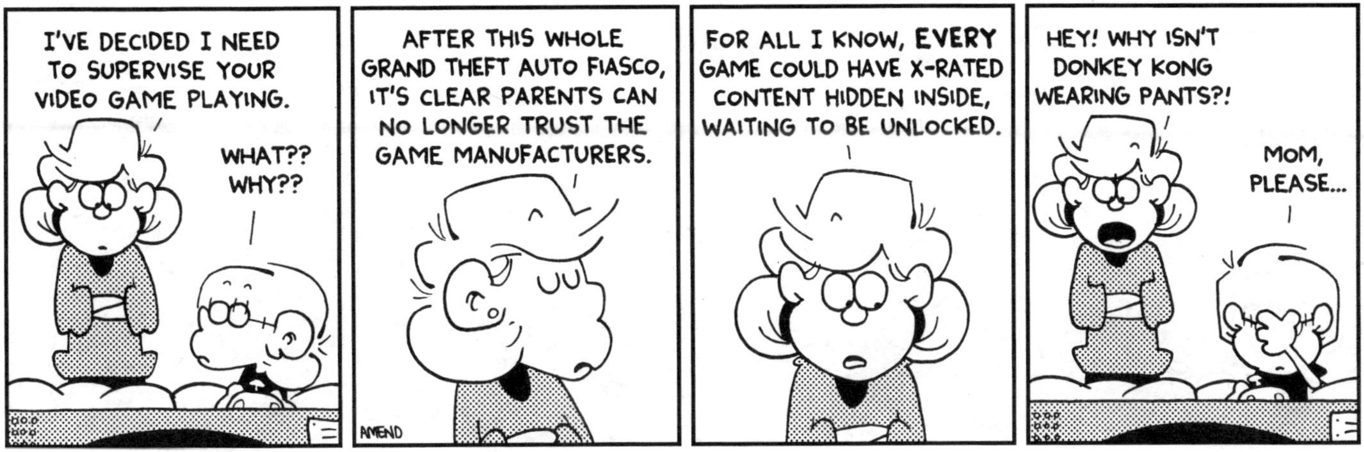
I'VE DECIDED I NEED TO SUPERVISE YOUR VIDEO GAME PLAYING.
WHAT?? WHY??
AFTER THIS WHOLE GRAND THEFT AUTO FIASCO, IT'S CLEAR PARENTS CAN NO LONGER TRUST THE GAME MANUFACTURERS.
AMEND
FOR ALL I KNOW, **EVERY** GAME COULD HAVE X-RATED CONTENT HIDDEN INSIDE, WAITING TO BE UNLOCKED.
HEY! WHY ISN'T DONKEY KONG WEARING PANTS?!
MOM, PLEASE...

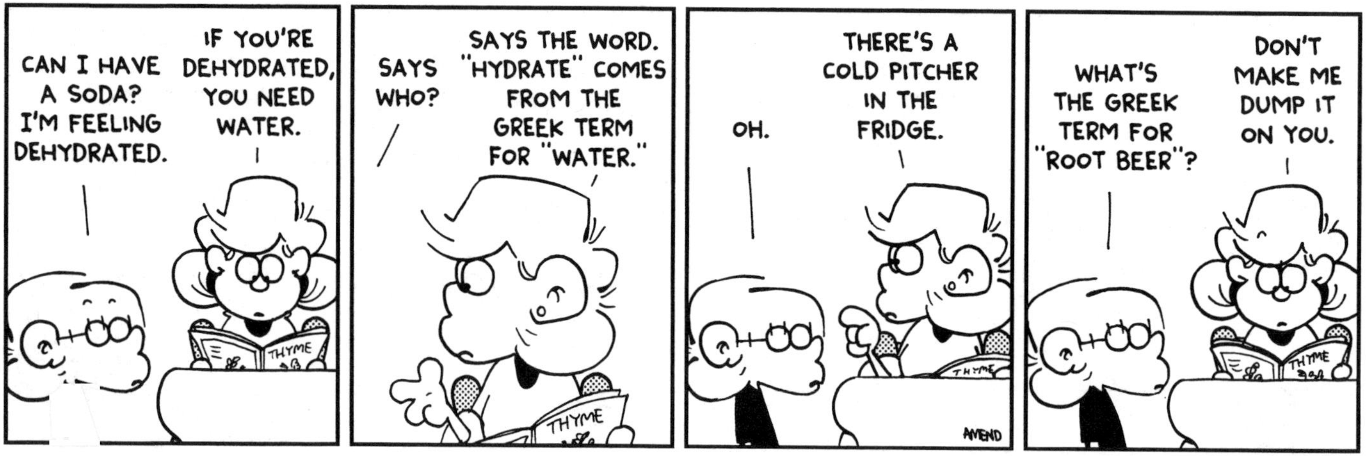
CAN I HAVE A SODA? I'M FEELING DEHYDRATED.
IF YOU'RE DEHYDRATED, YOU NEED WATER.
SAYS WHO?
SAYS THE WORD. "HYDRATE" COMES FROM THE GREEK TERM FOR "WATER."
OH.
THERE'S A COLD PITCHER IN THE FRIDGE.
WHAT'S THE GREEK TERM FOR "ROOT BEER"?
DON'T MAKE ME DUMP IT ON YOU.
THYME
AMEND

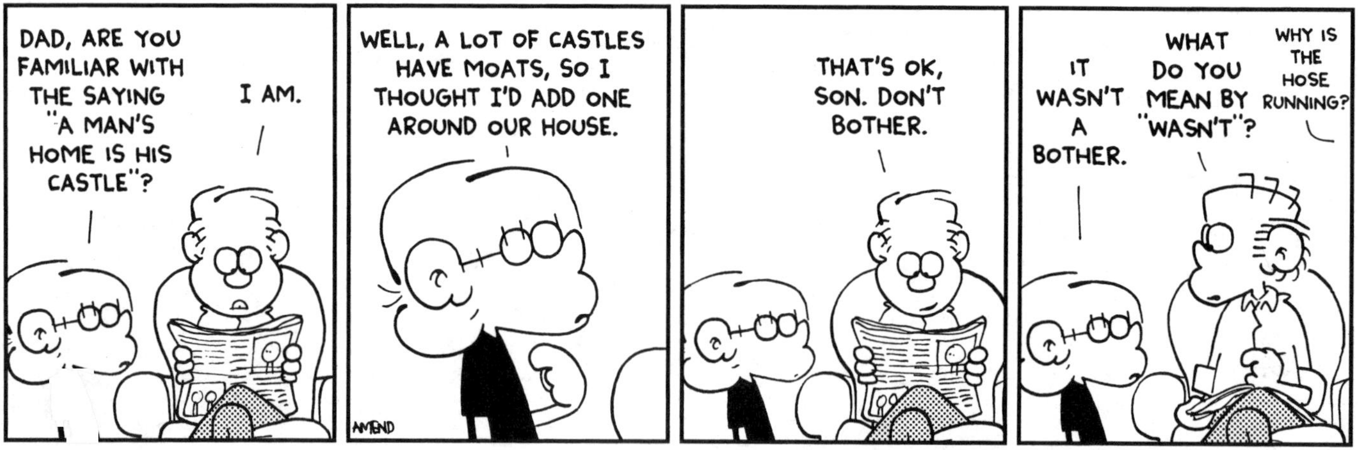
DAD, ARE YOU FAMILIAR WITH THE SAYING "A MAN'S HOME IS HIS CASTLE"?
I AM.
WELL, A LOT OF CASTLES HAVE MOATS, SO I THOUGHT I'D ADD ONE AROUND OUR HOUSE.
THAT'S OK, SON. DON'T BOTHER.
IT WASN'T A BOTHER.
WHAT DO YOU MEAN BY "WASN'T"?
WHY IS THE HOSE RUNNING?
AMEND

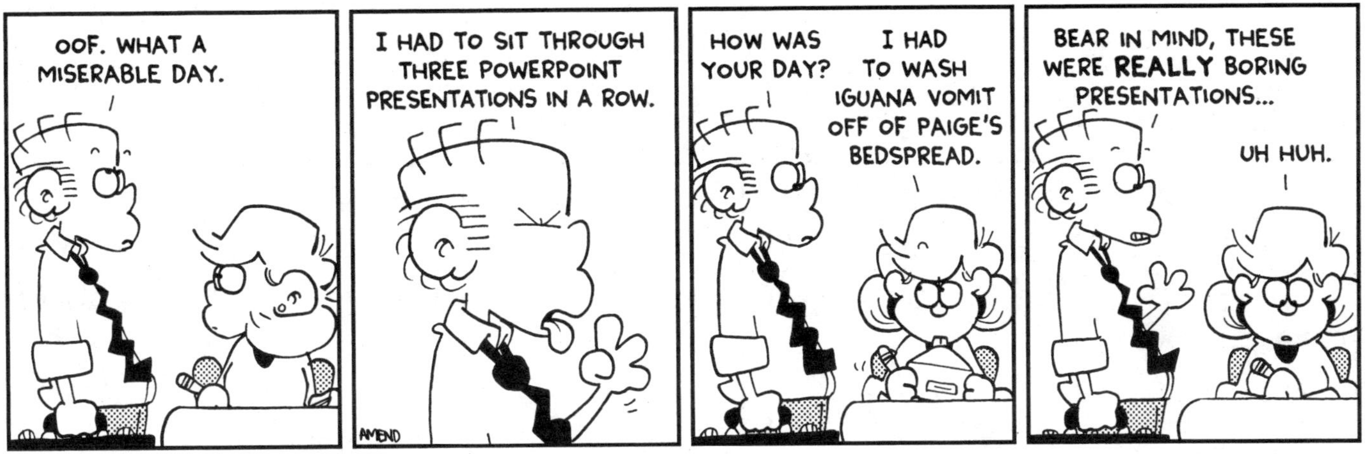
OOF. WHAT A MISERABLE DAY.
I HAD TO SIT THROUGH THREE POWERPOINT PRESENTATIONS IN A ROW.
AMEND
HOW WAS YOUR DAY?
I HAD TO WASH IGUANA VOMIT OFF OF PAIGE'S BEDSPREAD.
BEAR IN MIND, THESE WERE **REALLY** BORING PRESENTATIONS...
UH HUH.

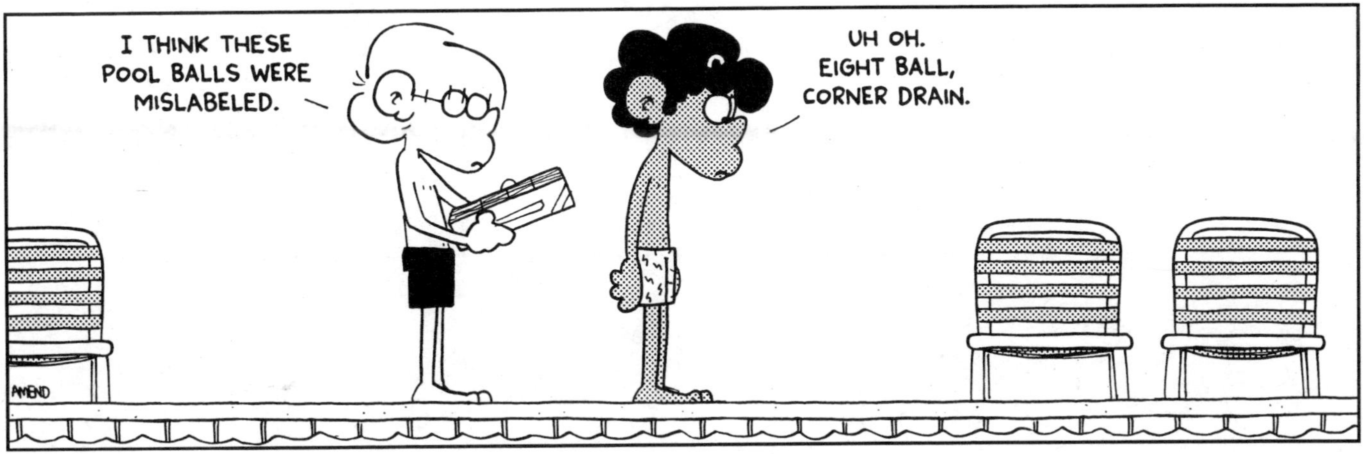
I THINK THESE POOL BALLS WERE MISLABELED.
UH OH. EIGHT BALL, CORNER DRAIN.
AMEND

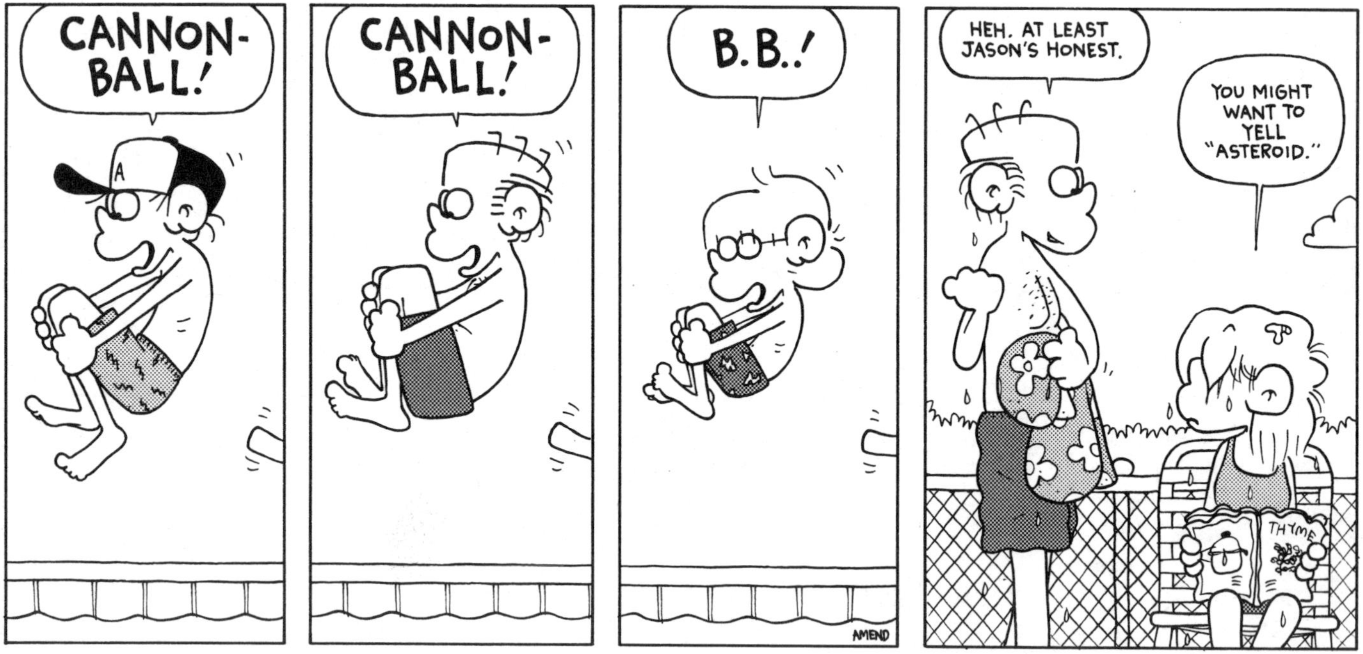
CANNON-BALL!
CANNON-BALL!
B.B.!
HEH. AT LEAST JASON'S HONEST.
YOU MIGHT WANT TO YELL "ASTEROID."
THYME
AMEND

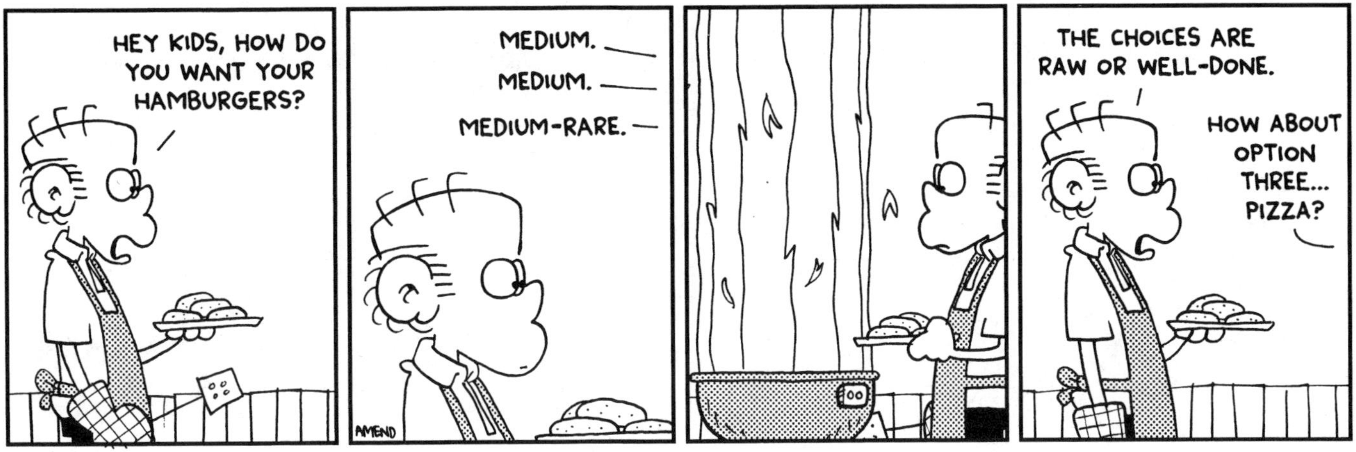
HEY KIDS, HOW DO YOU WANT YOUR HAMBURGERS?
MEDIUM.
MEDIUM.
MEDIUM-RARE.
AMEND
THE CHOICES ARE RAW OR WELL-DONE.
HOW ABOUT OPTION THREE... PIZZA?

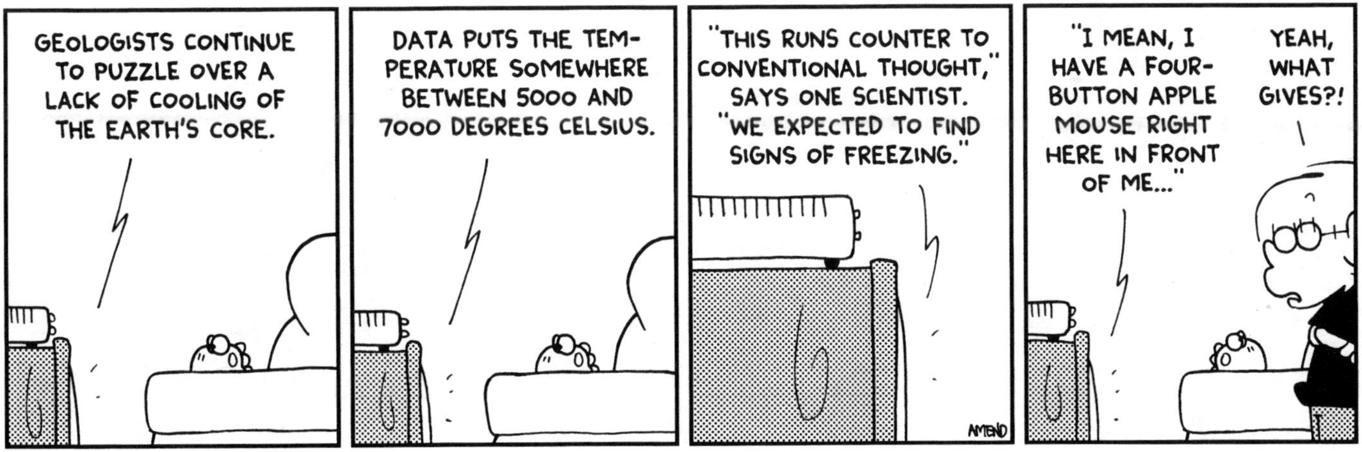
GEOLOGISTS CONTINUE TO PUZZLE OVER A LACK OF COOLING OF THE EARTH'S CORE.
DATA PUTS THE TEMPERATURE SOMEWHERE BETWEEN 5000 AND 7000 DEGREES CELSIUS.
"THIS RUNS COUNTER TO CONVENTIONAL THOUGHT," SAYS ONE SCIENTIST. "WE EXPECTED TO FIND SIGNS OF FREEZING."
AMEND
"I MEAN, I HAVE A FOUR-BUTTON APPLE MOUSE RIGHT HERE IN FRONT OF ME..."
YEAH, WHAT GIVES?!

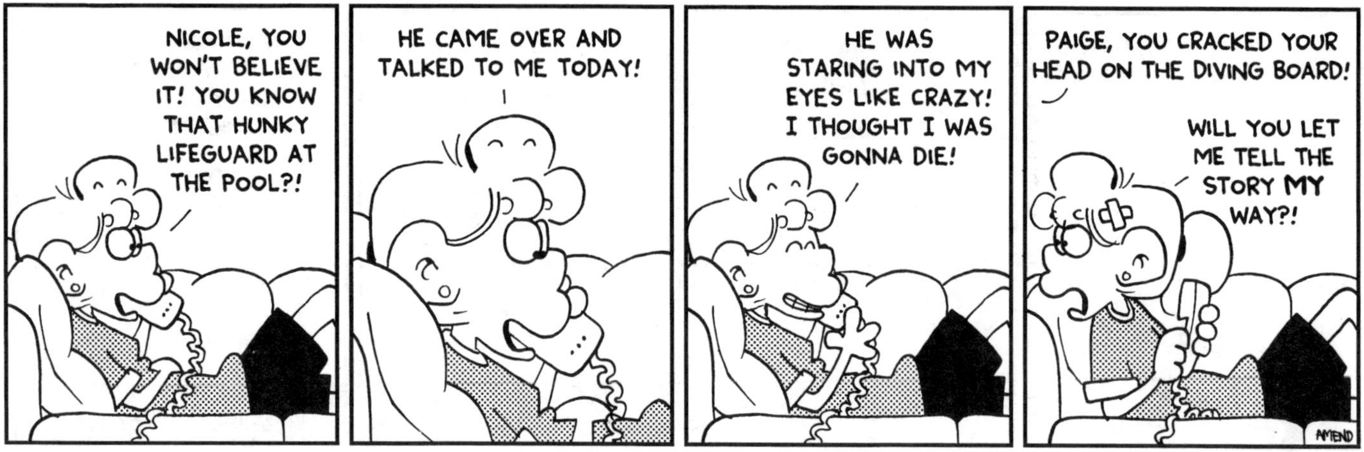
NICOLE, YOU WON'T BELIEVE IT! YOU KNOW THAT HUNKY LIFEGUARD AT THE POOL?!
HE CAME OVER AND TALKED TO ME TODAY!
HE WAS STARING INTO MY EYES LIKE CRAZY! I THOUGHT I WAS GONNA DIE!
PAIGE, YOU CRACKED YOUR HEAD ON THE DIVING BOARD!
WILL YOU LET ME TELL THE STORY MY WAY?!
AMEND

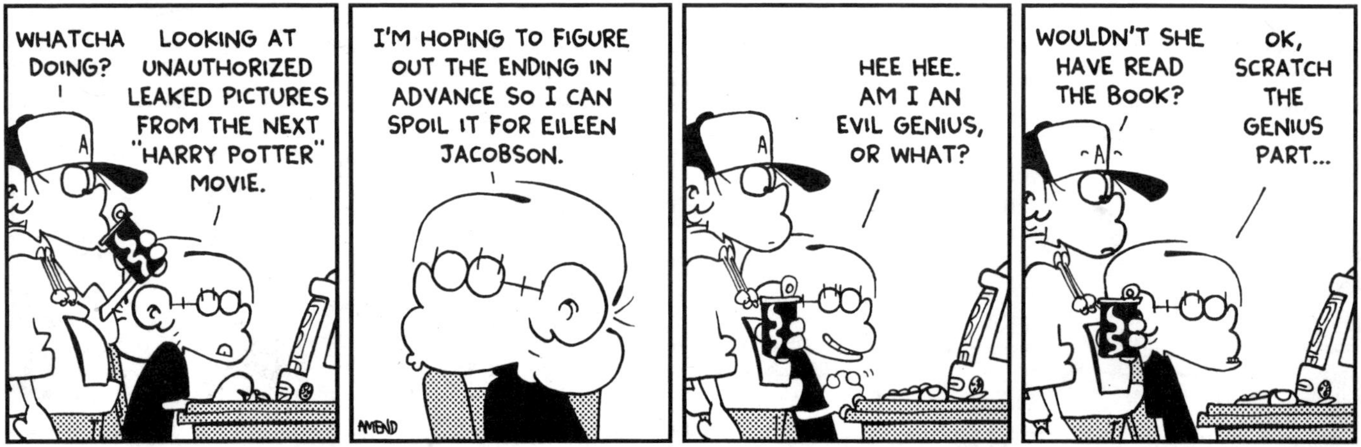
WHATCHA DOING?
LOOKING AT UNAUTHORIZED LEAKED PICTURES FROM THE NEXT "HARRY POTTER" MOVIE.
I'M HOPING TO FIGURE OUT THE ENDING IN ADVANCE SO I CAN SPOIL IT FOR EILEEN JACOBSON.
AMEND
HEE HEE. AM I AN EVIL GENIUS, OR WHAT?
WOULDN'T SHE HAVE READ THE BOOK?
OK, SCRATCH THE GENIUS PART...

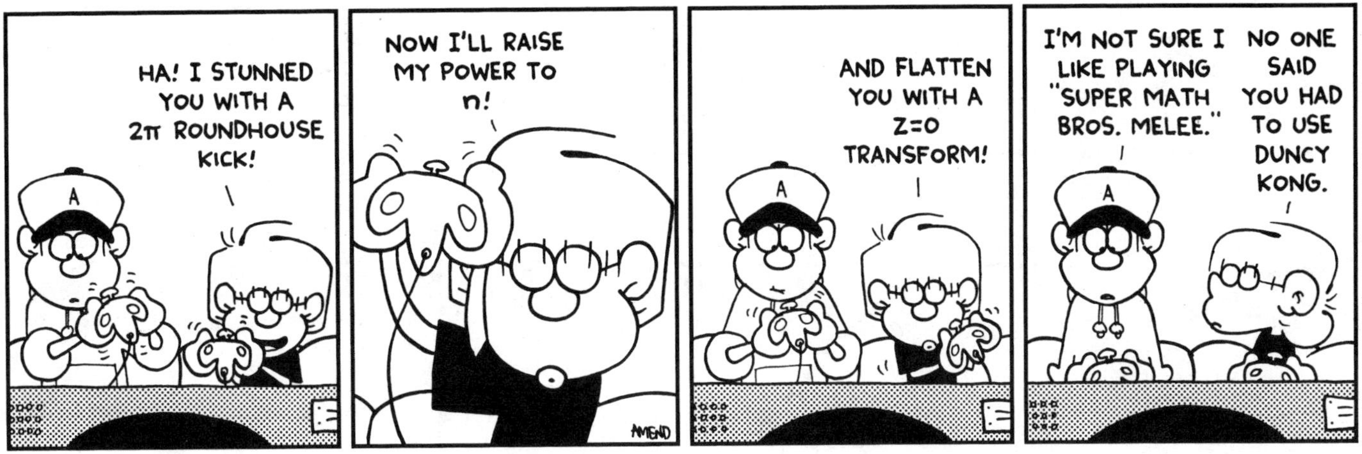
HA! I STUNNED YOU WITH A 2π ROUNDHOUSE KICK!
NOW I'LL RAISE MY POWER TO n!
AND FLATTEN YOU WITH A Z=0 TRANSFORM!
I'M NOT SURE I LIKE PLAYING "SUPER MATH BROS. MELEE."
NO ONE SAID YOU HAD TO USE DUNCY KONG.
AMEND

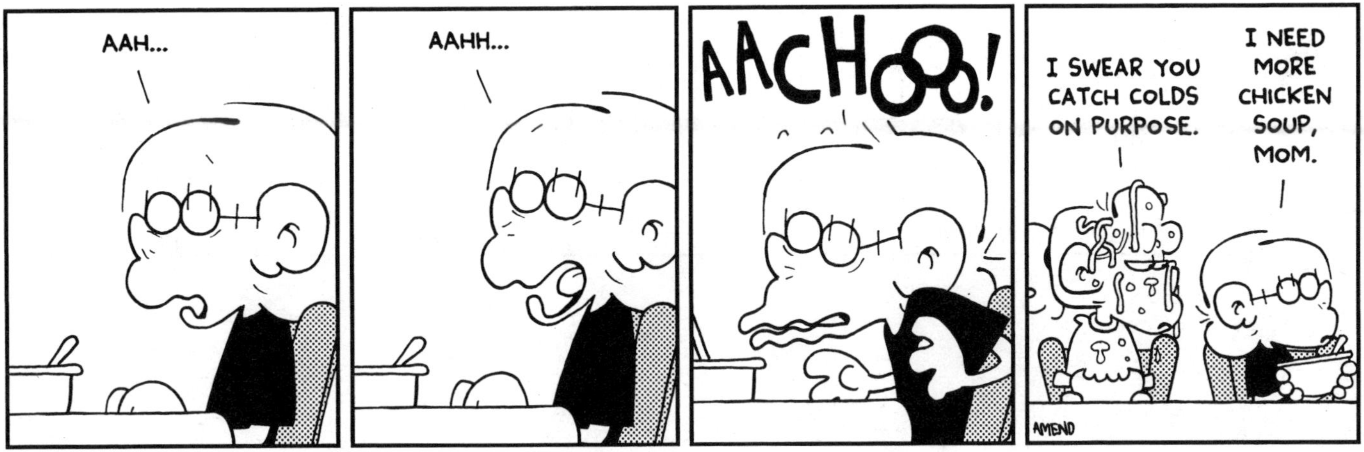
AAH...
AAHH...
AACHOOO!
I SWEAR YOU CATCH COLDS ON PURPOSE.
I NEED MORE CHICKEN SOUP, MOM.
AMEND

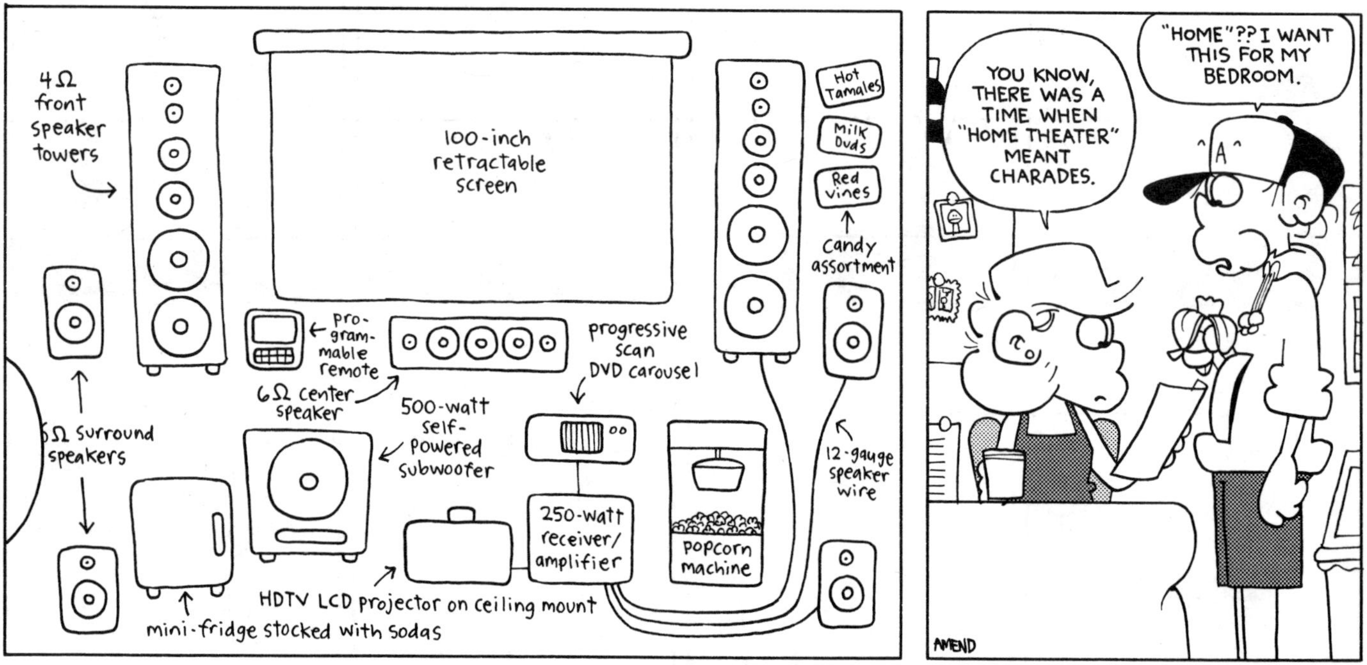
4Ω front speaker towers
100-inch retractable screen
Hot Tamales
Milk Duds
Red vines
candy assortment
pro-grammable remote
6Ω center speaker
progressive scan DVD carousel
500-watt self-powered subwoofer
6Ω surround speakers
12-gauge speaker wire
250-watt receiver/amplifier
popcorn machine
HDTV LCD projector on ceiling mount
mini-fridge stocked with sodas
YOU KNOW, THERE WAS A TIME WHEN "HOME THEATER" MEANT CHARADES.
"HOME"?? I WANT THIS FOR MY BEDROOM.
AMEND

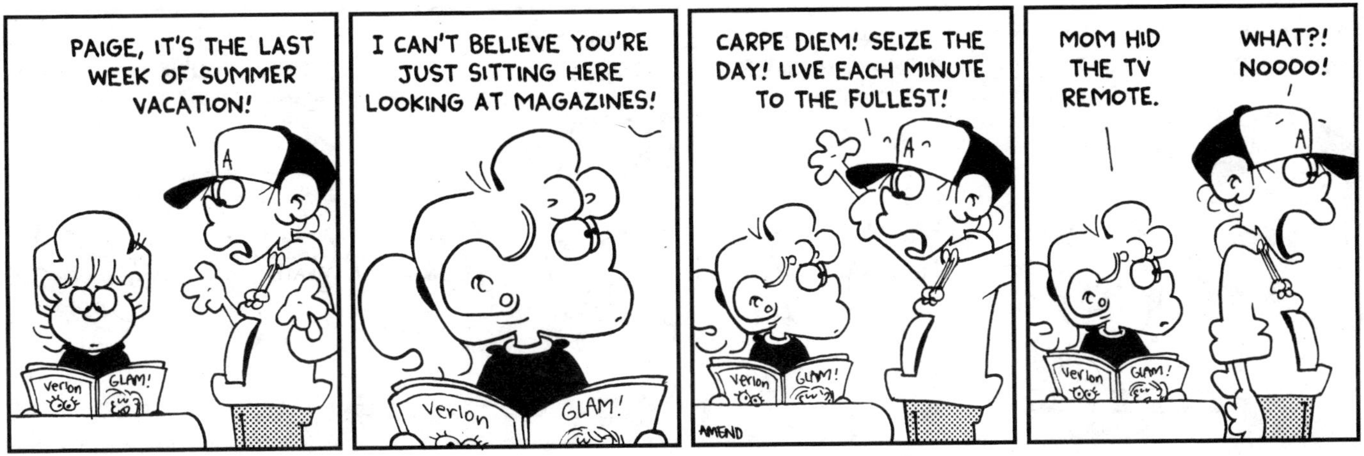
PAIGE, IT'S THE LAST WEEK OF SUMMER VACATION!
I CAN'T BELIEVE YOU'RE JUST SITTING HERE LOOKING AT MAGAZINES!
CARPE DIEM! SEIZE THE DAY! LIVE EACH MINUTE TO THE FULLEST!
MOM HID THE TV REMOTE.
WHAT?! NOOOO!

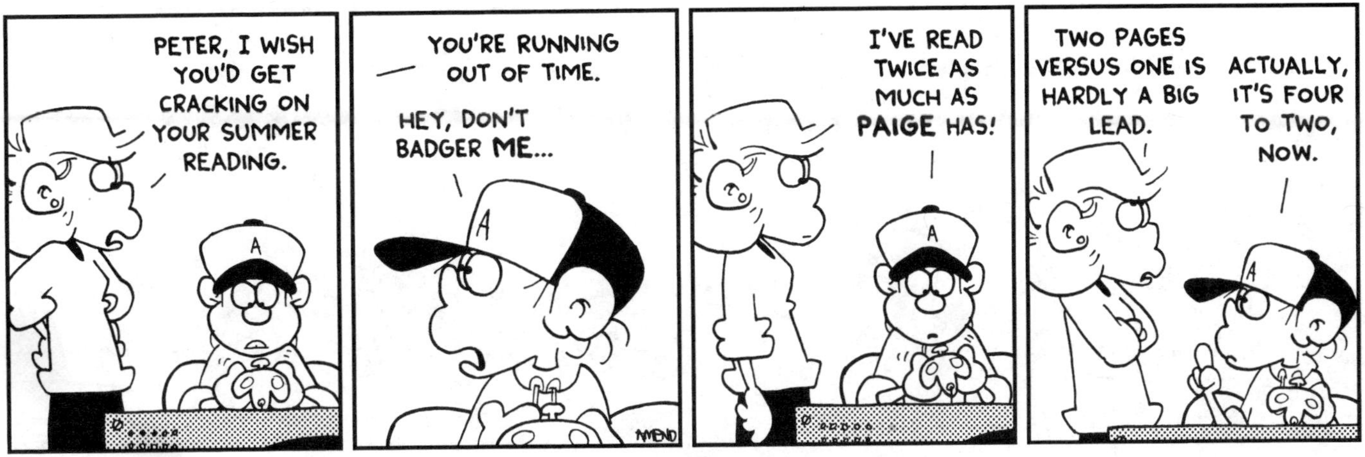
PETER, I WISH YOU'D GET CRACKING ON YOUR SUMMER READING.
YOU'RE RUNNING OUT OF TIME.
HEY, DON'T BADGER **ME**...
I'VE READ TWICE AS MUCH AS **PAIGE** HAS!
TWO PAGES VERSUS ONE IS HARDLY A BIG LEAD.
ACTUALLY, IT'S FOUR TO TWO, NOW.

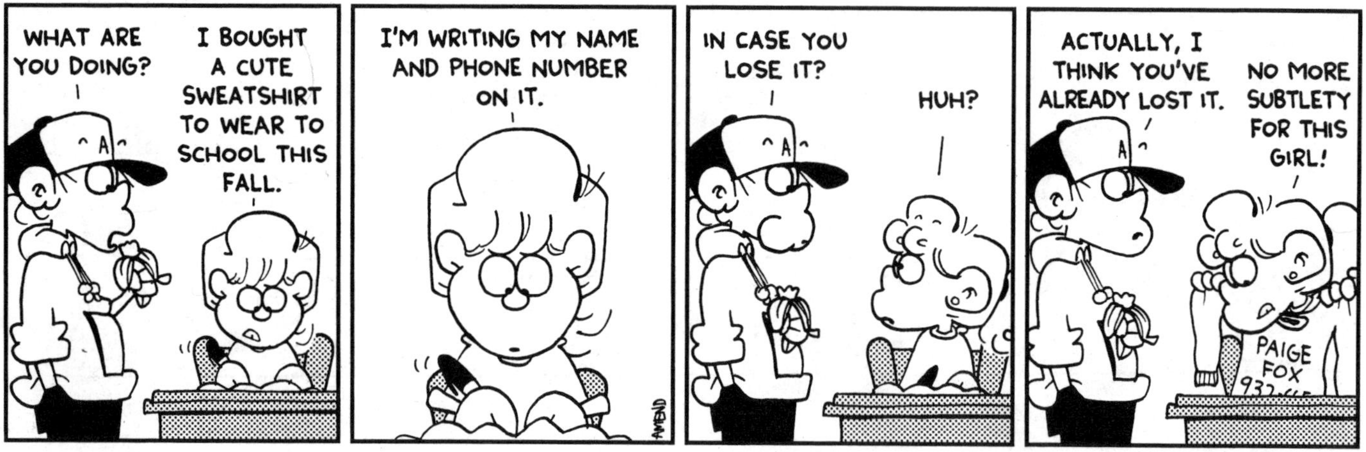
WHAT ARE YOU DOING?
I BOUGHT A CUTE SWEATSHIRT TO WEAR TO SCHOOL THIS FALL.
I'M WRITING MY NAME AND PHONE NUMBER ON IT.
AMEND
IN CASE YOU LOSE IT?
HUH?
ACTUALLY, I THINK YOU'VE ALREADY LOST IT.
NO MORE SUBTLETY FOR THIS GIRL!
PAIGE FOX

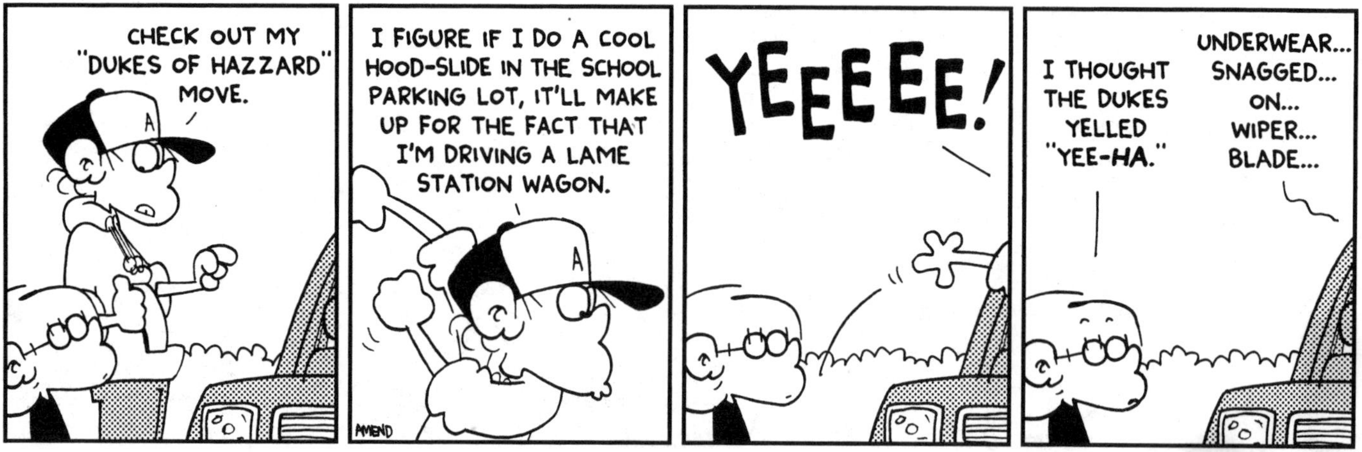
CHECK OUT MY "DUKES OF HAZZARD" MOVE.
I FIGURE IF I DO A COOL HOOD-SLIDE IN THE SCHOOL PARKING LOT, IT'LL MAKE UP FOR THE FACT THAT I'M DRIVING A LAME STATION WAGON.
AMEND
YEEEEE!
I THOUGHT THE DUKES YELLED "YEE-HA."
UNDERWEAR... SNAGGED... ON... WIPER... BLADE...

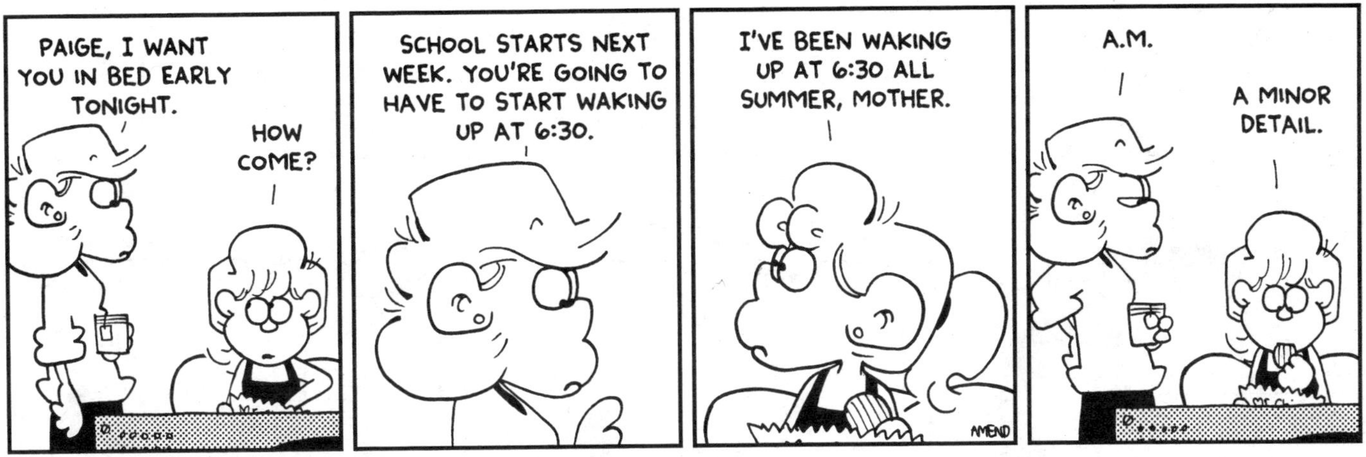
PAIGE, I WANT YOU IN BED EARLY TONIGHT.
HOW COME?
SCHOOL STARTS NEXT WEEK. YOU'RE GOING TO HAVE TO START WAKING UP AT 6:30.
I'VE BEEN WAKING UP AT 6:30 ALL SUMMER, MOTHER.
AMEND
A.M.
A MINOR DETAIL.

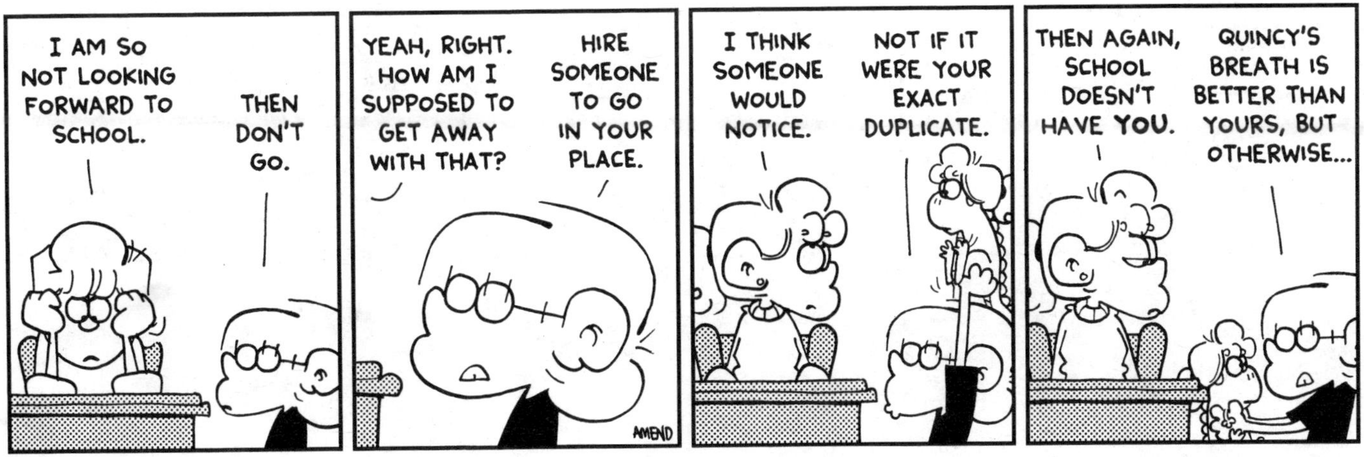
I AM SO NOT LOOKING FORWARD TO SCHOOL.
THEN DON'T GO.
YEAH, RIGHT. HOW AM I SUPPOSED TO GET AWAY WITH THAT?
HIRE SOMEONE TO GO IN YOUR PLACE.
AMEND
I THINK SOMEONE WOULD NOTICE.
NOT IF IT WERE YOUR EXACT DUPLICATE.
THEN AGAIN, SCHOOL DOESN'T HAVE YOU.
QUINCY'S BREATH IS BETTER THAN YOURS, BUT OTHERWISE...

CHECK IT OUT!
DAD SAID I COULD HAVE HIS OLD BRIEFCASE!
NOW I CAN KEEP MY HOMEWORK NICE AND CRISP WHEN I GO TO AND FROM SCHOOL!
AND I CAN CHANGE THE LOCK COMBINATION DAILY, TO THWART ANY WOULD-BE HOMEWORK THIEVES!
AND IF IT'S REALLY IMPORTANT HOMEWORK, I CAN HANDCUFF IT TO MY WRIST, LIKE THEY DO WITH THINGS LIKE NUCLEAR SECRETS.
AND WHEN YOUR CLASSMATES SHOOT SPITBALLS AT YOU FOR BEING SUCH A DWEEB, YOU CAN USE IT AS A SHIELD.
OOO— I HADN'T THOUGHT OF THAT!
AMEND

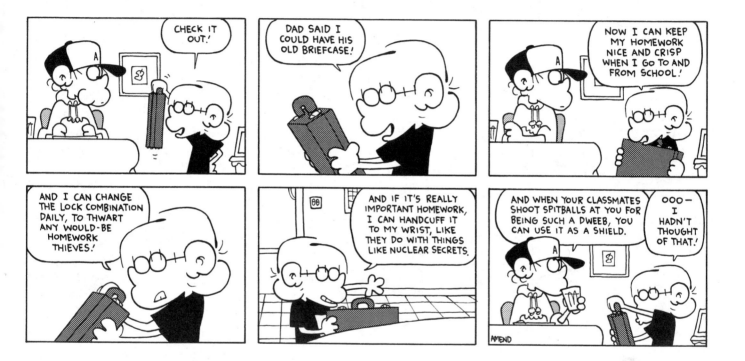

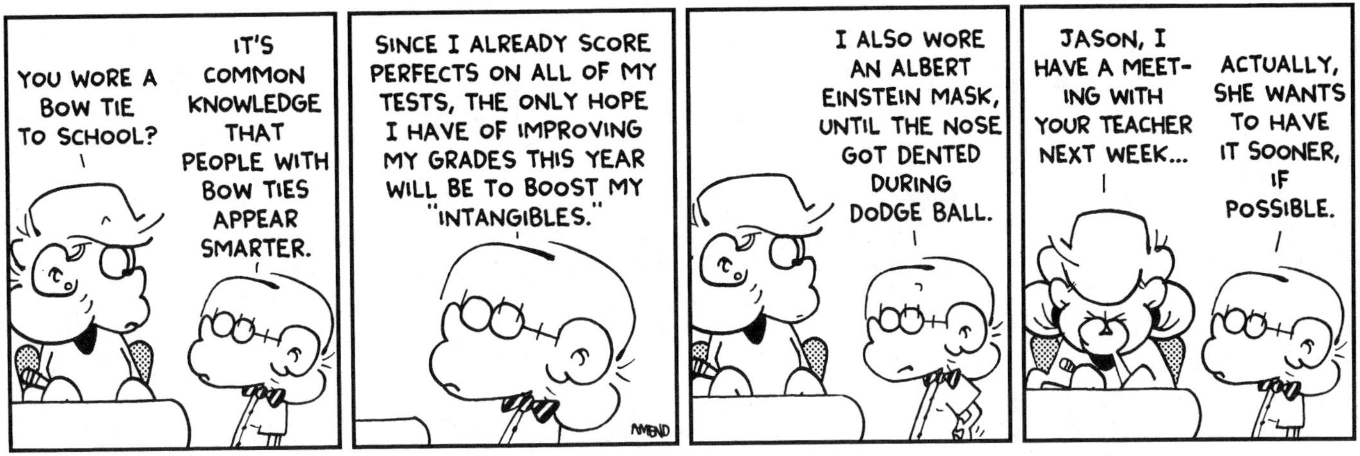
YOU WORE A BOW TIE TO SCHOOL?
IT'S COMMON KNOWLEDGE THAT PEOPLE WITH BOW TIES APPEAR SMARTER.
SINCE I ALREADY SCORE PERFECTS ON ALL OF MY TESTS, THE ONLY HOPE I HAVE OF IMPROVING MY GRADES THIS YEAR WILL BE TO BOOST MY "INTANGIBLES."
AMEND
I ALSO WORE AN ALBERT EINSTEIN MASK, UNTIL THE NOSE GOT DENTED DURING DODGE BALL.
JASON, I HAVE A MEETING WITH YOUR TEACHER NEXT WEEK...
ACTUALLY, SHE WANTS TO HAVE IT SOONER, IF POSSIBLE.

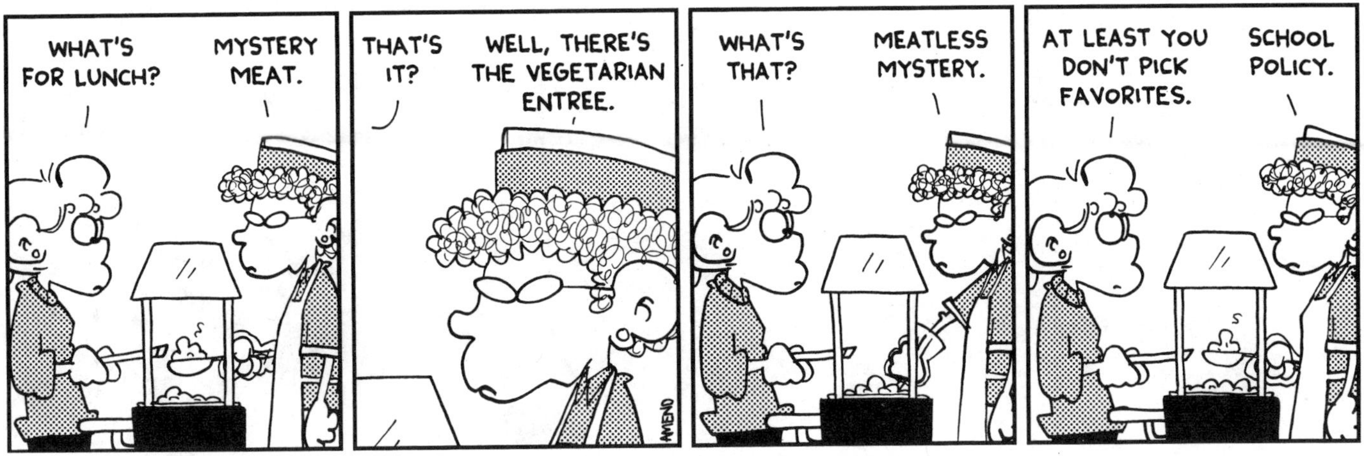
WHAT'S FOR LUNCH?
MYSTERY MEAT.
THAT'S IT?
WELL, THERE'S THE VEGETARIAN ENTREE.
AMEND
WHAT'S THAT?
MEATLESS MYSTERY.
AT LEAST YOU DON'T PICK FAVORITES.
SCHOOL POLICY.

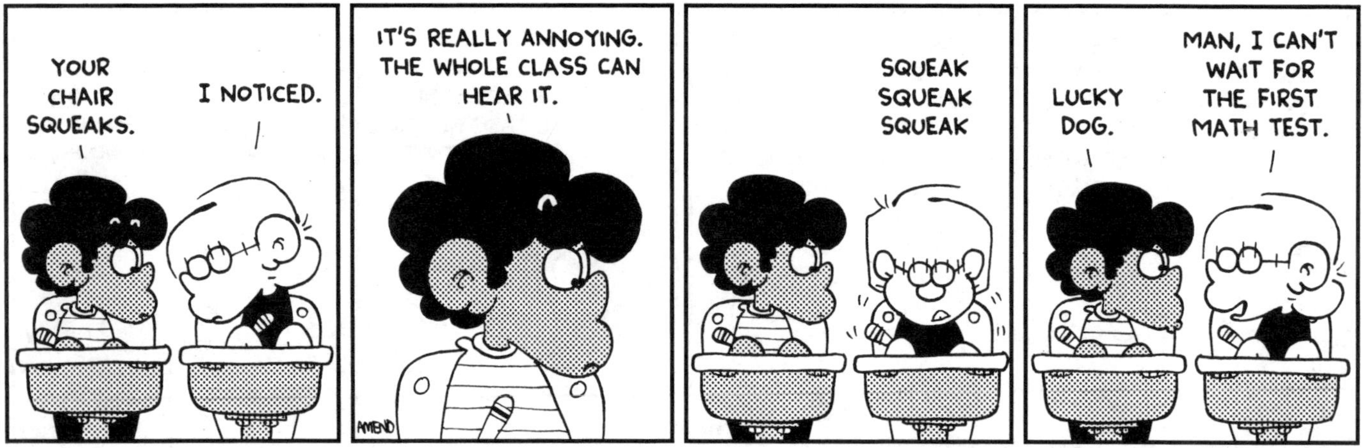
YOUR CHAIR SQUEAKS.
I NOTICED.
IT'S REALLY ANNOYING. THE WHOLE CLASS CAN HEAR IT.
AMEND
SQUEAK SQUEAK SQUEAK
LUCKY DOG.
MAN, I CAN'T WAIT FOR THE FIRST MATH TEST.

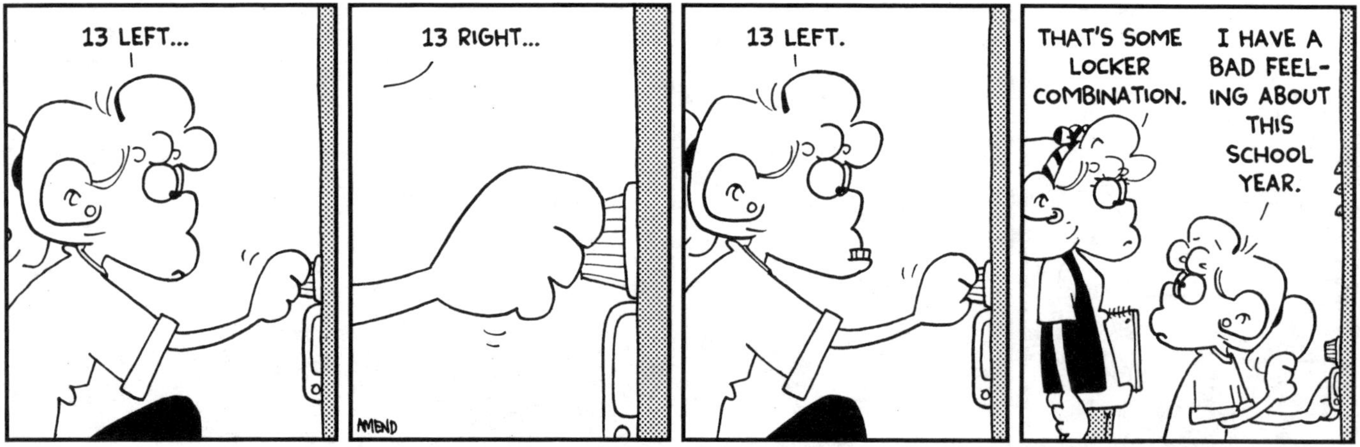
13 LEFT...
13 RIGHT...
AMEND
13 LEFT.
THAT'S SOME LOCKER COMBINATION.
I HAVE A BAD FEELING ABOUT THIS SCHOOL YEAR.

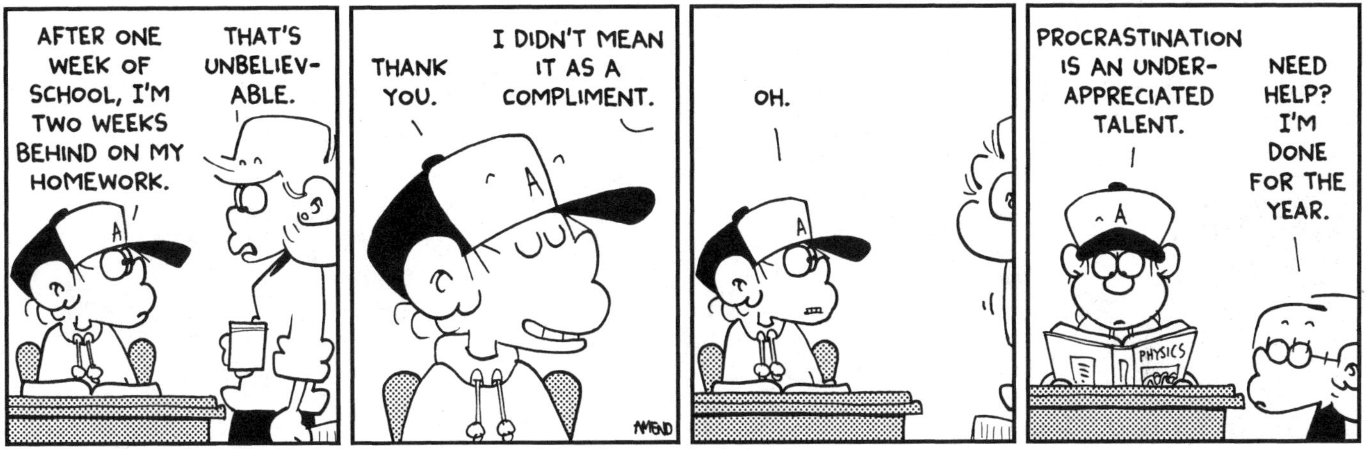
AFTER ONE WEEK OF SCHOOL, I'M TWO WEEKS BEHIND ON MY HOMEWORK.
THAT'S UNBELIEV-ABLE.
THANK YOU.
I DIDN'T MEAN IT AS A COMPLIMENT.
AMEND
OH.
PROCRASTINATION IS AN UNDER-APPRECIATED TALENT.
NEED HELP? I'M DONE FOR THE YEAR.
PHYSICS

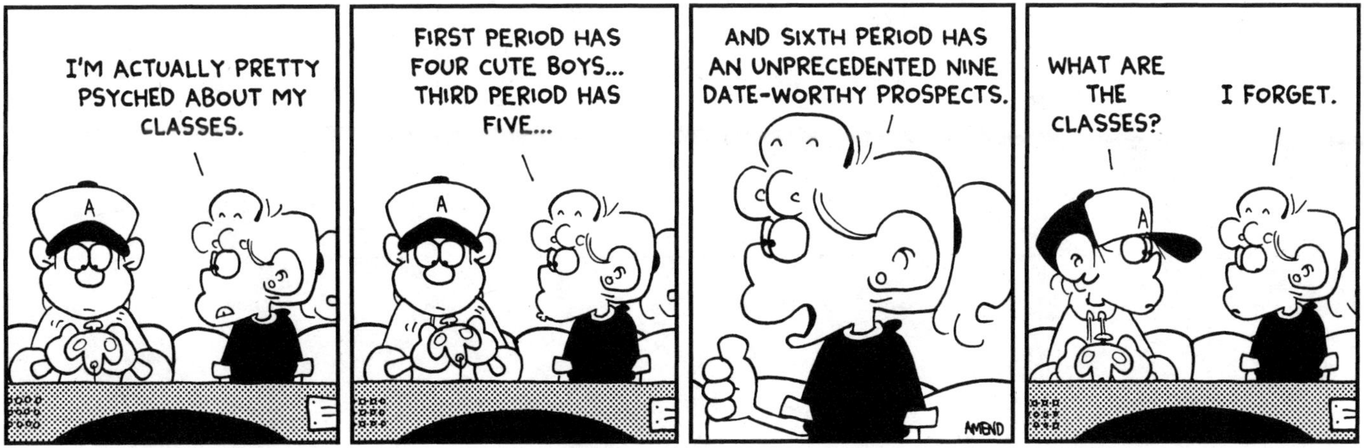
I'M ACTUALLY PRETTY PSYCHED ABOUT MY CLASSES.
FIRST PERIOD HAS FOUR CUTE BOYS... THIRD PERIOD HAS FIVE...
AND SIXTH PERIOD HAS AN UNPRECEDENTED NINE DATE-WORTHY PROSPECTS.
AMEND
WHAT ARE THE CLASSES?
I FORGET.

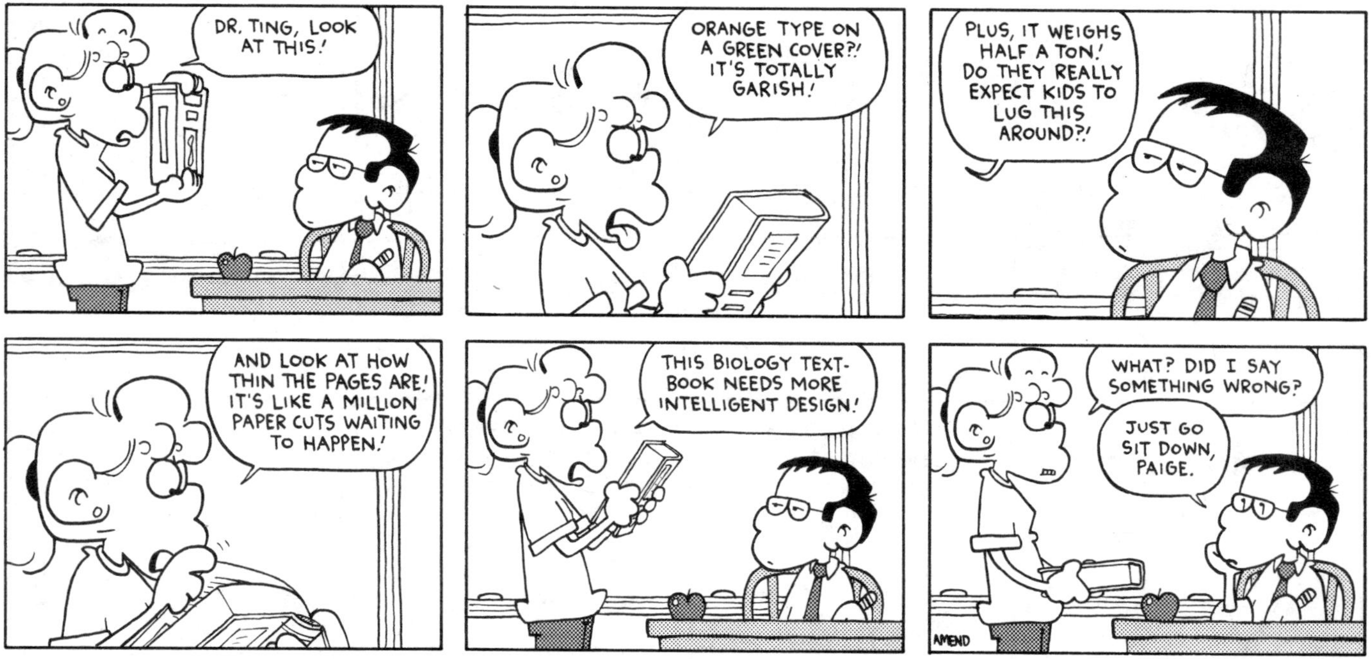

DR. TING, LOOK AT THIS!
ORANGE TYPE ON A GREEN COVER?! IT'S TOTALLY GARISH!
PLUS, IT WEIGHS HALF A TON! DO THEY REALLY EXPECT KIDS TO LUG THIS AROUND?!
AND LOOK AT HOW THIN THE PAGES ARE! IT'S LIKE A MILLION PAPER CUTS WAITING TO HAPPEN!
THIS BIOLOGY TEXT-BOOK NEEDS MORE INTELLIGENT DESIGN!
WHAT? DID I SAY SOMETHING WRONG?
JUST GO SIT DOWN, PAIGE.
AMEND

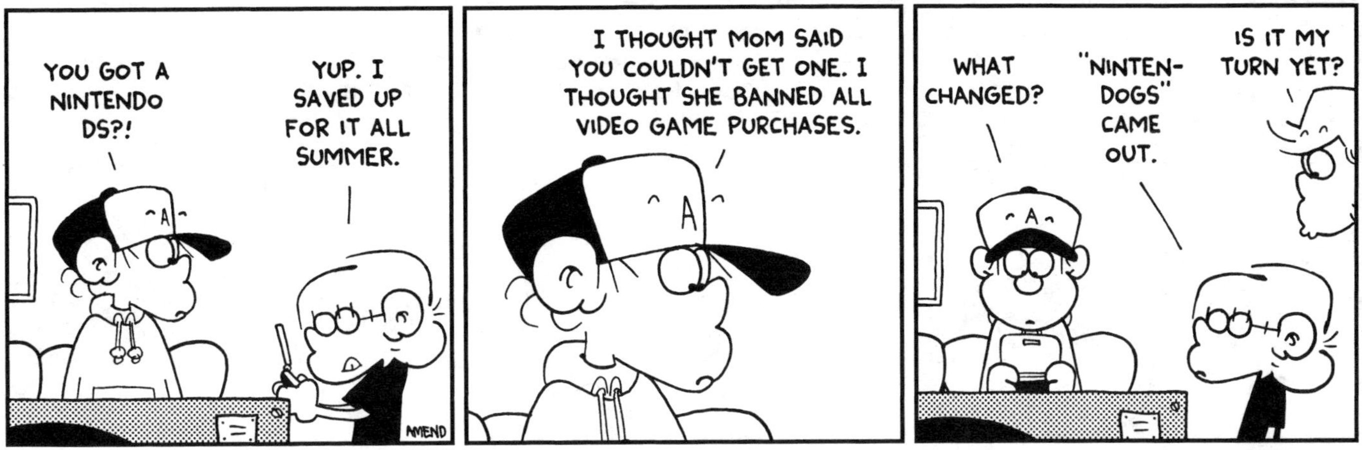
YOU GOT A NINTENDO DS?!
YUP. I SAVED UP FOR IT ALL SUMMER.
AMEND
I THOUGHT MOM SAID YOU COULDN'T GET ONE. I THOUGHT SHE BANNED ALL VIDEO GAME PURCHASES.
WHAT CHANGED?
"NINTEN-DOGS" CAME OUT.
IS IT MY TURN YET?

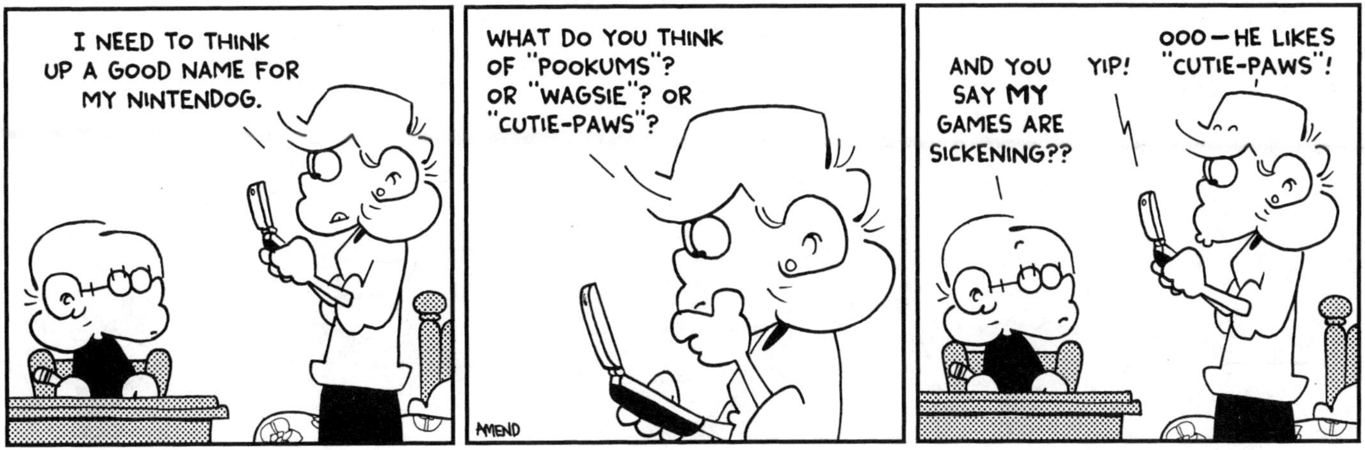
I NEED TO THINK UP A GOOD NAME FOR MY NINTENDOG.
WHAT DO YOU THINK OF "POOKUMS"? OR "WAGSIE"? OR "CUTIE-PAWS"?
AMEND
AND YOU SAY **MY** GAMES ARE SICKENING??
YIP!
OOO—HE LIKES "CUTIE-PAWS"!

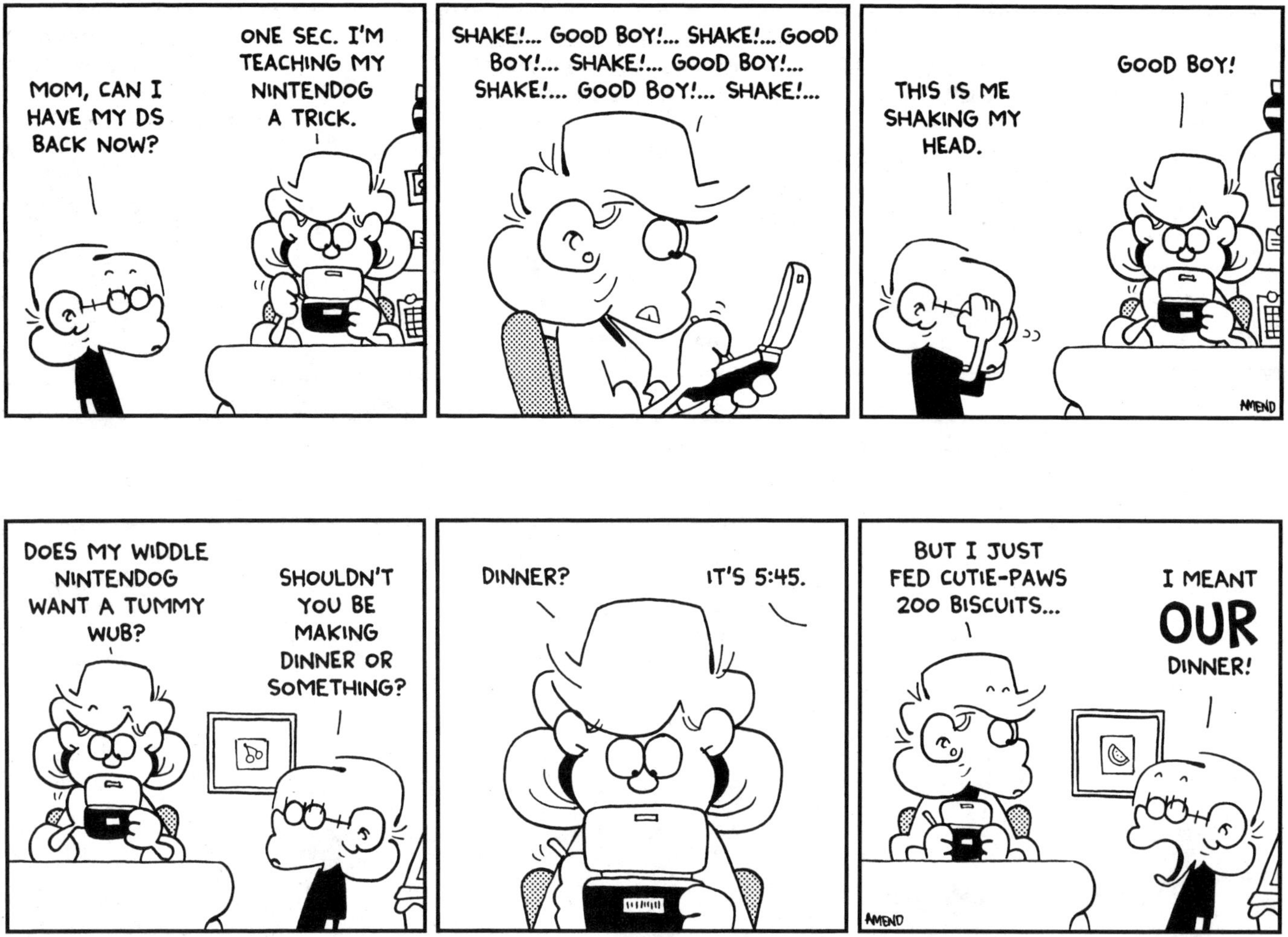
MOM, CAN I HAVE MY DS BACK NOW?
ONE SEC. I'M TEACHING MY NINTENDOG A TRICK.
SHAKE!... GOOD BOY!... SHAKE!... GOOD BOY!... SHAKE!... GOOD BOY!... SHAKE!... GOOD BOY!... SHAKE!...
THIS IS ME SHAKING MY HEAD.
GOOD BOY!
AMEND
DOES MY WIDDLE NINTENDOG WANT A TUMMY WUB?
SHOULDN'T YOU BE MAKING DINNER OR SOMETHING?
DINNER?
IT'S 5:45.
BUT I JUST FED CUTIE-PAWS 200 BISCUITS...
I MEANT **OUR** DINNER!
AMEND

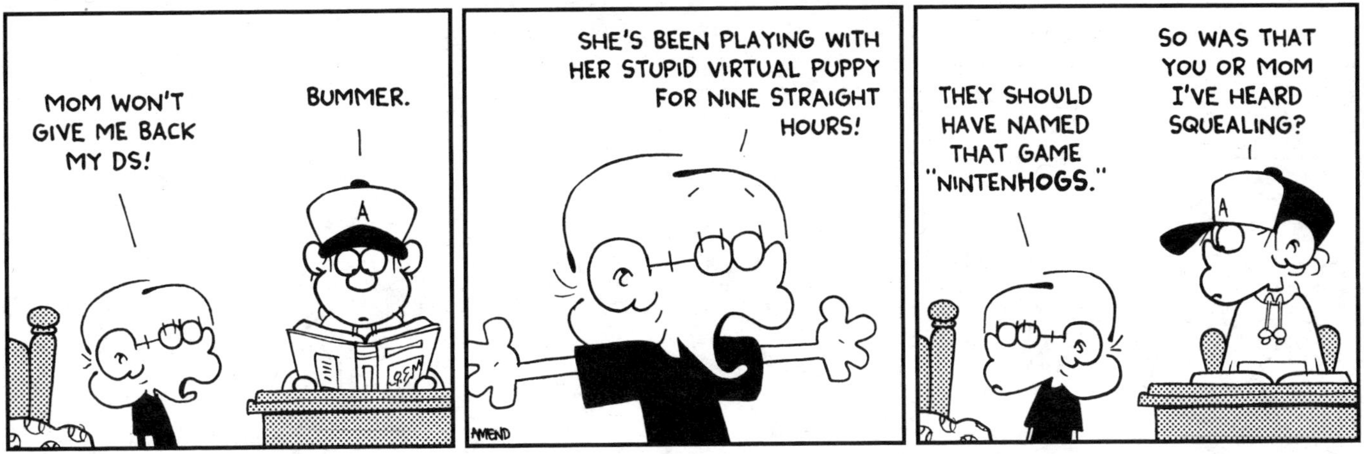
MOM WON'T GIVE ME BACK MY DS!
BUMMER.
SHE'S BEEN PLAYING WITH HER STUPID VIRTUAL PUPPY FOR NINE STRAIGHT HOURS!
AMEND
THEY SHOULD HAVE NAMED THAT GAME "NINTENHOGS."
SO WAS THAT YOU OR MOM I'VE HEARD SQUEALING?

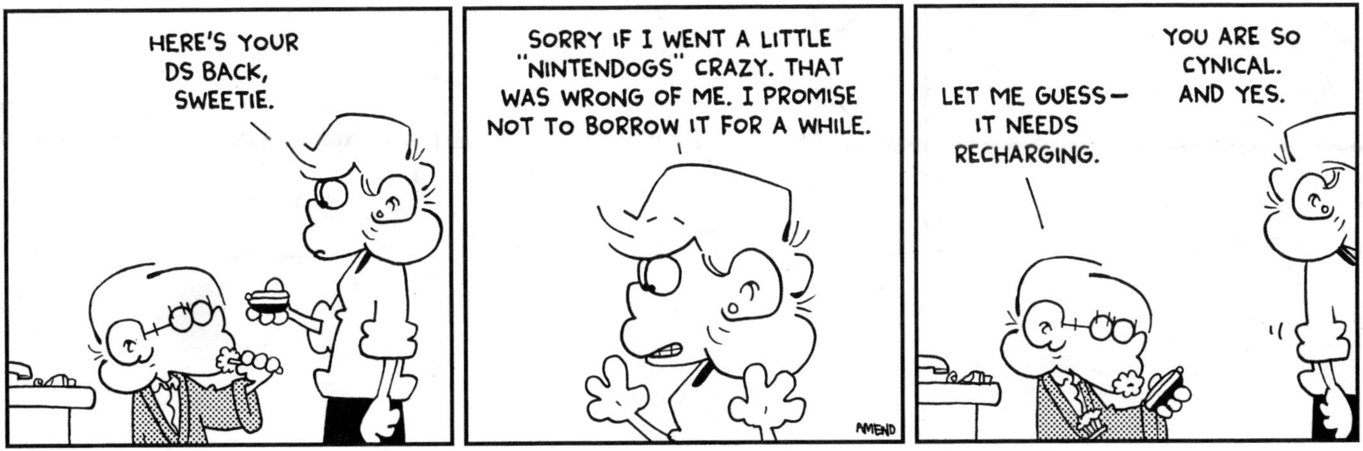
HERE'S YOUR DS BACK, SWEETIE.
SORRY IF I WENT A LITTLE "NINTENDOGS" CRAZY. THAT WAS WRONG OF ME. I PROMISE NOT TO BORROW IT FOR A WHILE.
AMEND
LET ME GUESS— IT NEEDS RECHARGING.
YOU ARE SO CYNICAL. AND YES.

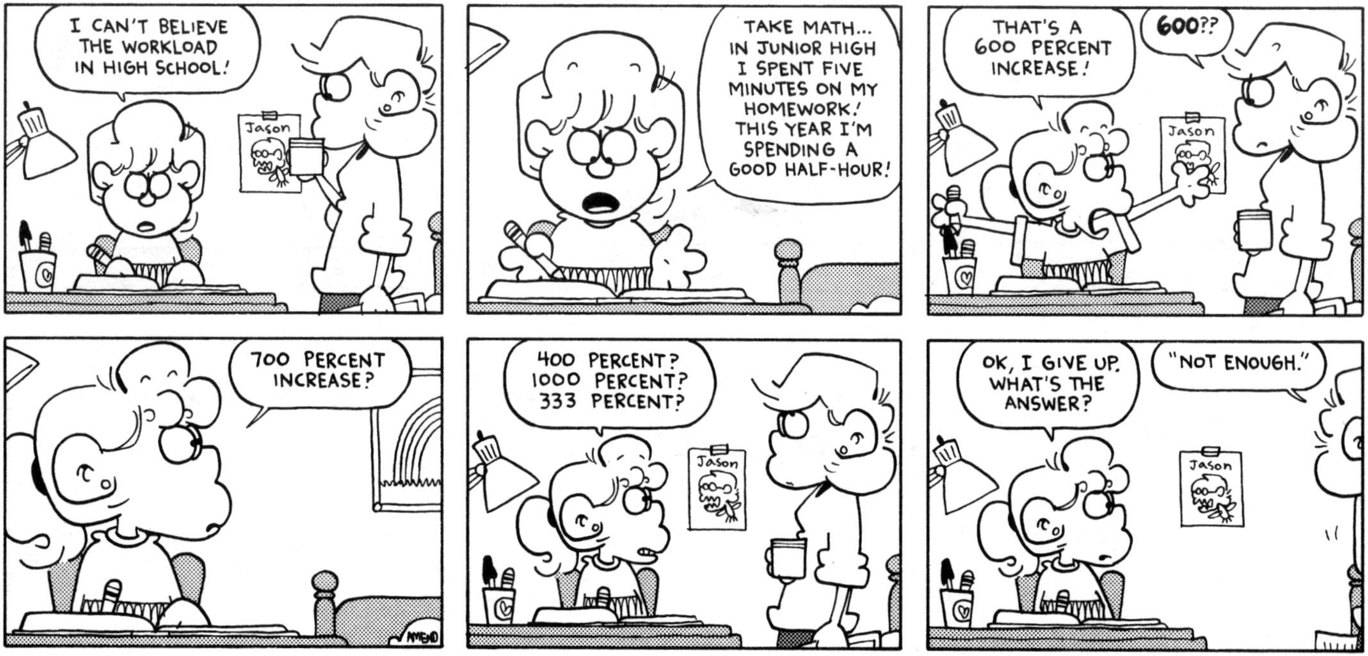
I CAN'T BELIEVE THE WORKLOAD IN HIGH SCHOOL!
Jason
TAKE MATH... IN JUNIOR HIGH I SPENT FIVE MINUTES ON MY HOMEWORK! THIS YEAR I'M SPENDING A GOOD HALF-HOUR!
THAT'S A 600 PERCENT INCREASE!
600??
Jason
700 PERCENT INCREASE?
400 PERCENT? 1000 PERCENT? 333 PERCENT?
Jason
OK, I GIVE UP. WHAT'S THE ANSWER?
"NOT ENOUGH."
Jason

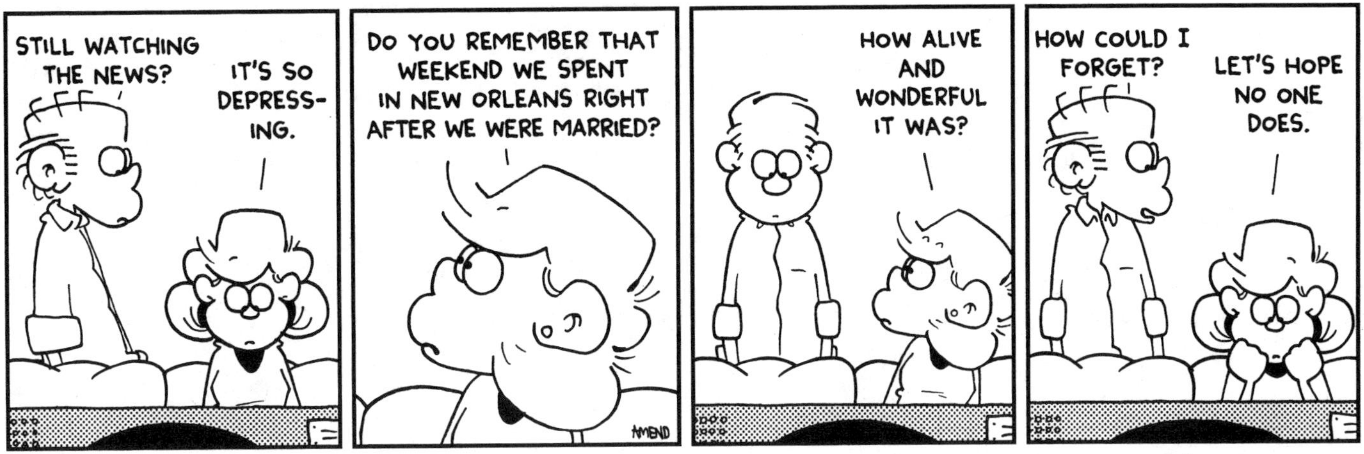
STILL WATCHING THE NEWS?
IT'S SO DEPRESS-ING.
DO YOU REMEMBER THAT WEEKEND WE SPENT IN NEW ORLEANS RIGHT AFTER WE WERE MARRIED?
HOW ALIVE AND WONDERFUL IT WAS?
HOW COULD I FORGET?
LET'S HOPE NO ONE DOES.
AMEND

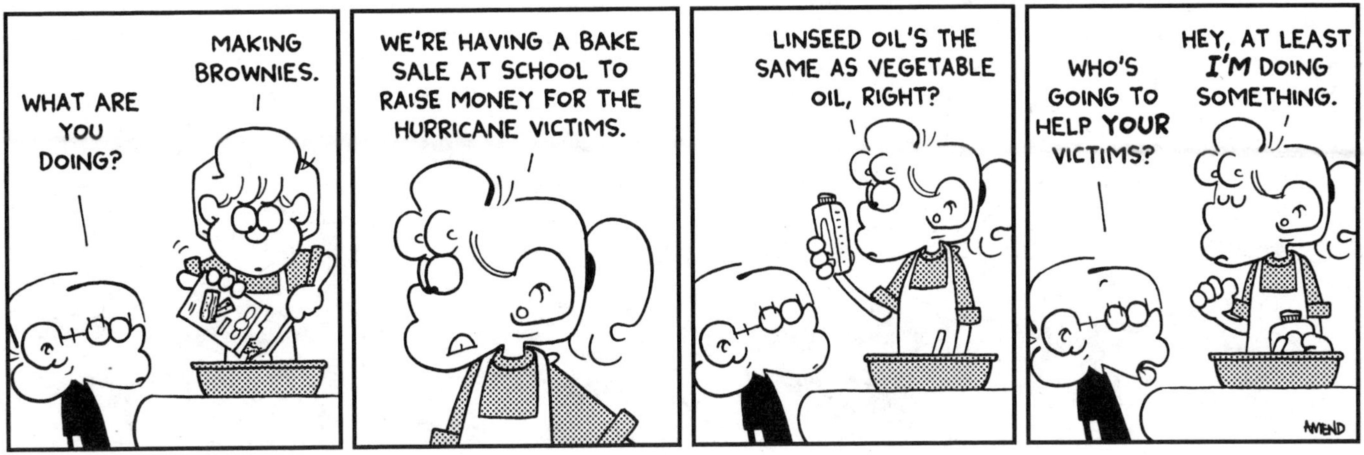
WHAT ARE YOU DOING?
MAKING BROWNIES.
WE'RE HAVING A BAKE SALE AT SCHOOL TO RAISE MONEY FOR THE HURRICANE VICTIMS.
LINSEED OIL'S THE SAME AS VEGETABLE OIL, RIGHT?
WHO'S GOING TO HELP **YOUR** VICTIMS?
HEY, AT LEAST ***I'M*** DOING SOMETHING.
AMEND

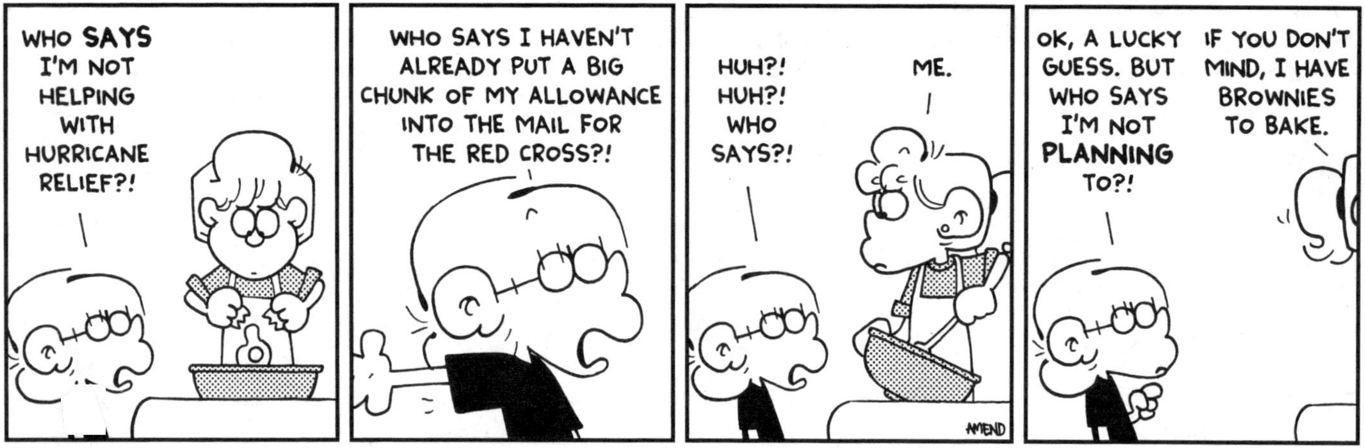
WHO SAYS I'M NOT HELPING WITH HURRICANE RELIEF?!
WHO SAYS I HAVEN'T ALREADY PUT A BIG CHUNK OF MY ALLOWANCE INTO THE MAIL FOR THE RED CROSS?!
HUH?! HUH?! WHO SAYS?!
ME.
AMEND
OK, A LUCKY GUESS. BUT WHO SAYS I'M NOT PLANNING TO?!
IF YOU DON'T MIND, I HAVE BROWNIES TO BAKE.

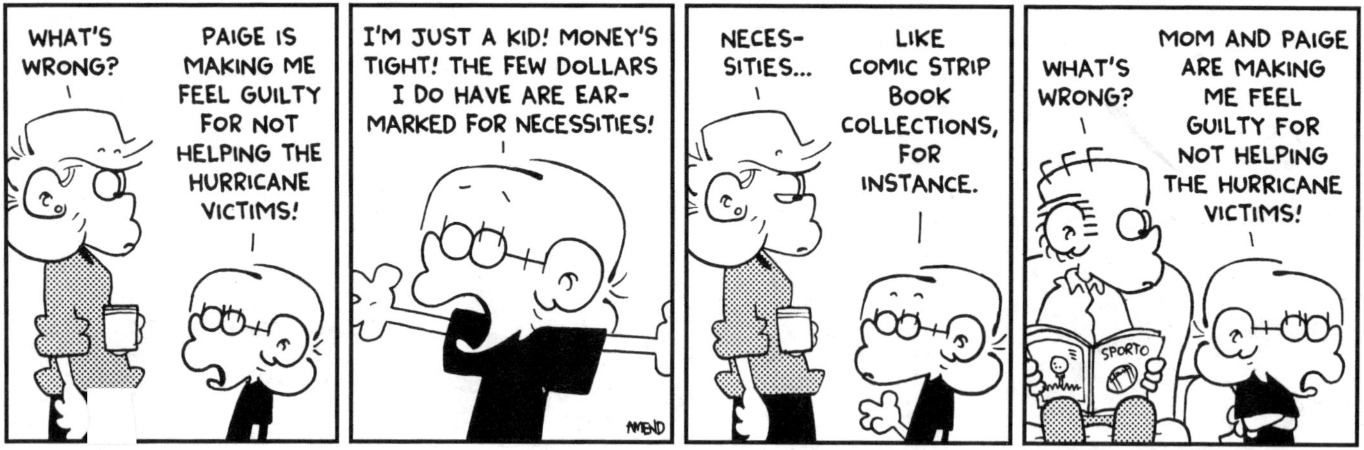
WHAT'S WRONG?
PAIGE IS MAKING ME FEEL GUILTY FOR NOT HELPING THE HURRICANE VICTIMS!
I'M JUST A KID! MONEY'S TIGHT! THE FEW DOLLARS I DO HAVE ARE EAR-MARKED FOR NECESSITIES!
AMEND
NECES-SITIES...
LIKE COMIC STRIP BOOK COLLECTIONS, FOR INSTANCE.
WHAT'S WRONG?
MOM AND PAIGE ARE MAKING ME FEEL GUILTY FOR NOT HELPING THE HURRICANE VICTIMS!
SPORTO

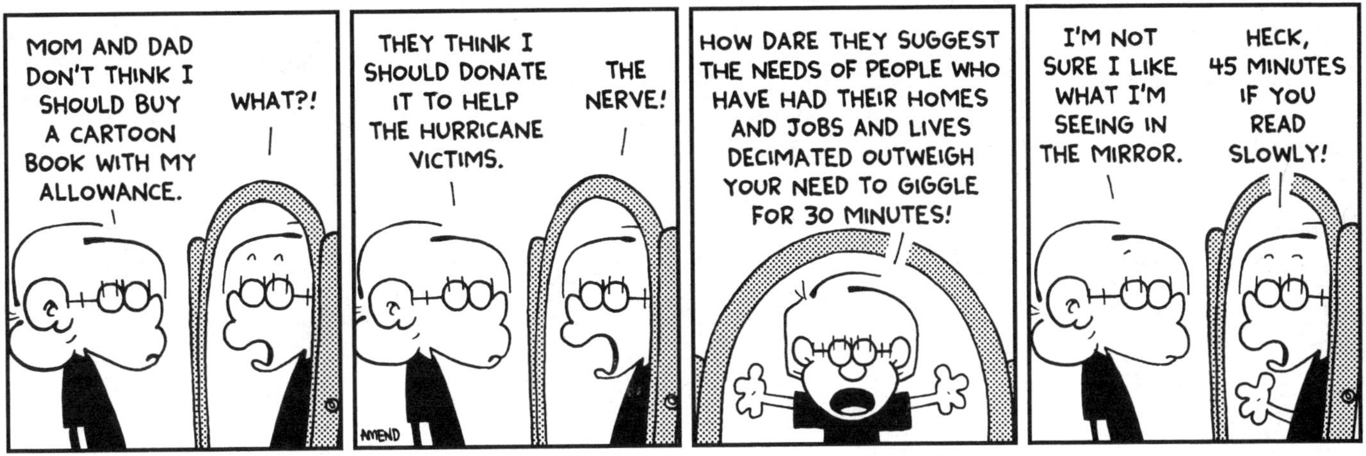
MOM AND DAD DON'T THINK I SHOULD BUY A CARTOON BOOK WITH MY ALLOWANCE.
WHAT?!
THEY THINK I SHOULD DONATE IT TO HELP THE HURRICANE VICTIMS.
THE NERVE!
AMEND
HOW DARE THEY SUGGEST THE NEEDS OF PEOPLE WHO HAVE HAD THEIR HOMES AND JOBS AND LIVES DECIMATED OUTWEIGH YOUR NEED TO GIGGLE FOR 30 MINUTES!
I'M NOT SURE I LIKE WHAT I'M SEEING IN THE MIRROR.
HECK, 45 MINUTES IF YOU READ SLOWLY!

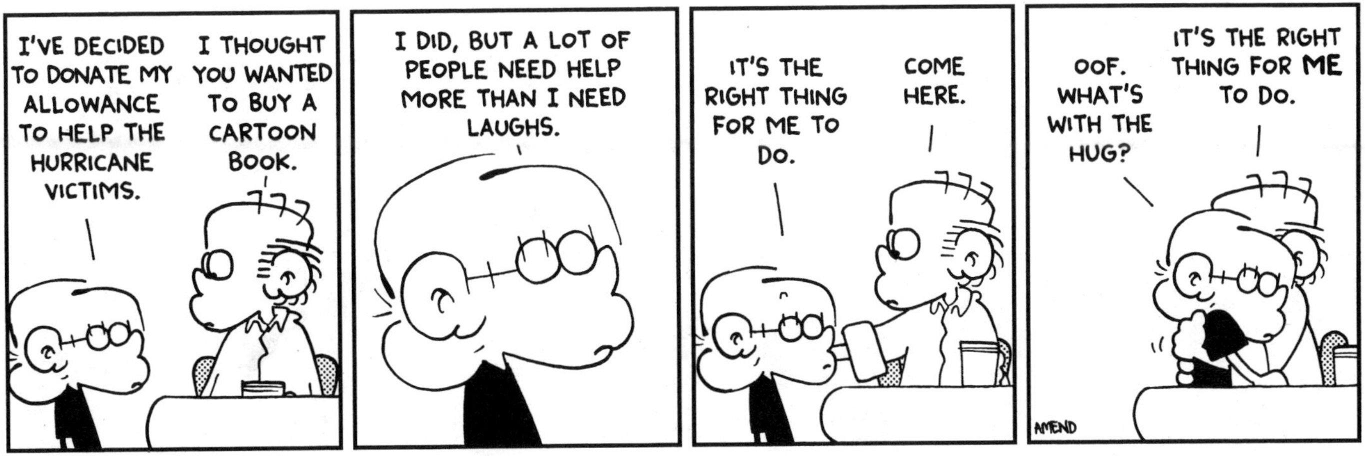
I'VE DECIDED TO DONATE MY ALLOWANCE TO HELP THE HURRICANE VICTIMS.
I THOUGHT YOU WANTED TO BUY A CARTOON BOOK.
I DID, BUT A LOT OF PEOPLE NEED HELP MORE THAN I NEED LAUGHS.
IT'S THE RIGHT THING FOR ME TO DO.
COME HERE.
OOF. WHAT'S WITH THE HUG?
IT'S THE RIGHT THING FOR ME TO DO.
AMEND

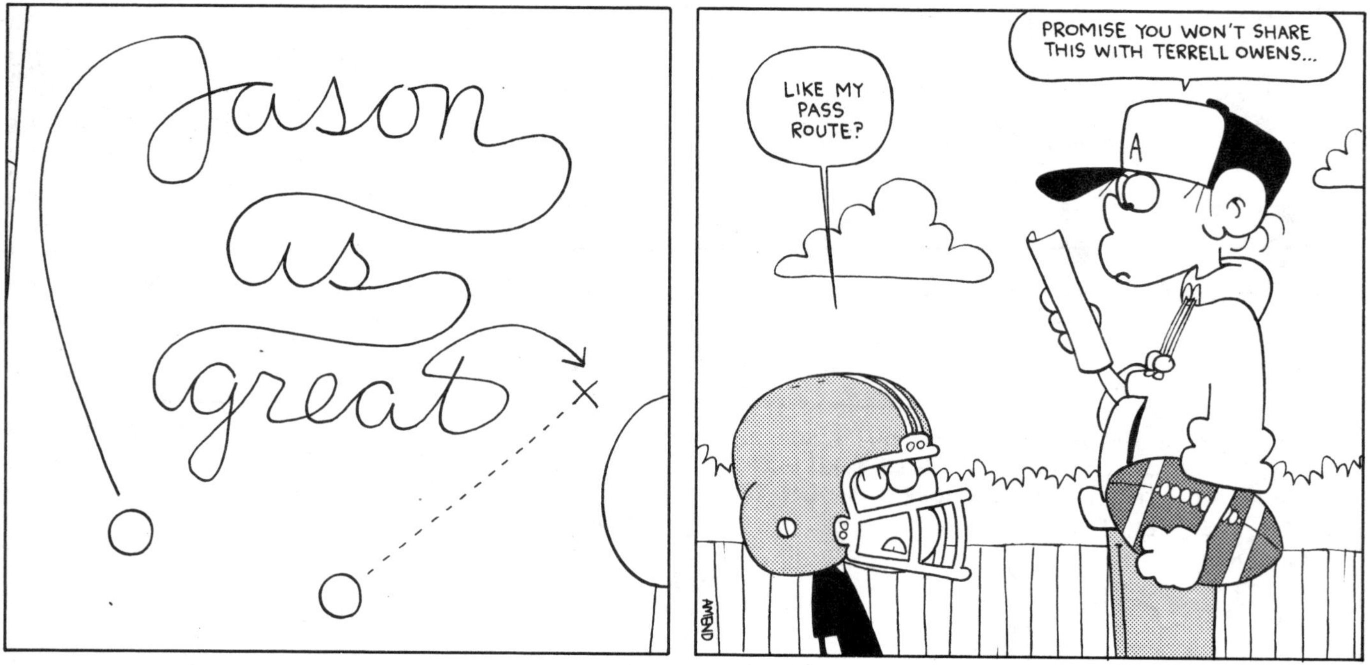
Jason is great
LIKE MY PASS ROUTE?
PROMISE YOU WON'T SHARE THIS WITH TERRELL OWENS...
AMEND

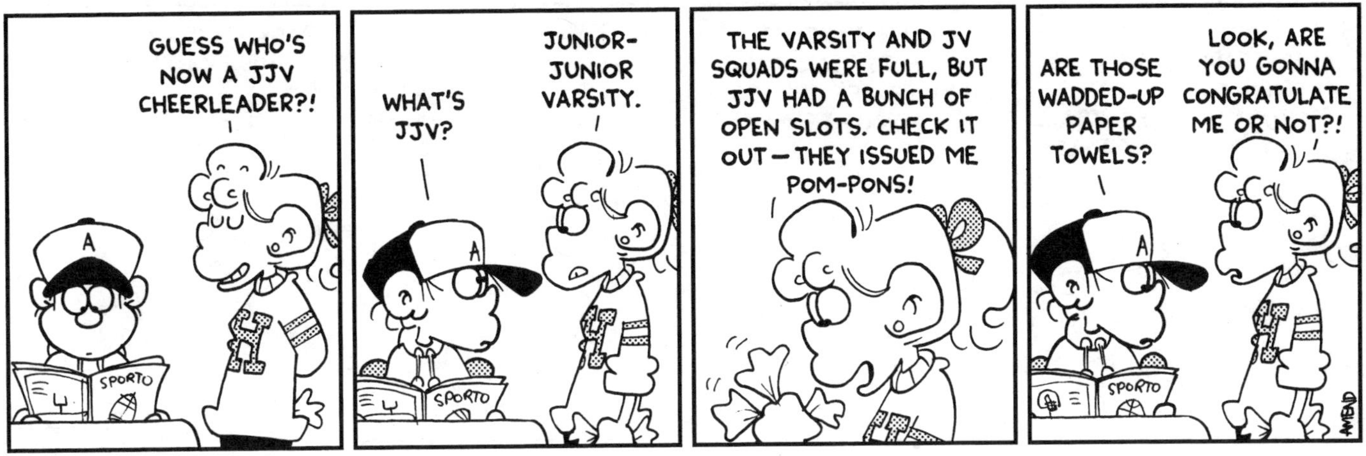
GUESS WHO'S NOW A JJV CHEERLEADER?!
SPORTO
WHAT'S JJV?
JUNIOR-JUNIOR VARSITY.
SPORTO
THE VARSITY AND JV SQUADS WERE FULL, BUT JJV HAD A BUNCH OF OPEN SLOTS. CHECK IT OUT — THEY ISSUED ME POM-PONS!
ARE THOSE WADDED-UP PAPER TOWELS?
LOOK, ARE YOU GONNA CONGRATULATE ME OR NOT?!
SPORTO

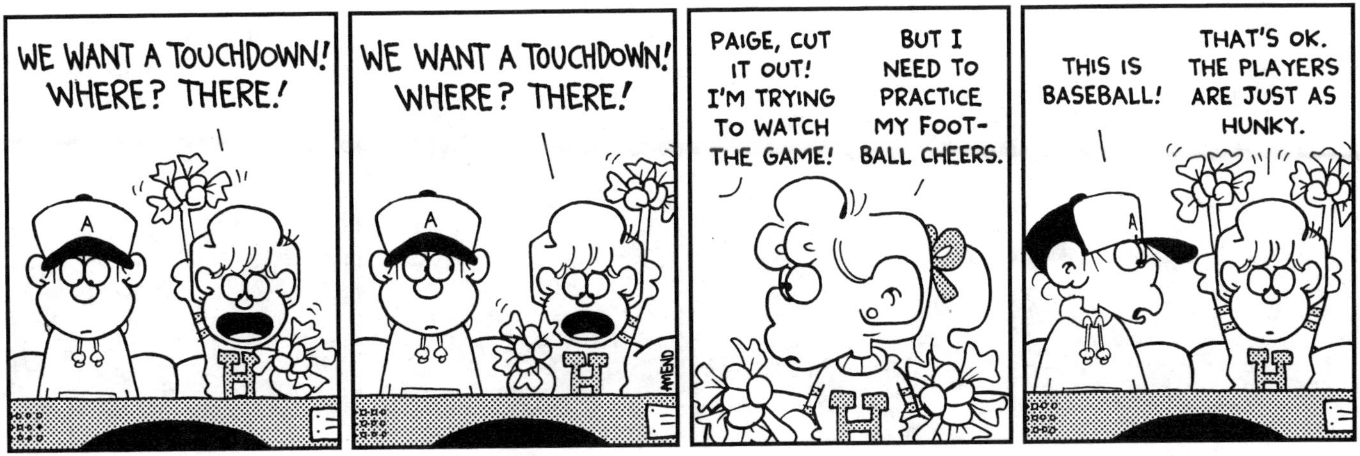
WE WANT A TOUCHDOWN! WHERE? THERE!
WE WANT A TOUCHDOWN! WHERE? THERE!
PAIGE, CUT IT OUT! I'M TRYING TO WATCH THE GAME!
BUT I NEED TO PRACTICE MY FOOT-BALL CHEERS.
THIS IS BASEBALL!
THAT'S OK. THE PLAYERS ARE JUST AS HUNKY.

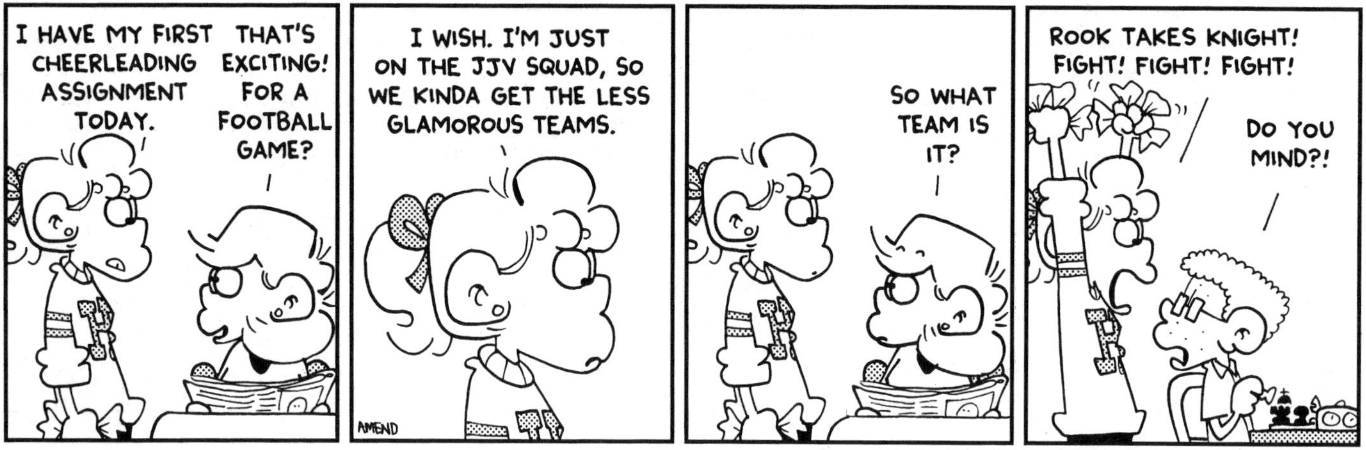
I HAVE MY FIRST CHEERLEADING ASSIGNMENT TODAY.
THAT'S EXCITING! FOR A FOOTBALL GAME?
I WISH. I'M JUST ON THE JJV SQUAD, SO WE KINDA GET THE LESS GLAMOROUS TEAMS.
AMEND
SO WHAT TEAM IS IT?
ROOK TAKES KNIGHT! FIGHT! FIGHT! FIGHT!
DO YOU MIND?!

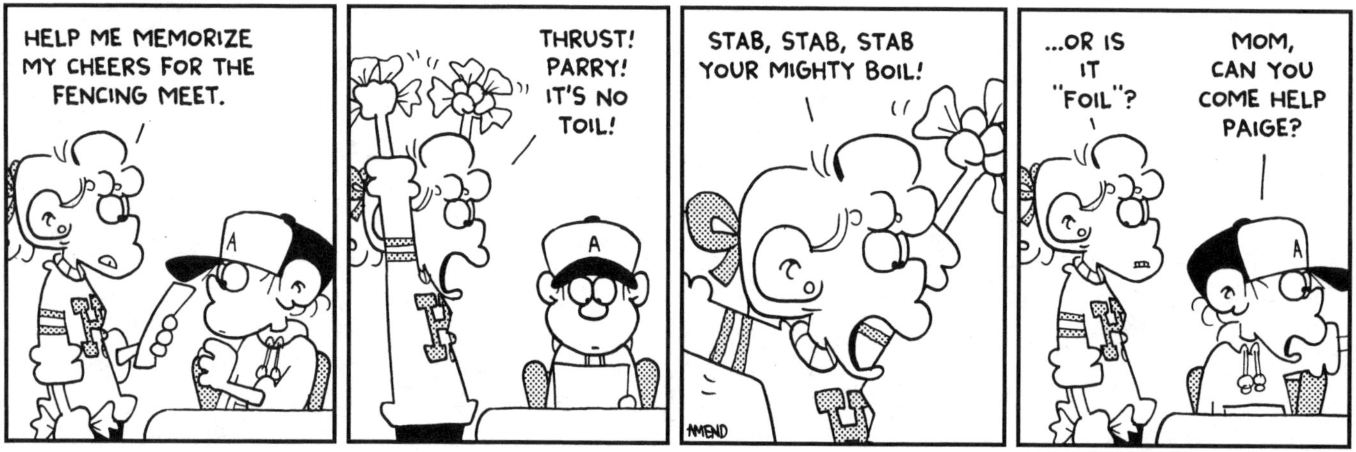
HELP ME MEMORIZE MY CHEERS FOR THE FENCING MEET.
THRUST! PARRY! IT'S NO TOIL!
STAB, STAB, STAB YOUR MIGHTY BOIL!
AMEND
...OR IS IT "FOIL"?
MOM, CAN YOU COME HELP PAIGE?

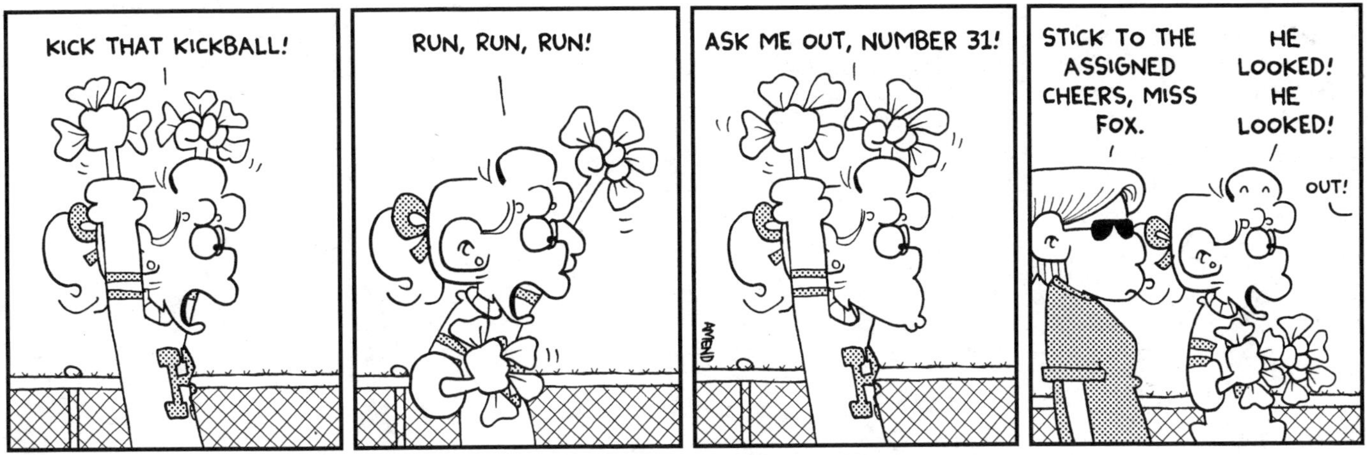
KICK THAT KICKBALL!
RUN, RUN, RUN!
ASK ME OUT, NUMBER 31!
STICK TO THE ASSIGNED CHEERS, MISS FOX.
HE LOOKED! HE LOOKED!
OUT!
AMEND

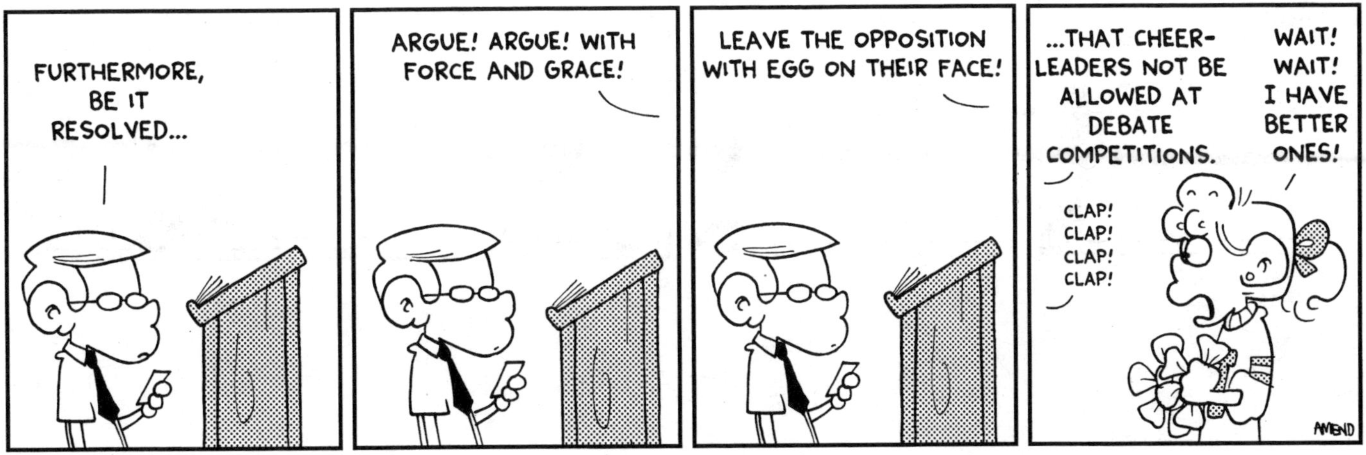
FURTHERMORE, BE IT RESOLVED...
ARGUE! ARGUE! WITH FORCE AND GRACE!
LEAVE THE OPPOSITION WITH EGG ON THEIR FACE!
...THAT CHEER-LEADERS NOT BE ALLOWED AT DEBATE COMPETITIONS.
CLAP! CLAP! CLAP! CLAP!
WAIT! WAIT! I HAVE BETTER ONES!
AMEND

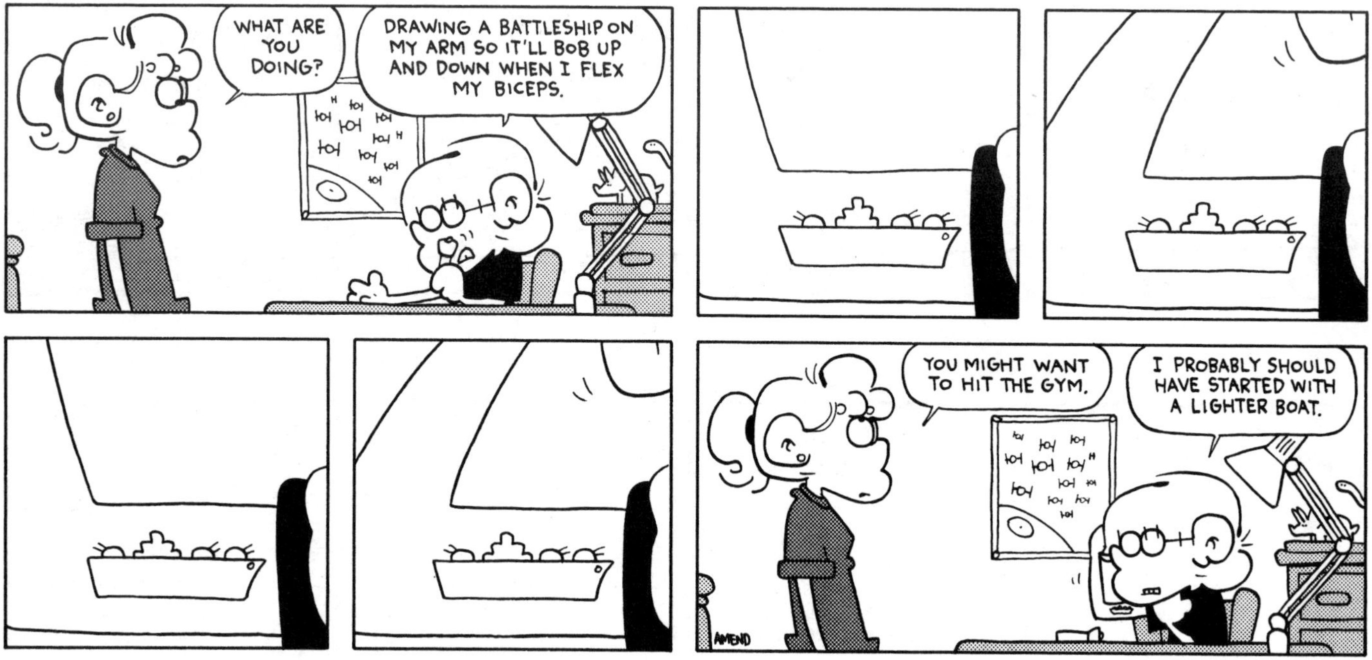
WHAT ARE YOU DOING?
DRAWING A BATTLESHIP ON MY ARM SO IT'LL BOB UP AND DOWN WHEN I FLEX MY BICEPS.
YOU MIGHT WANT TO HIT THE GYM.
I PROBABLY SHOULD HAVE STARTED WITH A LIGHTER BOAT.
AMEND

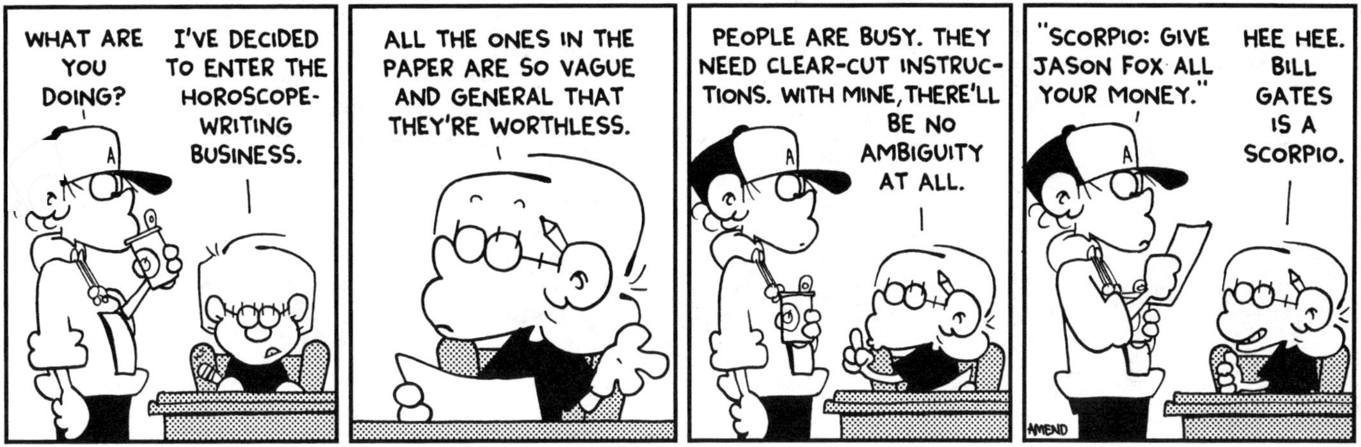
WHAT ARE YOU DOING?
I'VE DECIDED TO ENTER THE HOROSCOPE-WRITING BUSINESS.
ALL THE ONES IN THE PAPER ARE SO VAGUE AND GENERAL THAT THEY'RE WORTHLESS.
PEOPLE ARE BUSY. THEY NEED CLEAR-CUT INSTRUCTIONS. WITH MINE, THERE'LL BE NO AMBIGUITY AT ALL.
"SCORPIO: GIVE JASON FOX ALL YOUR MONEY."
HEE HEE. BILL GATES IS A SCORPIO.
AMEND

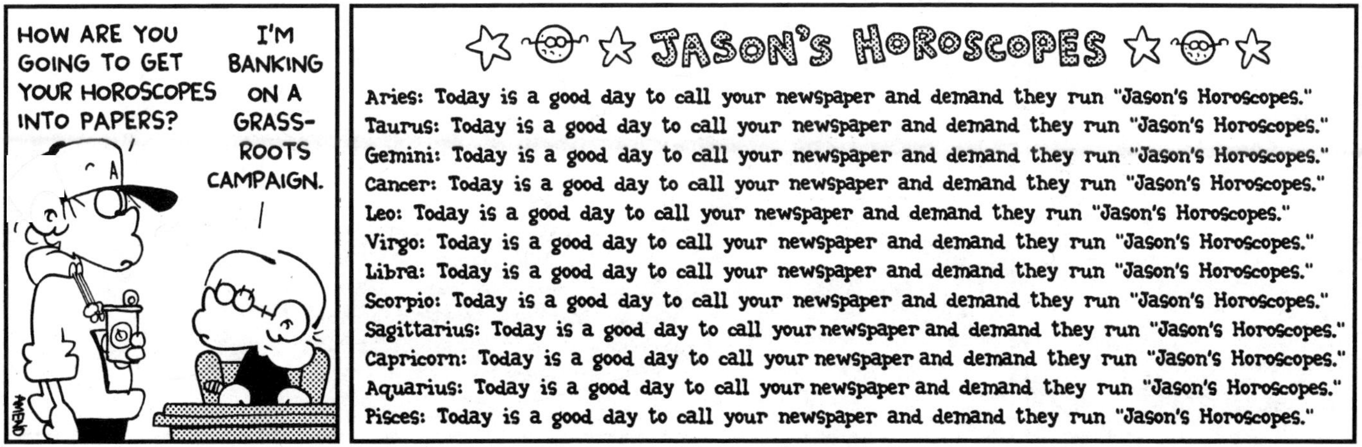
HOW ARE YOU GOING TO GET YOUR HOROSCOPES INTO PAPERS?
I'M BANKING ON A GRASS-ROOTS CAMPAIGN.
AMEND
JASON'S HOROSCOPES
Aries: Today is a good day to call your newspaper and demand they run "Jason's Horoscopes."
Taurus: Today is a good day to call your newspaper and demand they run "Jason's Horoscopes."
Gemini: Today is a good day to call your newspaper and demand they run "Jason's Horoscopes."
Cancer: Today is a good day to call your newspaper and demand they run "Jason's Horoscopes."
Leo: Today is a good day to call your newspaper and demand they run "Jason's Horoscopes."
Virgo: Today is a good day to call your newspaper and demand they run "Jason's Horoscopes."
Libra: Today is a good day to call your newspaper and demand they run "Jason's Horoscopes."
Scorpio: Today is a good day to call your newspaper and demand they run "Jason's Horoscopes."
Sagittarius: Today is a good day to call your newspaper and demand they run "Jason's Horoscopes."
Capricorn: Today is a good day to call your newspaper and demand they run "Jason's Horoscopes."
Aquarius: Today is a good day to call your newspaper and demand they run "Jason's Horoscopes."
Pisces: Today is a good day to call your newspaper and demand they run "Jason's Horoscopes."

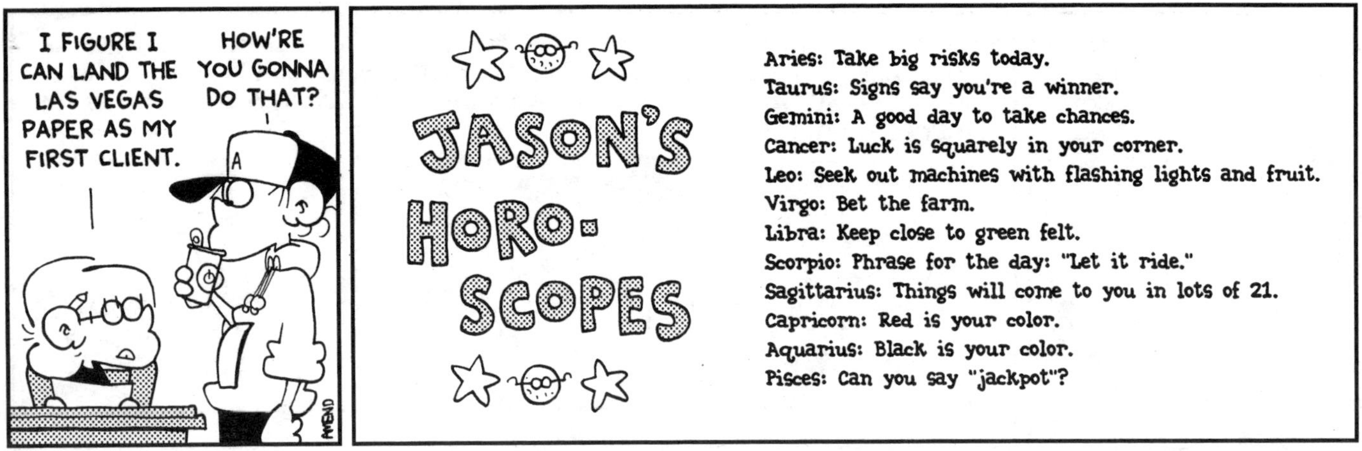
I FIGURE I CAN LAND THE LAS VEGAS PAPER AS MY FIRST CLIENT.
HOW'RE YOU GONNA DO THAT?
JASON'S HORO-SCOPES
Aries: Take big risks today.
Taurus: Signs say you're a winner.
Gemini: A good day to take chances.
Cancer: Luck is squarely in your corner.
Leo: Seek out machines with flashing lights and fruit.
Virgo: Bet the farm.
Libra: Keep close to green felt.
Scorpio: Phrase for the day: "Let it ride."
Sagittarius: Things will come to you in lots of 21.
Capricorn: Red is your color.
Aquarius: Black is your color.
Pisces: Can you say "jackpot"?

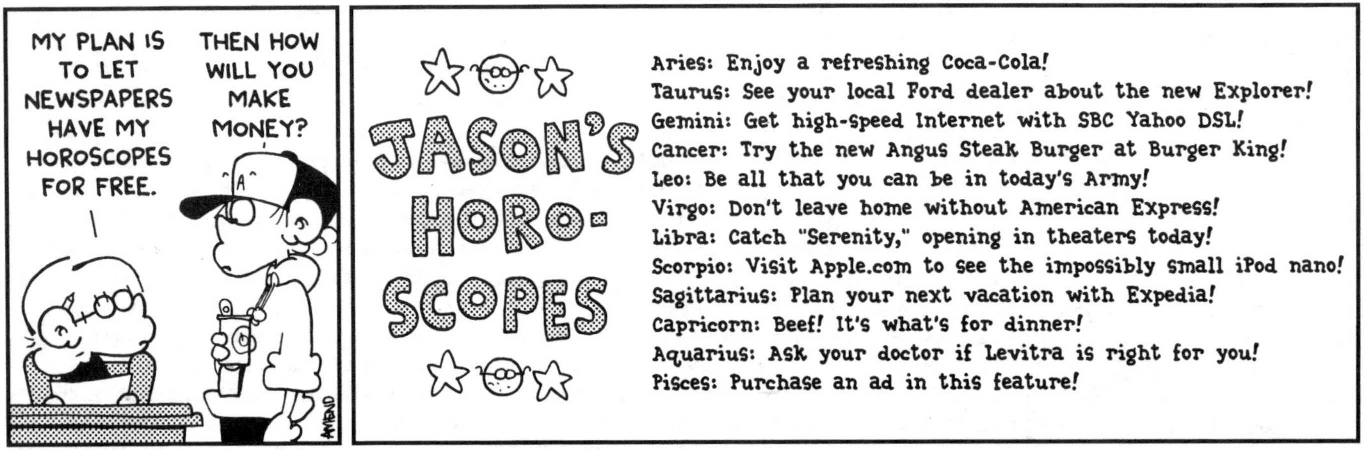
MY PLAN IS TO LET NEWSPAPERS HAVE MY HOROSCOPES FOR FREE.
THEN HOW WILL YOU MAKE MONEY?
JASON'S HORO-SCOPES
Aries: Enjoy a refreshing Coca-Cola!
Taurus: See your local Ford dealer about the new Explorer!
Gemini: Get high-speed Internet with SBC Yahoo DSL!
Cancer: Try the new Angus Steak Burger at Burger King!
Leo: Be all that you can be in today's Army!
Virgo: Don't leave home without American Express!
Libra: Catch "Serenity," opening in theaters today!
Scorpio: Visit Apple.com to see the impossibly small iPod nano!
Sagittarius: Plan your next vacation with Expedia!
Capricorn: Beef! It's what's for dinner!
Aquarius: Ask your doctor if Levitra is right for you!
Pisces: Purchase an ad in this feature!

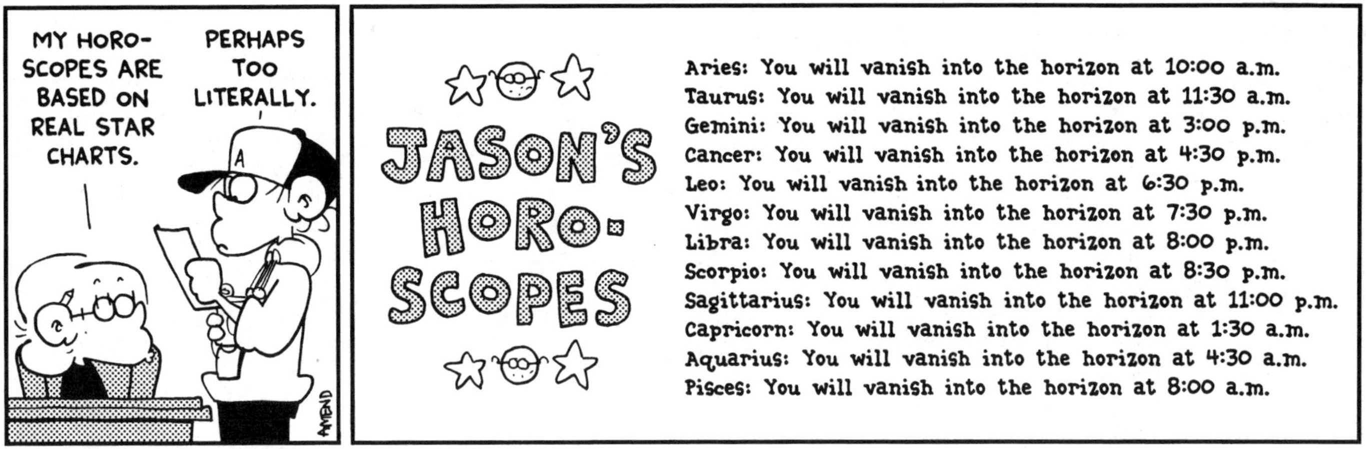
MY HORO-SCOPES ARE BASED ON REAL STAR CHARTS.
PERHAPS TOO LITERALLY.
JASON'S HORO-SCOPES
Aries: You will vanish into the horizon at 10:00 a.m.
Taurus: You will vanish into the horizon at 11:30 a.m.
Gemini: You will vanish into the horizon at 3:00 p.m.
Cancer: You will vanish into the horizon at 4:30 p.m.
Leo: You will vanish into the horizon at 6:30 p.m.
Virgo: You will vanish into the horizon at 7:30 p.m.
Libra: You will vanish into the horizon at 8:00 p.m.
Scorpio: You will vanish into the horizon at 8:30 p.m.
Sagittarius: You will vanish into the horizon at 11:00 p.m.
Capricorn: You will vanish into the horizon at 1:30 a.m.
Aquarius: You will vanish into the horizon at 4:30 a.m.
Pisces: You will vanish into the horizon at 8:00 a.m.

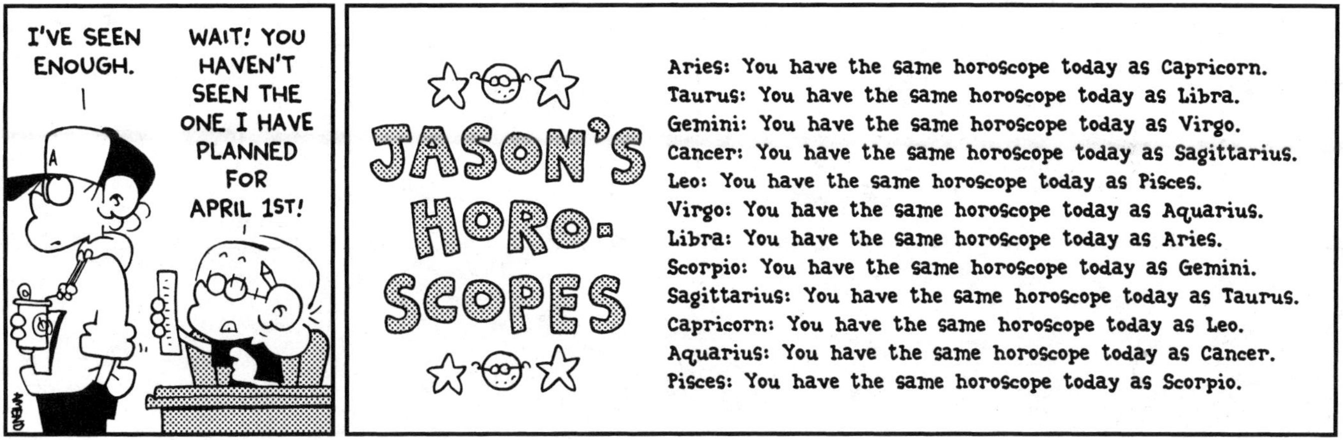
I'VE SEEN ENOUGH.
WAIT! YOU HAVEN'T SEEN THE ONE I HAVE PLANNED FOR APRIL 1ST!
JASON'S HORO-SCOPES
Aries: You have the same horoscope today as Capricorn.
Taurus: You have the same horoscope today as Libra.
Gemini: You have the same horoscope today as Virgo.
Cancer: You have the same horoscope today as Sagittarius.
Leo: You have the same horoscope today as Pisces.
Virgo: You have the same horoscope today as Aquarius.
Libra: You have the same horoscope today as Aries.
Scorpio: You have the same horoscope today as Gemini.
Sagittarius: You have the same horoscope today as Taurus.
Capricorn: You have the same horoscope today as Leo.
Aquarius: You have the same horoscope today as Cancer.
Pisces: You have the same horoscope today as Scorpio.

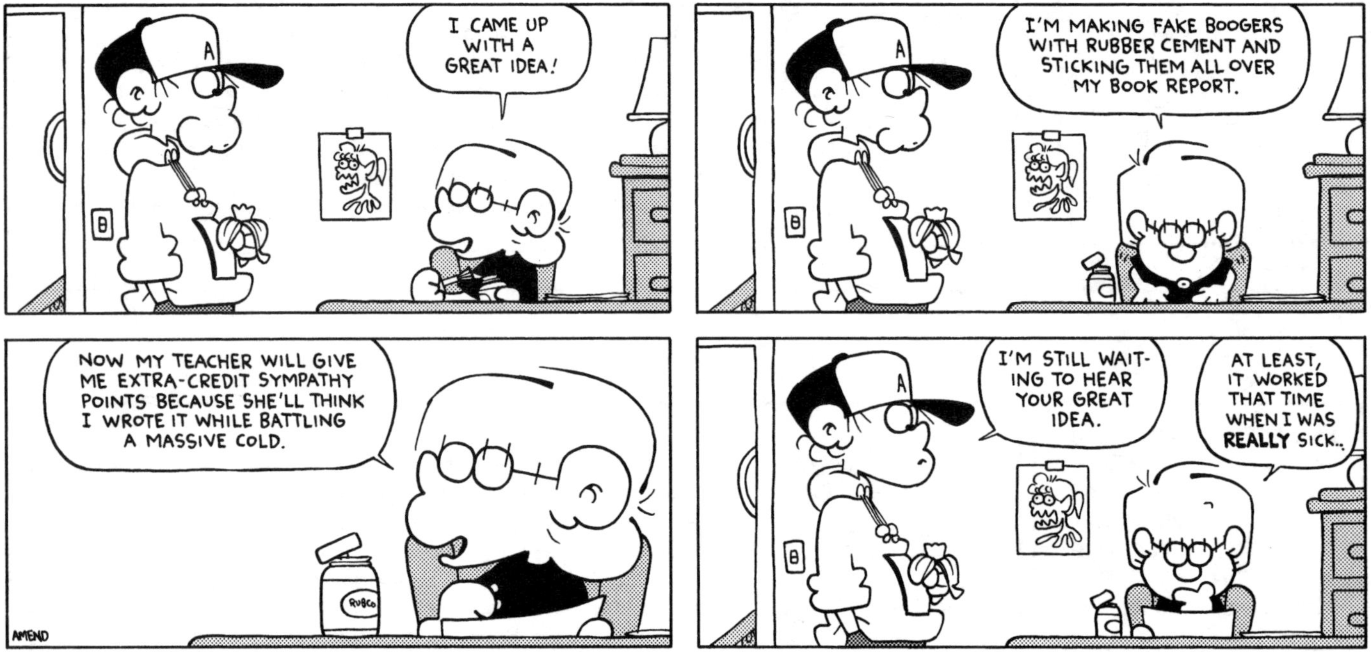

I CAME UP WITH A GREAT IDEA!
I'M MAKING FAKE BOOGERS WITH RUBBER CEMENT AND STICKING THEM ALL OVER MY BOOK REPORT.
NOW MY TEACHER WILL GIVE ME EXTRA-CREDIT SYMPATHY POINTS BECAUSE SHE'LL THINK I WROTE IT WHILE BATTLING A MASSIVE COLD.
RUBCO
AMEND
I'M STILL WAITING TO HEAR YOUR GREAT IDEA.
AT LEAST, IT WORKED THAT TIME WHEN I WAS **REALLY** SICK..

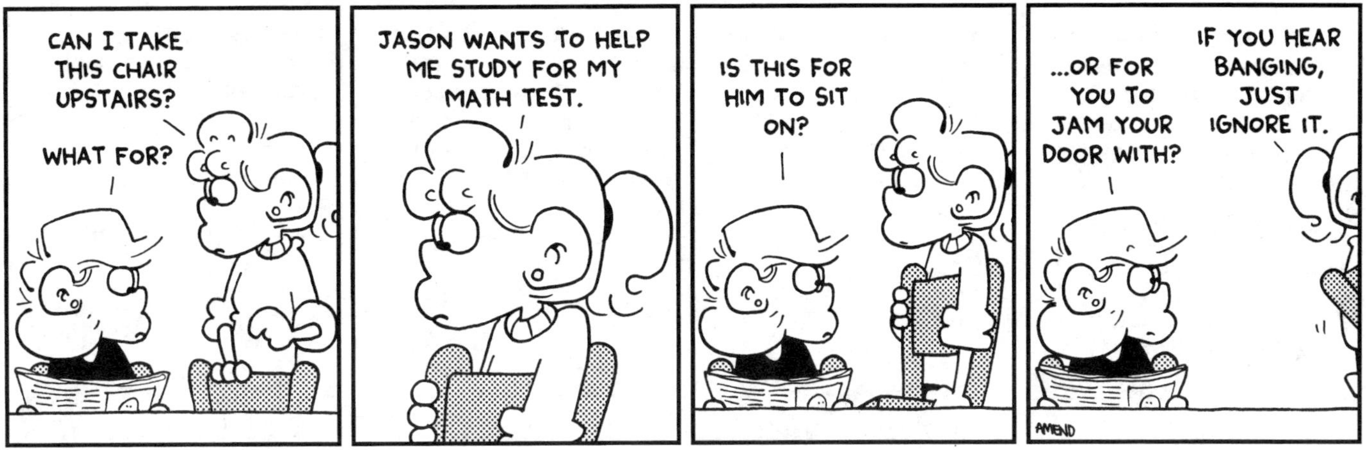
CAN I TAKE THIS CHAIR UPSTAIRS?
WHAT FOR?
JASON WANTS TO HELP ME STUDY FOR MY MATH TEST.
IS THIS FOR HIM TO SIT ON?
...OR FOR YOU TO JAM YOUR DOOR WITH?
IF YOU HEAR BANGING, JUST IGNORE IT.
AMEND

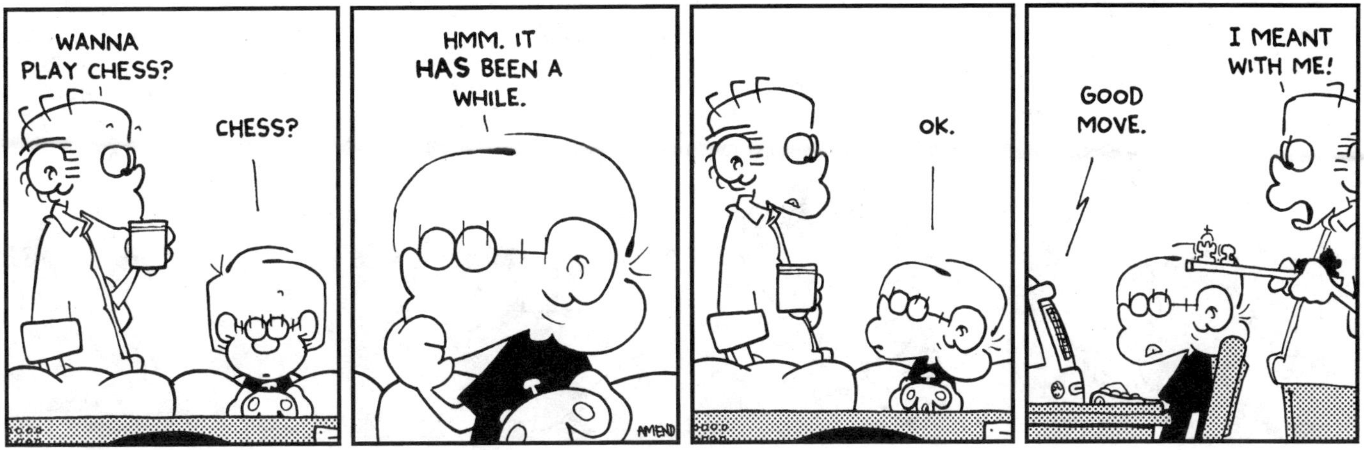
WANNA PLAY CHESS?
CHESS?
HMM. IT HAS BEEN A WHILE.
AMEND
OK.
GOOD MOVE.
I MEANT WITH ME!

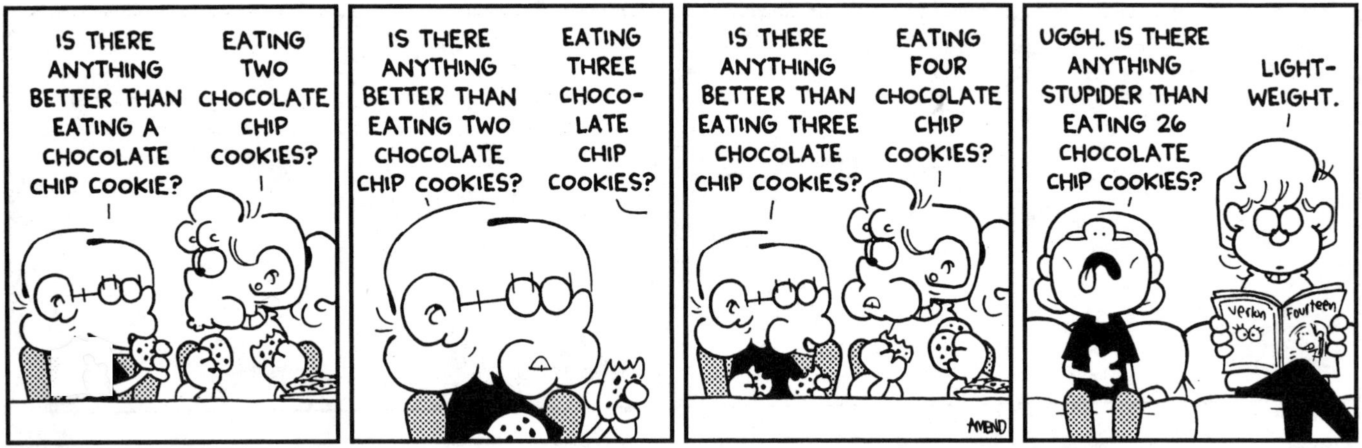
IS THERE ANYTHING BETTER THAN EATING A CHOCOLATE CHIP COOKIE?
EATING TWO CHOCOLATE CHIP COOKIES?
IS THERE ANYTHING BETTER THAN EATING TWO CHOCOLATE CHIP COOKIES?
EATING THREE CHOCO-LATE CHIP COOKIES?
IS THERE ANYTHING BETTER THAN EATING THREE CHOCOLATE CHIP COOKIES?
EATING FOUR CHOCOLATE CHIP COOKIES?
UGGH. IS THERE ANYTHING STUPIDER THAN EATING 26 CHOCOLATE CHIP COOKIES?
LIGHT-WEIGHT.
AMEND

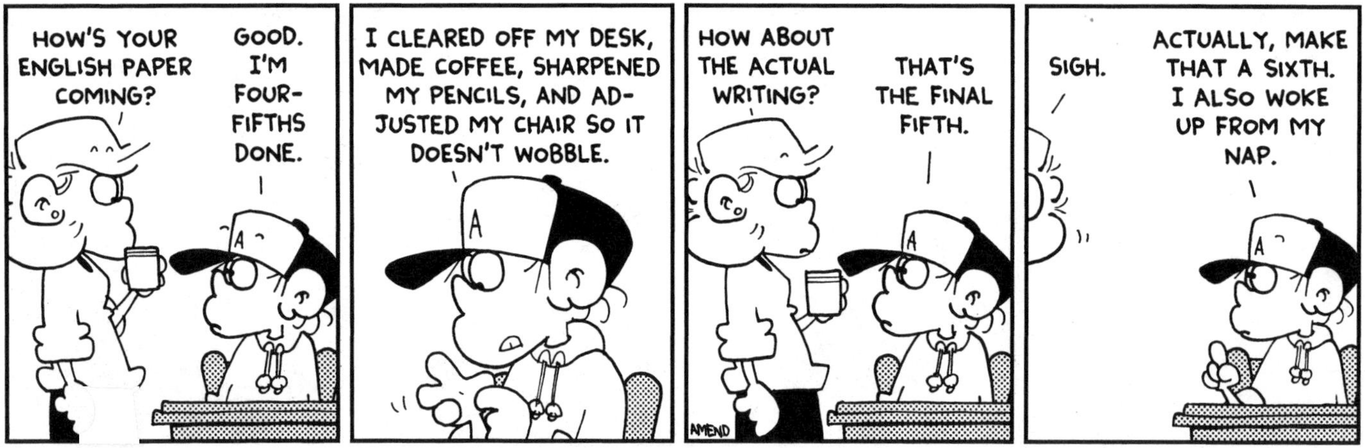
HOW'S YOUR ENGLISH PAPER COMING?
GOOD. I'M FOUR-FIFTHS DONE.
I CLEARED OFF MY DESK, MADE COFFEE, SHARPENED MY PENCILS, AND AD-JUSTED MY CHAIR SO IT DOESN'T WOBBLE.
HOW ABOUT THE ACTUAL WRITING?
THAT'S THE FINAL FIFTH.
AMEND
SIGH.
ACTUALLY, MAKE THAT A SIXTH. I ALSO WOKE UP FROM MY NAP.

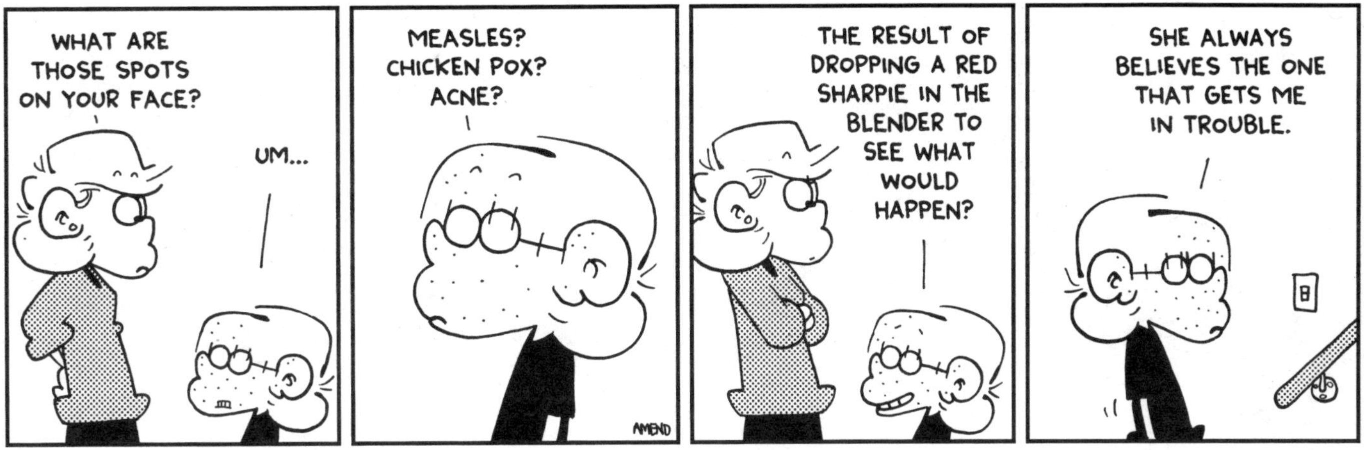
WHAT ARE THOSE SPOTS ON YOUR FACE?
UM...
MEASLES? CHICKEN POX? ACNE?
THE RESULT OF DROPPING A RED SHARPIE IN THE BLENDER TO SEE WHAT WOULD HAPPEN?
SHE ALWAYS BELIEVES THE ONE THAT GETS ME IN TROUBLE.
AMEND

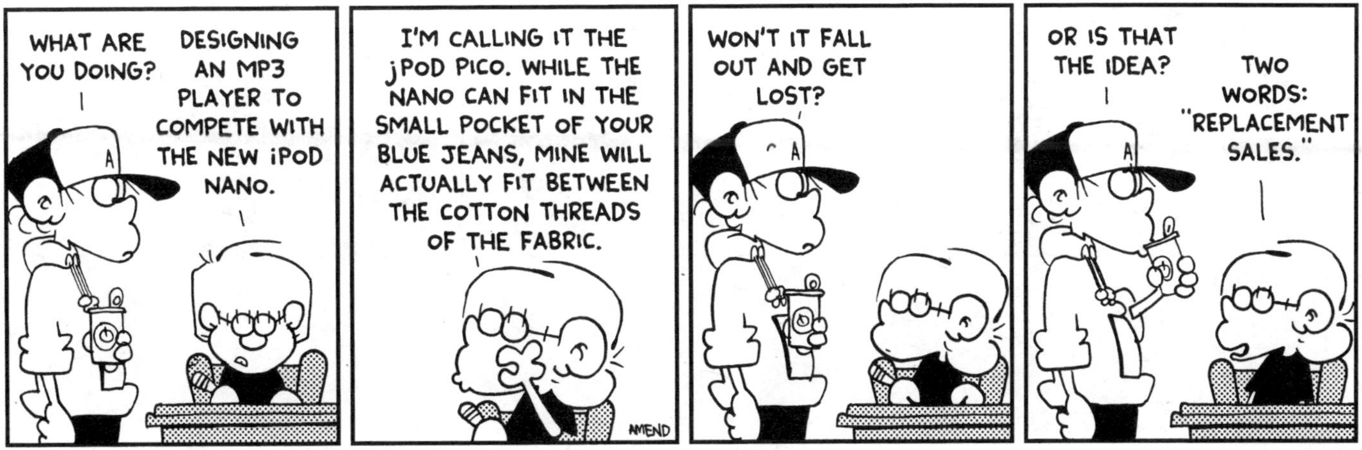
WHAT ARE YOU DOING?
DESIGNING AN MP3 PLAYER TO COMPETE WITH THE NEW iPOD NANO.
I'M CALLING IT THE jPOD PICO. WHILE THE NANO CAN FIT IN THE SMALL POCKET OF YOUR BLUE JEANS, MINE WILL ACTUALLY FIT BETWEEN THE COTTON THREADS OF THE FABRIC.
AMEND
WON'T IT FALL OUT AND GET LOST?
OR IS THAT THE IDEA?
TWO WORDS: "REPLACEMENT SALES."

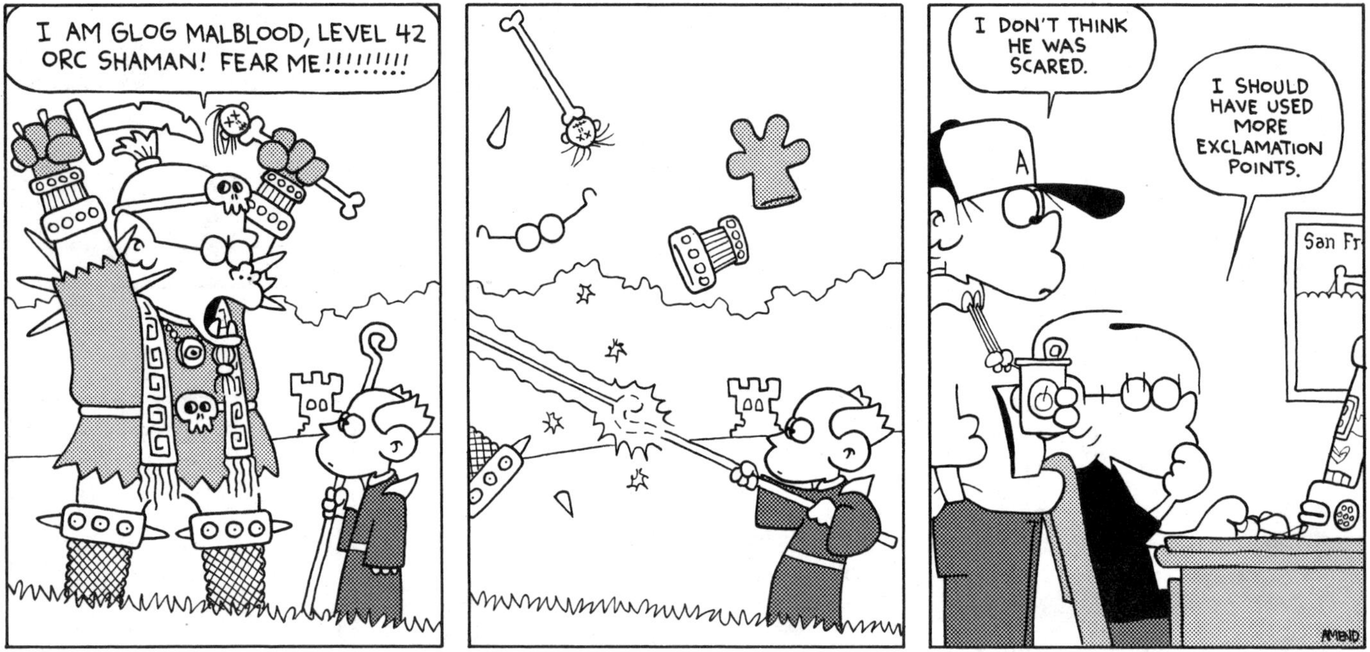
I AM GLOG MALBLOOD, LEVEL 42 ORC SHAMAN! FEAR ME!!!!!!!!!
I DON'T THINK HE WAS SCARED.
I SHOULD HAVE USED MORE EXCLAMATION POINTS.
San Fr
AMEND

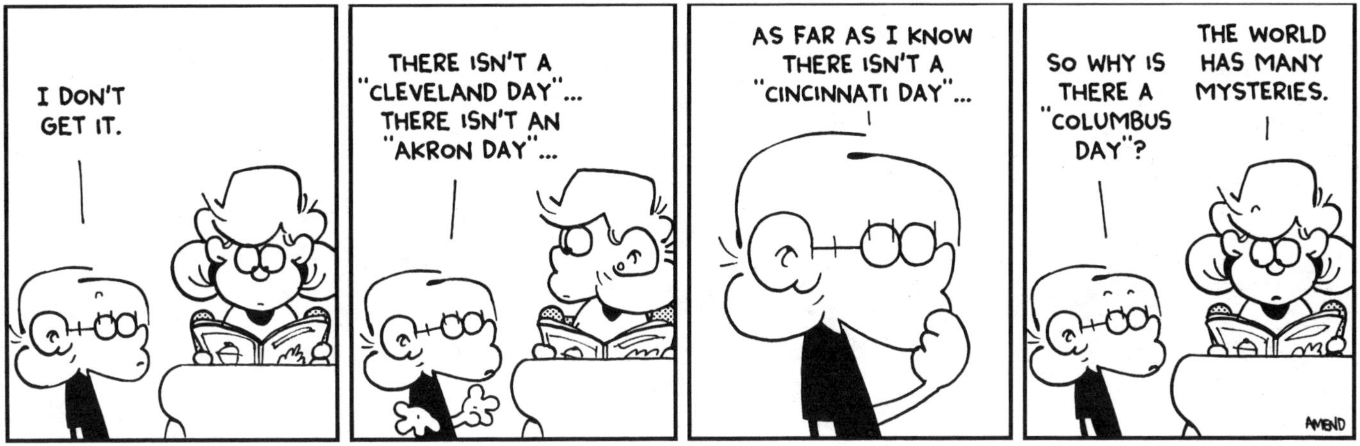
I DON'T GET IT.
THERE ISN'T A "CLEVELAND DAY"... THERE ISN'T AN "AKRON DAY"...
AS FAR AS I KNOW THERE ISN'T A "CINCINNATI DAY"...
SO WHY IS THERE A "COLUMBUS DAY"?
THE WORLD HAS MANY MYSTERIES.
AMEND

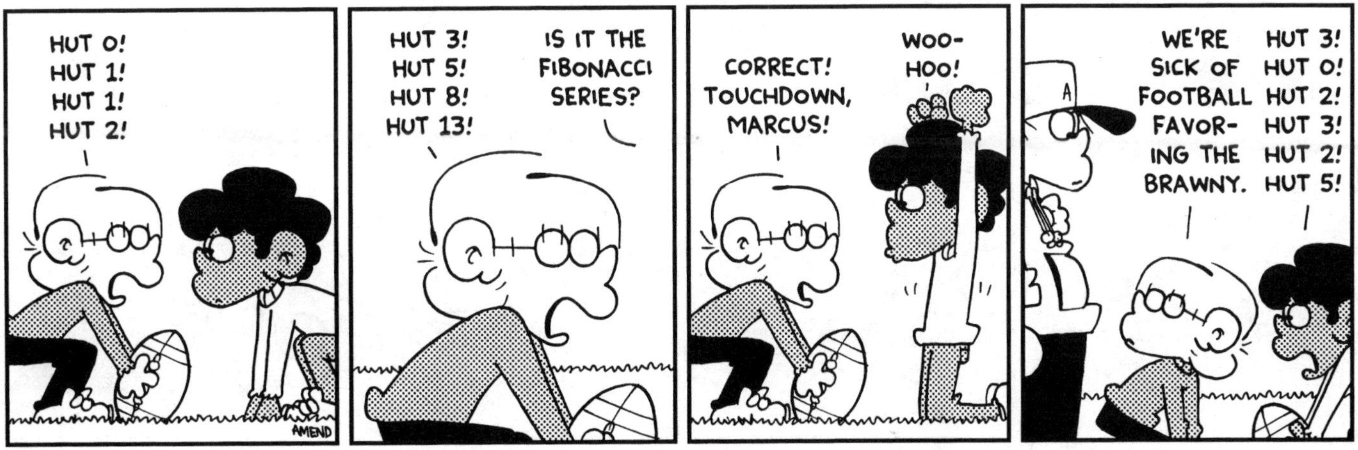
HUT 0! HUT 1! HUT 1! HUT 2!
AMEND
HUT 3! HUT 5! HUT 8! HUT 13!
IS IT THE FIBONACCI SERIES?
CORRECT! TOUCHDOWN, MARCUS!
WOO-HOO!
WE'RE SICK OF FOOTBALL FAVOR-ING THE BRAWNY.
HUT 3! HUT 0! HUT 2! HUT 3! HUT 2! HUT 5!

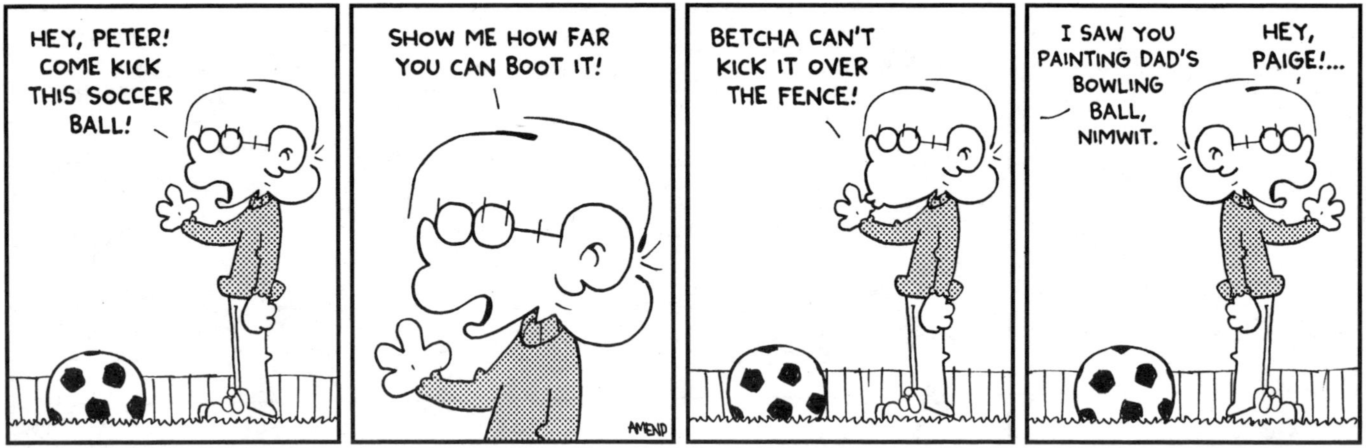
HEY, PETER! COME KICK THIS SOCCER BALL!
SHOW ME HOW FAR YOU CAN BOOT IT!
AMEND
BETCHA CAN'T KICK IT OVER THE FENCE!
I SAW YOU PAINTING DAD'S BOWLING BALL, NIMWIT.
HEY, PAIGE!...

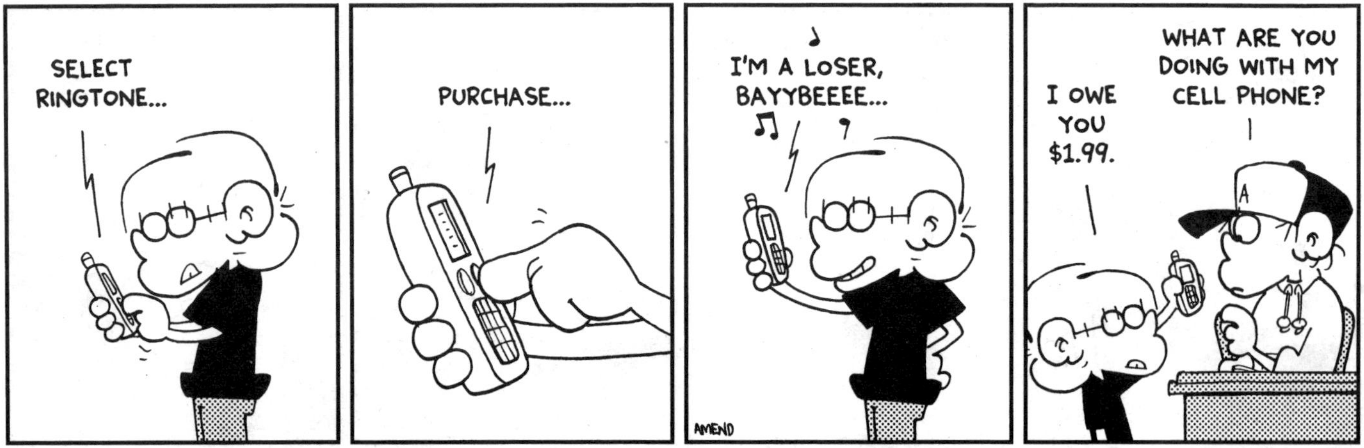
SELECT RINGTONE...
PURCHASE...
I'M A LOSER, BAYYBEEEE...
AMEND
I OWE YOU $1.99.
WHAT ARE YOU DOING WITH MY CELL PHONE?

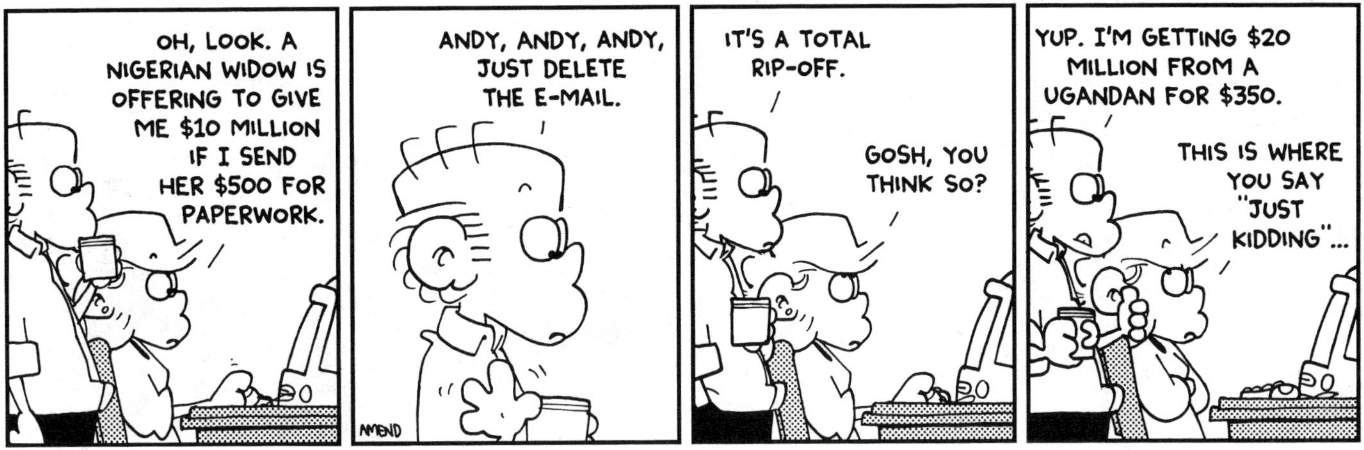
OH, LOOK. A NIGERIAN WIDOW IS OFFERING TO GIVE ME $10 MILLION IF I SEND HER $500 FOR PAPERWORK.
ANDY, ANDY, ANDY, JUST DELETE THE E-MAIL.
AMEND
IT'S A TOTAL RIP-OFF.
GOSH, YOU THINK SO?
YUP. I'M GETTING $20 MILLION FROM A UGANDAN FOR $350.
THIS IS WHERE YOU SAY "JUST KIDDING"...

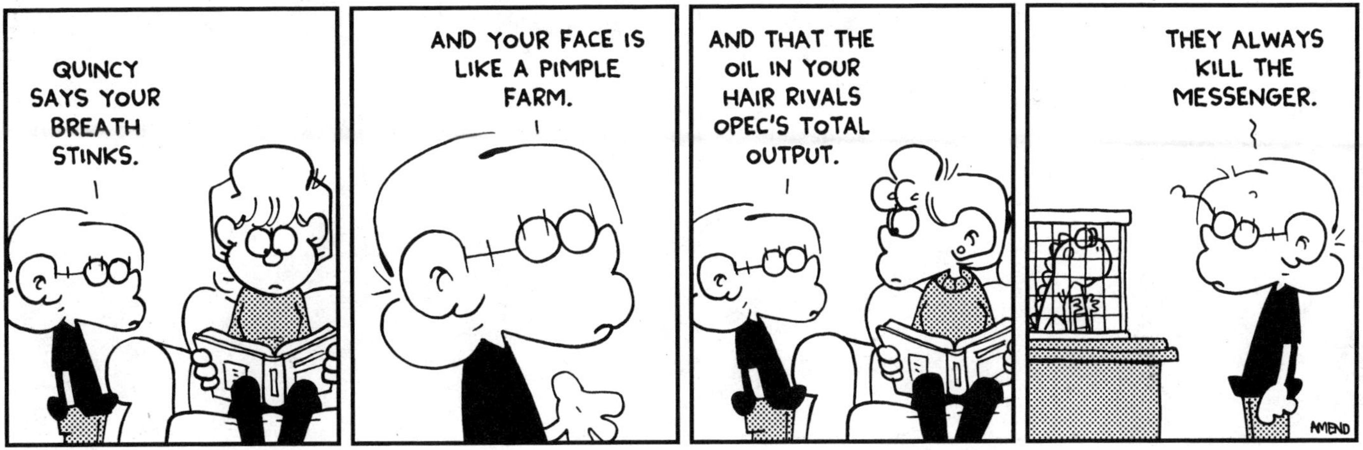
QUINCY SAYS YOUR BREATH STINKS.
AND YOUR FACE IS LIKE A PIMPLE FARM.
AND THAT THE OIL IN YOUR HAIR RIVALS OPEC'S TOTAL OUTPUT.
THEY ALWAYS KILL THE MESSENGER.
AMEND

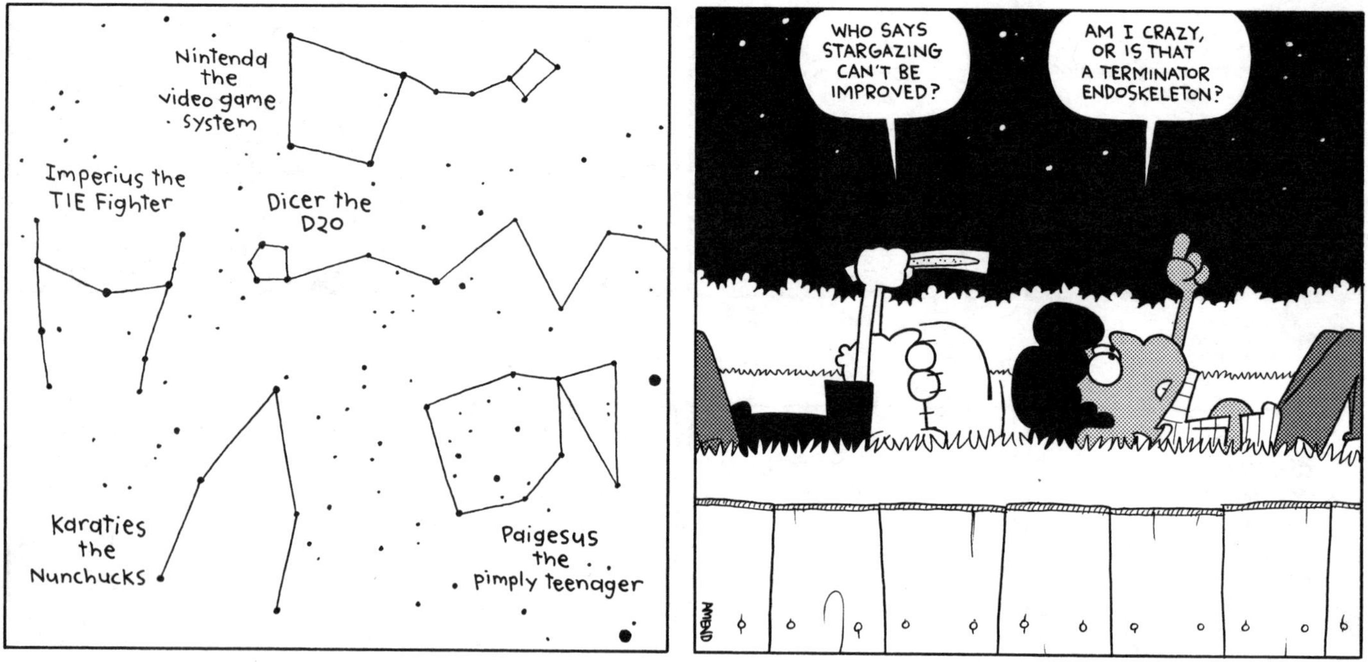

Nintenda the video game system
Imperius the TIE Fighter
Dicer the D20
Karaties the Nunchucks
Paigesus the pimply teenager
WHO SAYS STARGAZING CAN'T BE IMPROVED?
AM I CRAZY, OR IS THAT A TERMINATOR ENDOSKELETON?

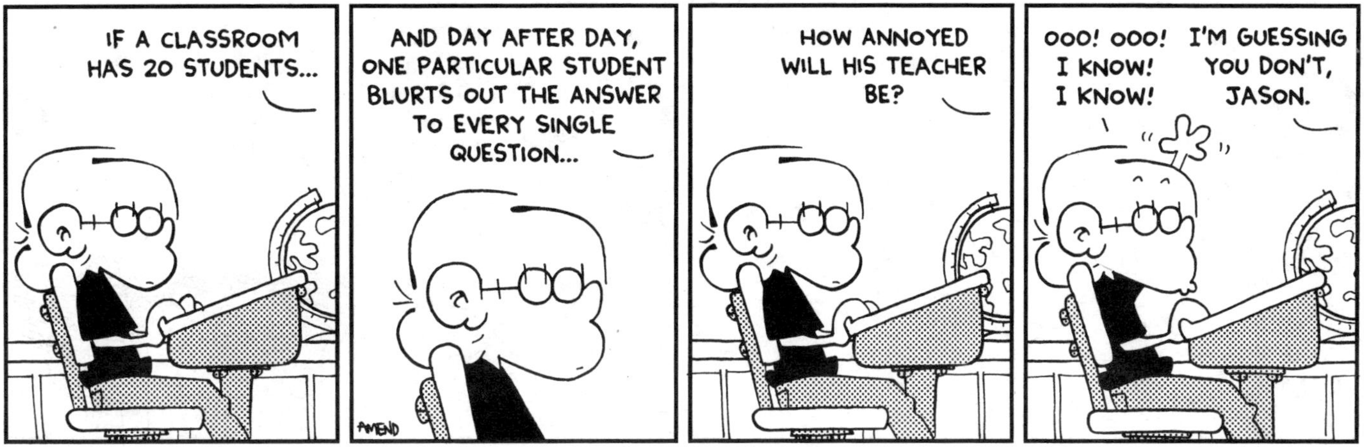
IF A CLASSROOM HAS 20 STUDENTS...
AND DAY AFTER DAY, ONE PARTICULAR STUDENT BLURTS OUT THE ANSWER TO EVERY SINGLE QUESTION...
AMEND
HOW ANNOYED WILL HIS TEACHER BE?
OOO! OOO! I KNOW! I KNOW!
I'M GUESSING YOU DON'T, JASON.

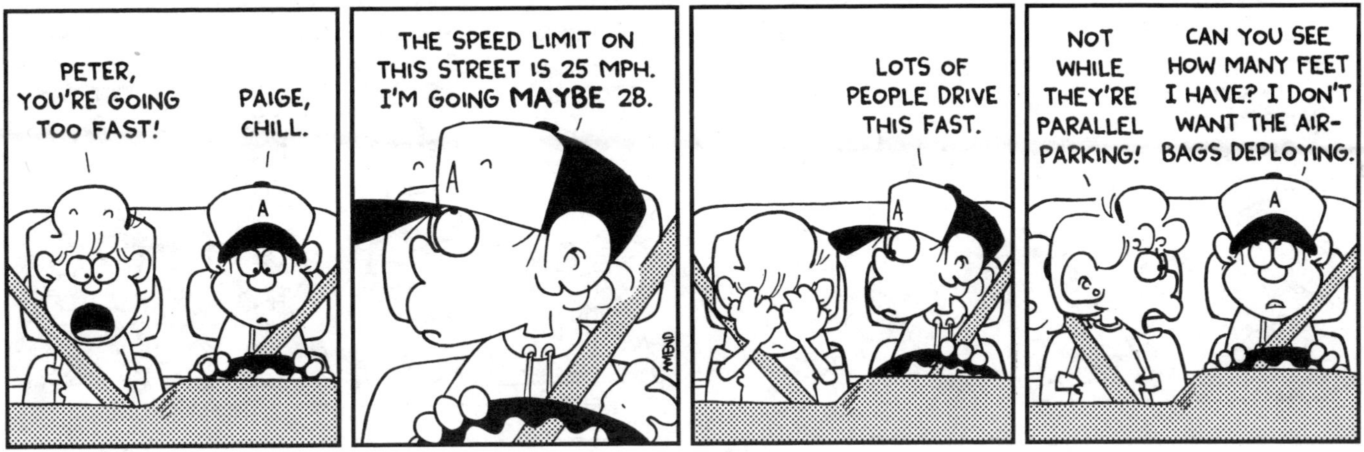
PETER, YOU'RE GOING TOO FAST!
PAIGE, CHILL.
THE SPEED LIMIT ON THIS STREET IS 25 MPH. I'M GOING MAYBE 28.
AMEND
LOTS OF PEOPLE DRIVE THIS FAST.
NOT WHILE THEY'RE PARALLEL PARKING!
CAN YOU SEE HOW MANY FEET I HAVE? I DON'T WANT THE AIR-BAGS DEPLOYING.

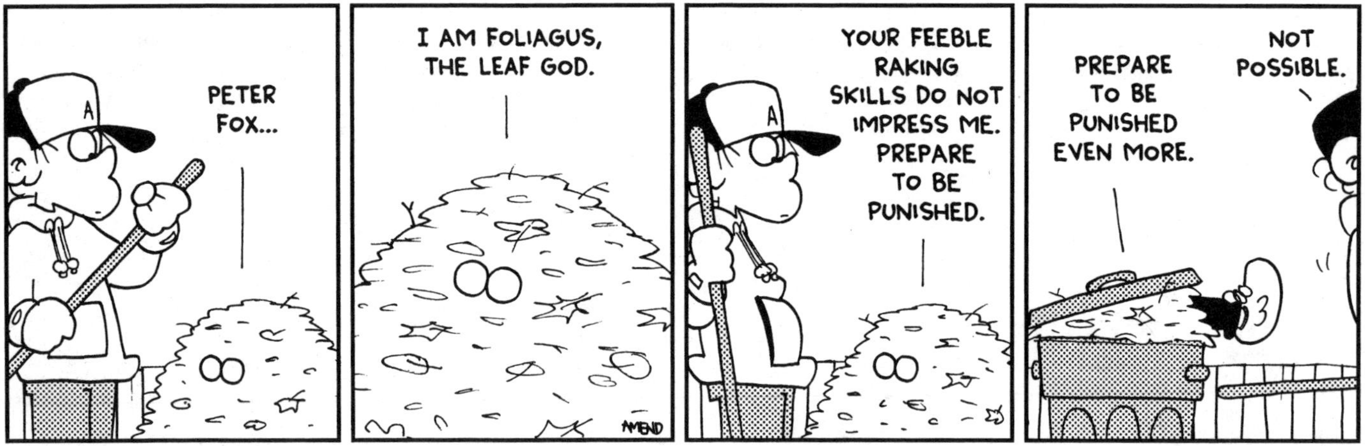
PETER FOX...
I AM FOLIAGUS, THE LEAF GOD.
YOUR FEEBLE RAKING SKILLS DO NOT IMPRESS ME. PREPARE TO BE PUNISHED.
PREPARE TO BE PUNISHED EVEN MORE.
NOT POSSIBLE.
AMEND

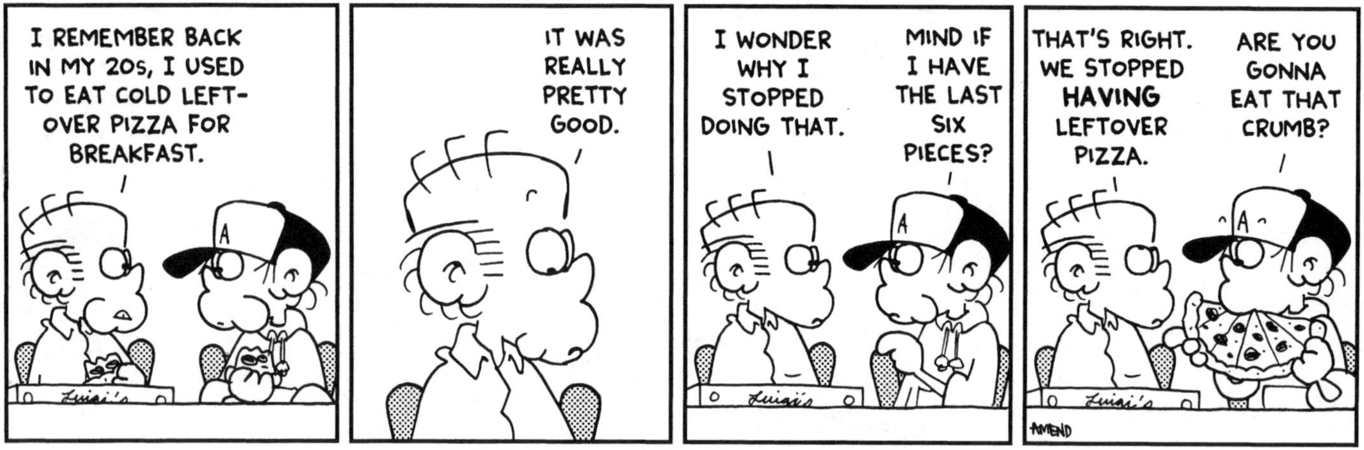
I REMEMBER BACK IN MY 20s, I USED TO EAT COLD LEFT-OVER PIZZA FOR BREAKFAST.
IT WAS REALLY PRETTY GOOD.
I WONDER WHY I STOPPED DOING THAT.
MIND IF I HAVE THE LAST SIX PIECES?
THAT'S RIGHT. WE STOPPED **HAVING** LEFTOVER PIZZA.
ARE YOU GONNA EAT THAT CRUMB?
AMEND

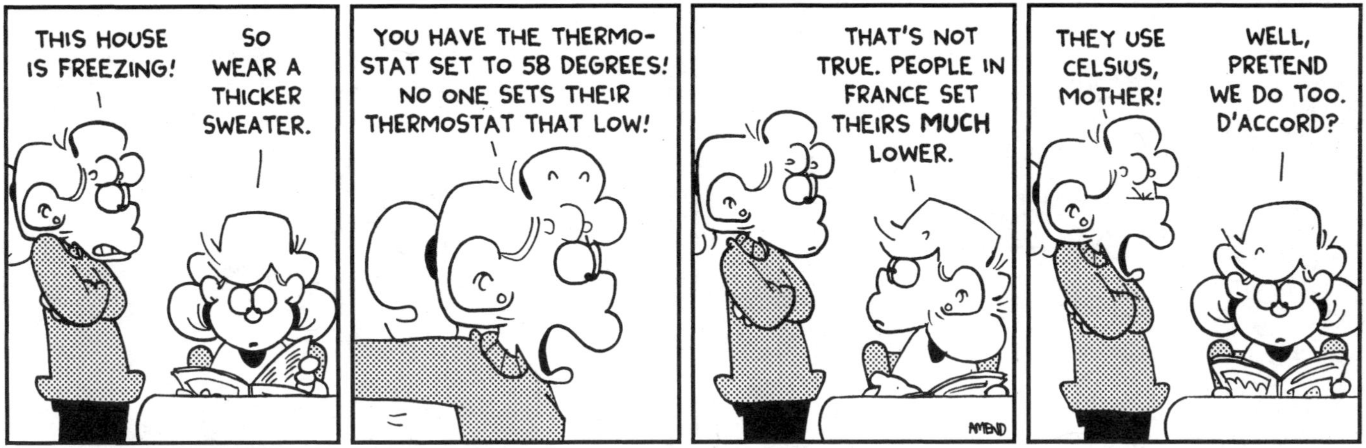
THIS HOUSE IS FREEZING!
SO WEAR A THICKER SWEATER.
YOU HAVE THE THERMOSTAT SET TO 58 DEGREES! NO ONE SETS THEIR THERMOSTAT THAT LOW!
THAT'S NOT TRUE. PEOPLE IN FRANCE SET THEIRS MUCH LOWER.
AMEND
THEY USE CELSIUS, MOTHER!
WELL, PRETEND WE DO TOO. D'ACCORD?

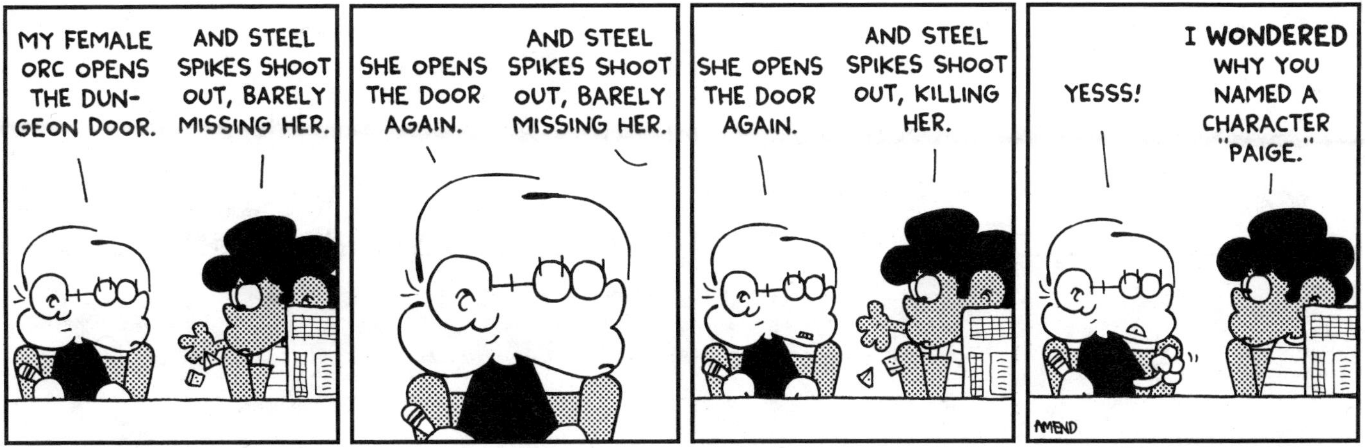
MY FEMALE ORC OPENS THE DUNGEON DOOR.
AND STEEL SPIKES SHOOT OUT, BARELY MISSING HER.
SHE OPENS THE DOOR AGAIN.
AND STEEL SPIKES SHOOT OUT, BARELY MISSING HER.
SHE OPENS THE DOOR AGAIN.
AND STEEL SPIKES SHOOT OUT, KILLING HER.
YESSS!
I WONDERED WHY YOU NAMED A CHARACTER "PAIGE."
AMEND

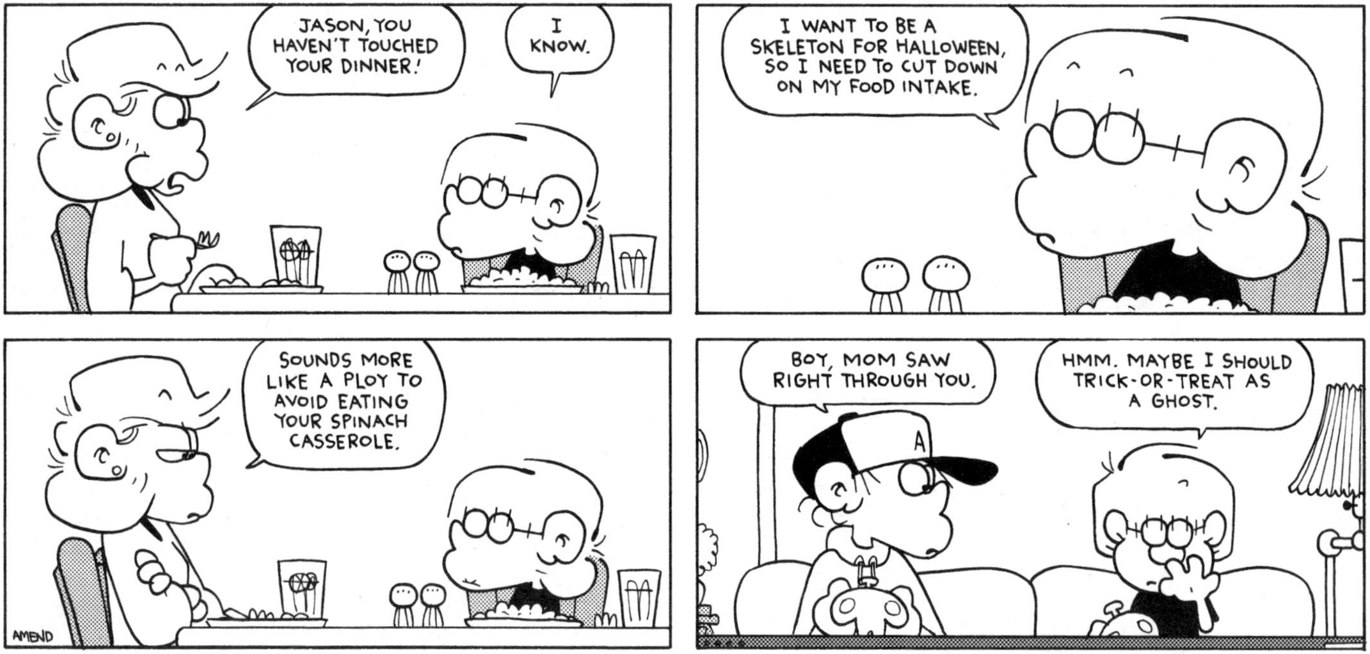
JASON, YOU HAVEN'T TOUCHED YOUR DINNER!
I KNOW.
I WANT TO BE A SKELETON FOR HALLOWEEN, SO I NEED TO CUT DOWN ON MY FOOD INTAKE.
SOUNDS MORE LIKE A PLOY TO AVOID EATING YOUR SPINACH CASSEROLE.
AMEND
BOY, MOM SAW RIGHT THROUGH YOU.
HMM. MAYBE I SHOULD TRICK-OR-TREAT AS A GHOST.

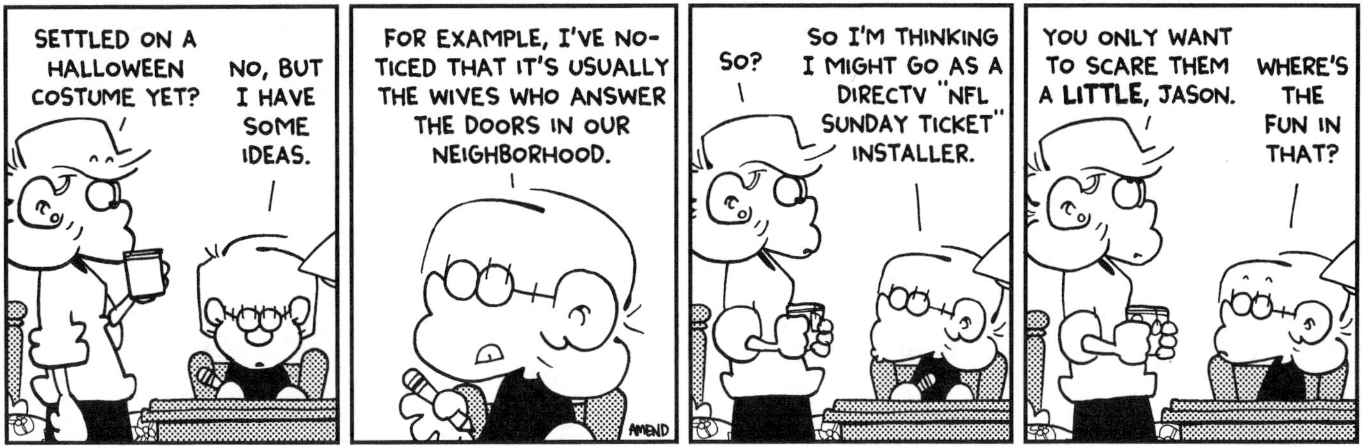
SETTLED ON A HALLOWEEN COSTUME YET?
NO, BUT I HAVE SOME IDEAS.
FOR EXAMPLE, I'VE NOTICED THAT IT'S USUALLY THE WIVES WHO ANSWER THE DOORS IN OUR NEIGHBORHOOD.
AMEND
SO?
SO I'M THINKING I MIGHT GO AS A DIRECTV "NFL SUNDAY TICKET" INSTALLER.
YOU ONLY WANT TO SCARE THEM A LITTLE, JASON.
WHERE'S THE FUN IN THAT?

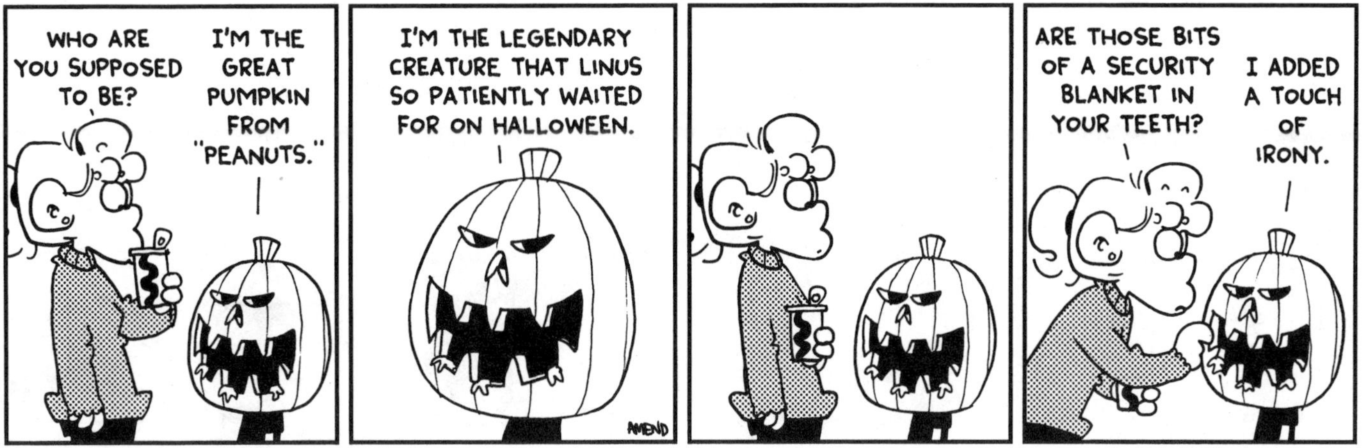
WHO ARE YOU SUPPOSED TO BE?
I'M THE GREAT PUMPKIN FROM "PEANUTS."
I'M THE LEGENDARY CREATURE THAT LINUS SO PATIENTLY WAITED FOR ON HALLOWEEN.
AMEND
ARE THOSE BITS OF A SECURITY BLANKET IN YOUR TEETH?
I ADDED A TOUCH OF IRONY.

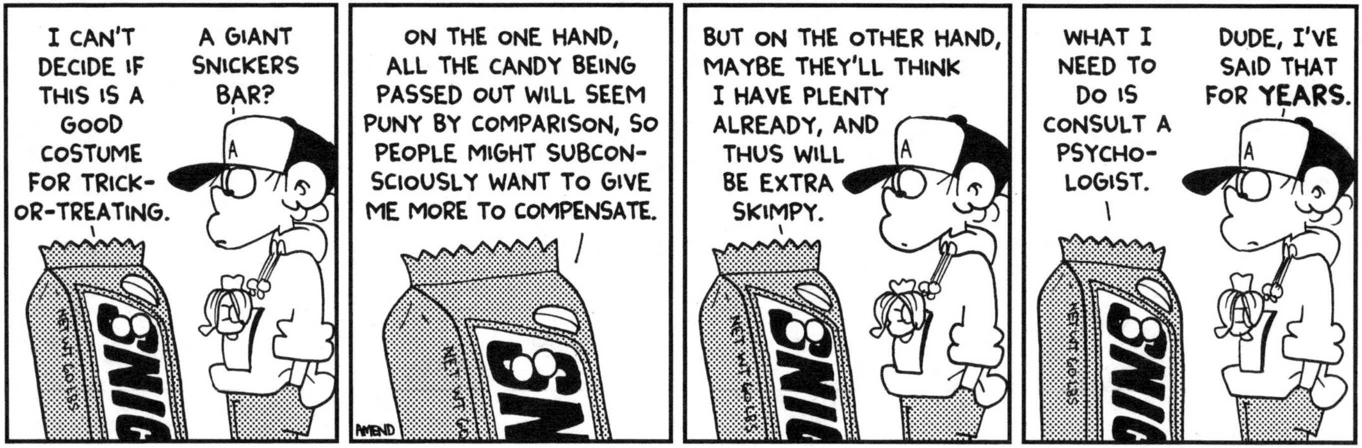
I CAN'T DECIDE IF THIS IS A GOOD COSTUME FOR TRICK-OR-TREATING.
A GIANT SNICKERS BAR?
ON THE ONE HAND, ALL THE CANDY BEING PASSED OUT WILL SEEM PUNY BY COMPARISON, SO PEOPLE MIGHT SUBCONSCIOUSLY WANT TO GIVE ME MORE TO COMPENSATE.
BUT ON THE OTHER HAND, MAYBE THEY'LL THINK I HAVE PLENTY ALREADY, AND THUS WILL BE EXTRA SKIMPY.
WHAT I NEED TO DO IS CONSULT A PSYCHOLOGIST.
DUDE, I'VE SAID THAT FOR **YEARS**.
AMEND

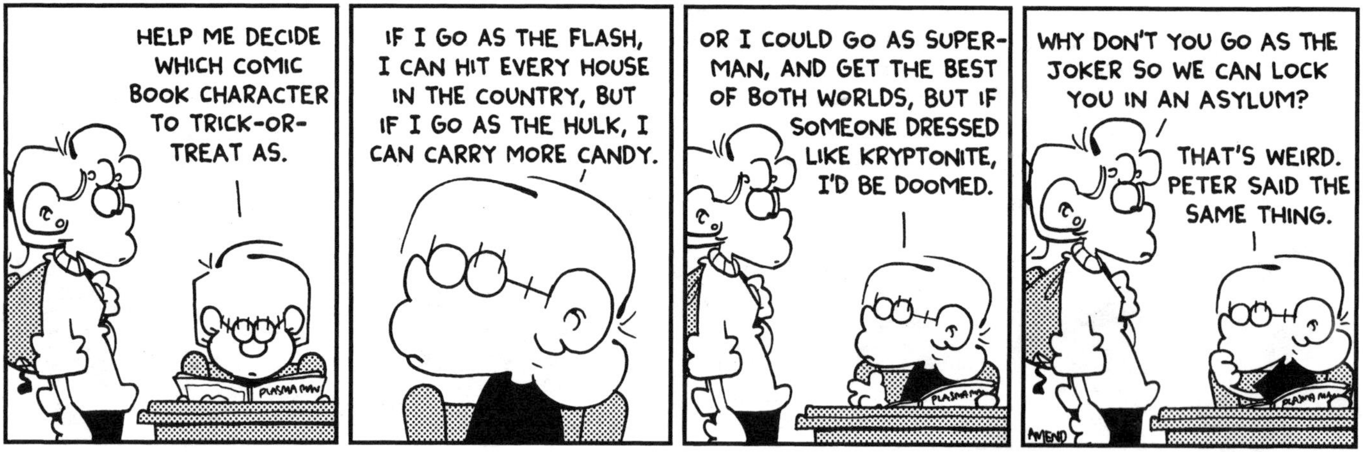
HELP ME DECIDE WHICH COMIC BOOK CHARACTER TO TRICK-OR-TREAT AS.
PLASMA MAN
IF I GO AS THE FLASH, I CAN HIT EVERY HOUSE IN THE COUNTRY, BUT IF I GO AS THE HULK, I CAN CARRY MORE CANDY.
OR I COULD GO AS SUPERMAN, AND GET THE BEST OF BOTH WORLDS, BUT IF SOMEONE DRESSED LIKE KRYPTONITE, I'D BE DOOMED.
WHY DON'T YOU GO AS THE JOKER SO WE CAN LOCK YOU IN AN ASYLUM?
THAT'S WEIRD. PETER SAID THE SAME THING.
AMEND

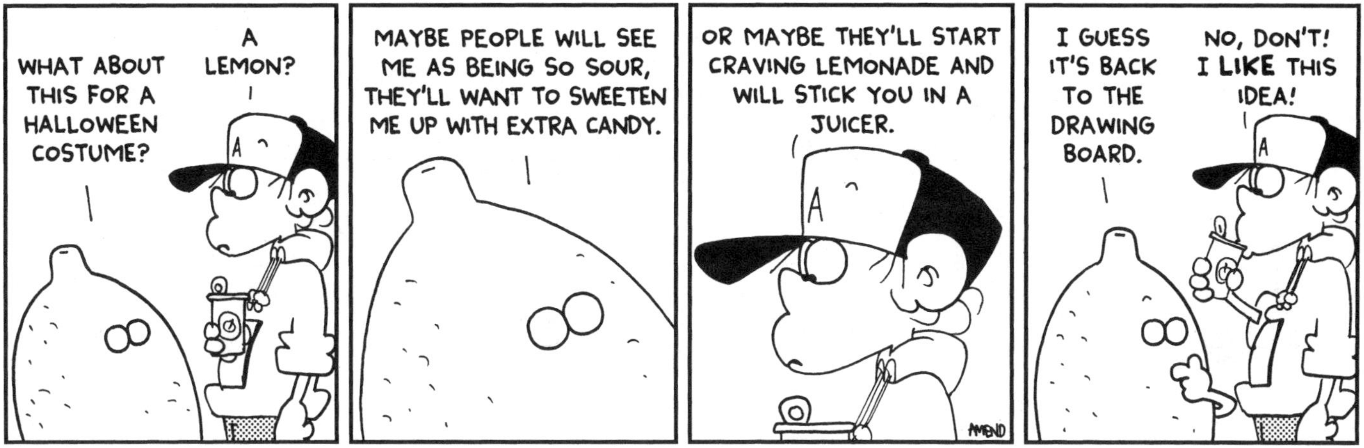
WHAT ABOUT THIS FOR A HALLOWEEN COSTUME?
A LEMON?
MAYBE PEOPLE WILL SEE ME AS BEING SO SOUR, THEY'LL WANT TO SWEETEN ME UP WITH EXTRA CANDY.
OR MAYBE THEY'LL START CRAVING LEMONADE AND WILL STICK YOU IN A JUICER.
AMEND
I GUESS IT'S BACK TO THE DRAWING BOARD.
NO, DON'T! I **LIKE** THIS IDEA!

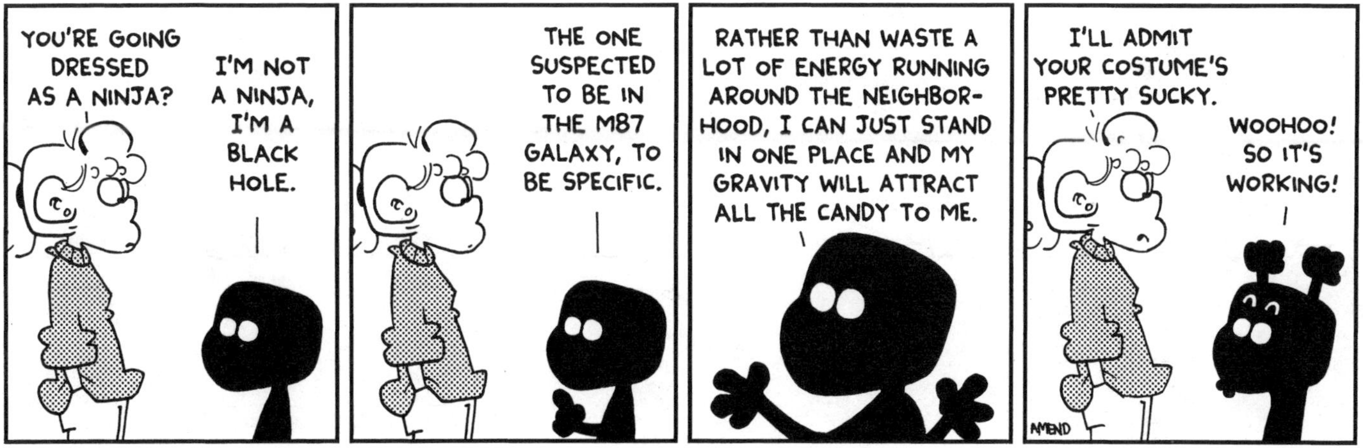
YOU'RE GOING DRESSED AS A NINJA?
I'M NOT A NINJA, I'M A BLACK HOLE.
THE ONE SUSPECTED TO BE IN THE M87 GALAXY, TO BE SPECIFIC.
RATHER THAN WASTE A LOT OF ENERGY RUNNING AROUND THE NEIGHBORHOOD, I CAN JUST STAND IN ONE PLACE AND MY GRAVITY WILL ATTRACT ALL THE CANDY TO ME.
I'LL ADMIT YOUR COSTUME'S PRETTY SUCKY.
WOOHOO! SO IT'S WORKING!
AMEND

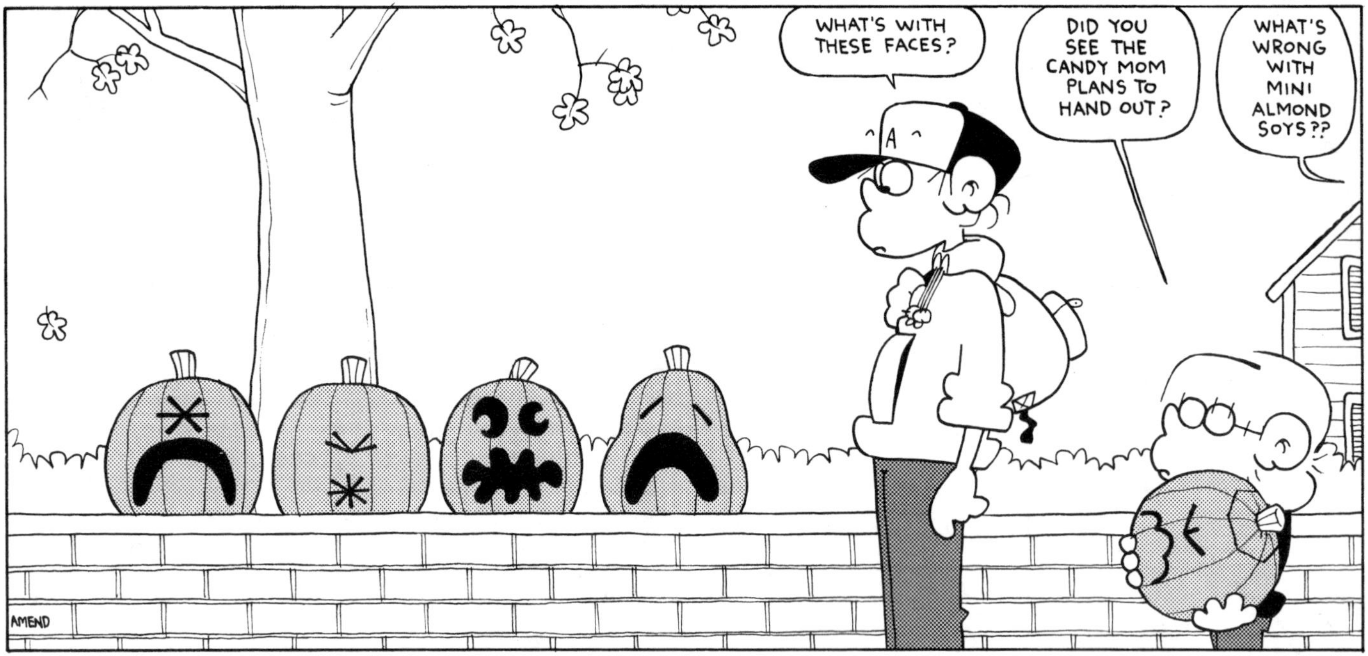
WHAT'S WITH THESE FACES?
DID YOU SEE THE CANDY MOM PLANS TO HAND OUT?
WHAT'S WRONG WITH MINI ALMOND SOYS??
AMEND

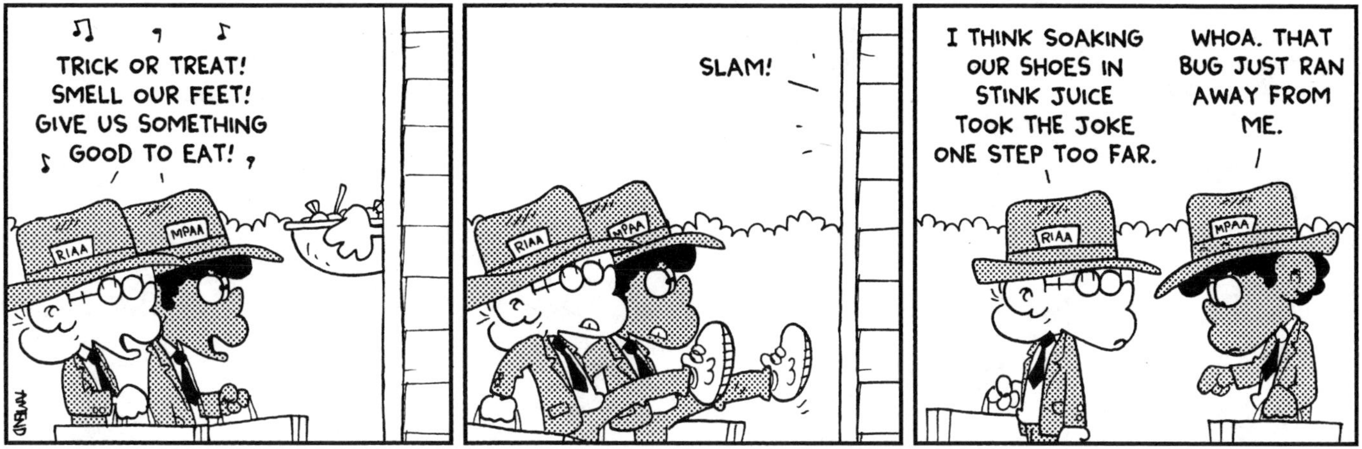
TRICK OR TREAT! SMELL OUR FEET! GIVE US SOMETHING GOOD TO EAT!
RIAA
MPAA
SLAM!
I THINK SOAKING OUR SHOES IN STINK JUICE TOOK THE JOKE ONE STEP TOO FAR.
WHOA. THAT BUG JUST RAN AWAY FROM ME.

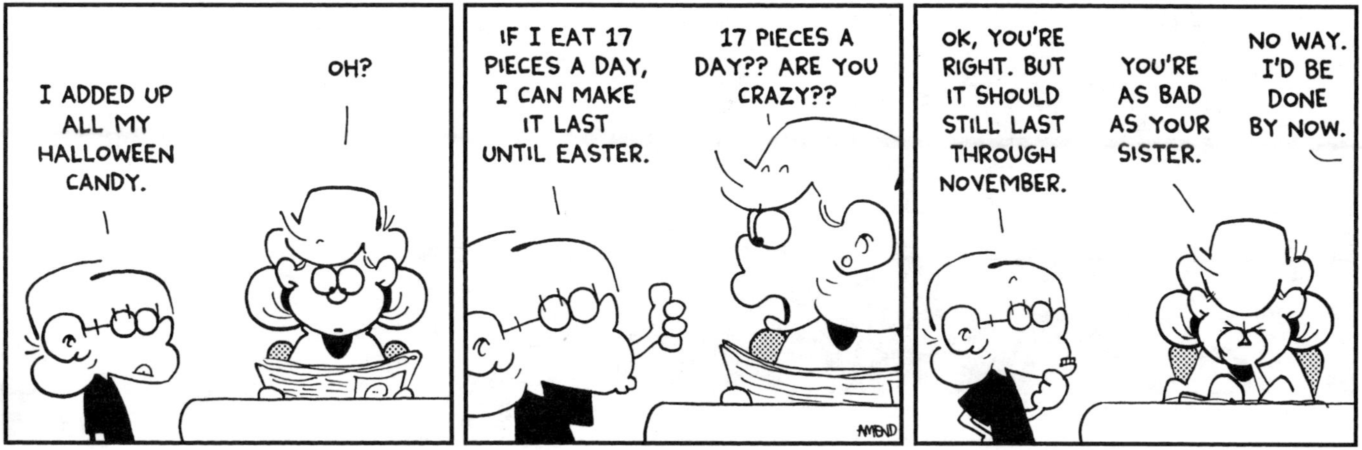
I ADDED UP ALL MY HALLOWEEN CANDY.
OH?
IF I EAT 17 PIECES A DAY, I CAN MAKE IT LAST UNTIL EASTER.
17 PIECES A DAY?? ARE YOU CRAZY??
AMEND
OK, YOU'RE RIGHT. BUT IT SHOULD STILL LAST THROUGH NOVEMBER.
YOU'RE AS BAD AS YOUR SISTER.
NO WAY. I'D BE DONE BY NOW.

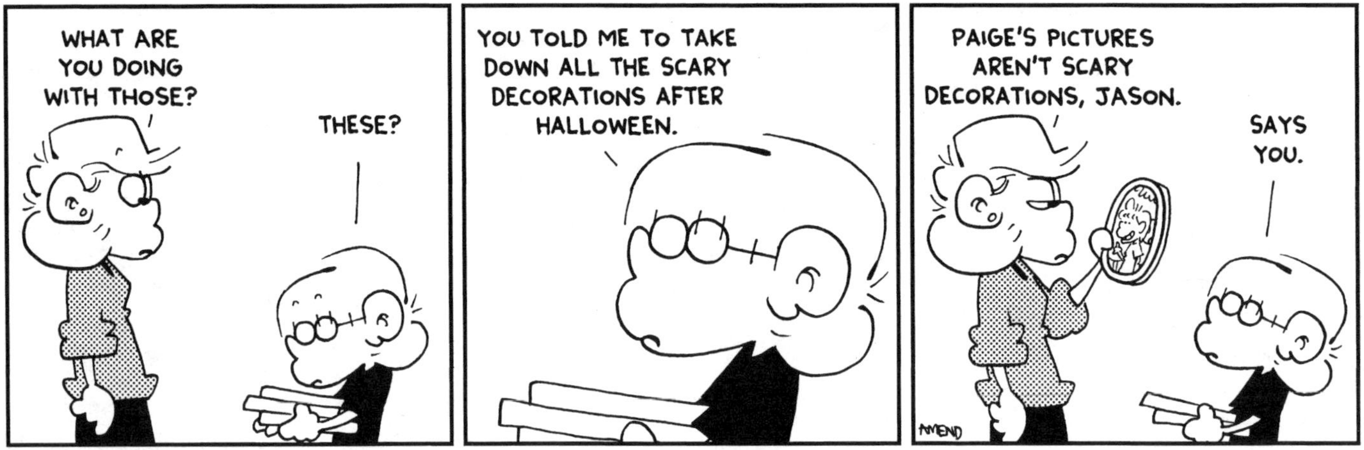
WHAT ARE YOU DOING WITH THOSE?
THESE?
YOU TOLD ME TO TAKE DOWN ALL THE SCARY DECORATIONS AFTER HALLOWEEN.
PAIGE'S PICTURES AREN'T SCARY DECORATIONS, JASON.
SAYS YOU.
AMEND

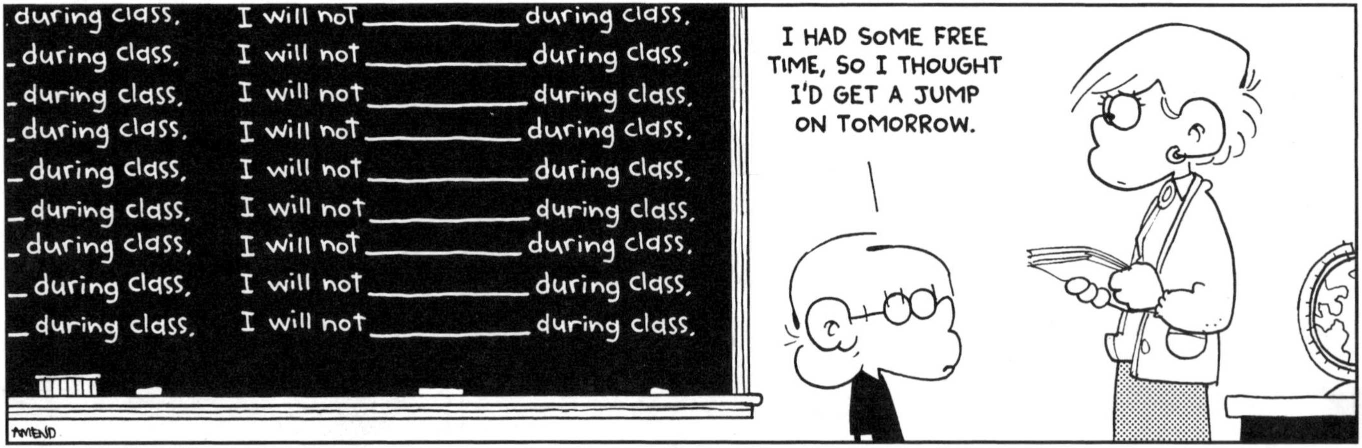
I will not ____ during class.
I HAD SOME FREE TIME, SO I THOUGHT I'D GET A JUMP ON TOMORROW.
AMEND

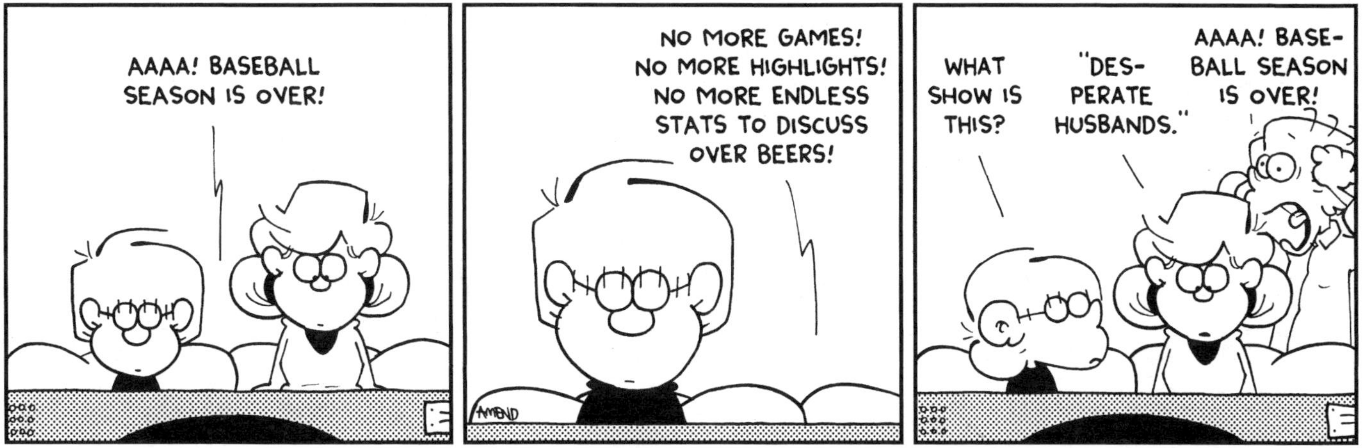
AAAA! BASEBALL SEASON IS OVER!
NO MORE GAMES! NO MORE HIGHLIGHTS! NO MORE ENDLESS STATS TO DISCUSS OVER BEERS!
WHAT SHOW IS THIS?
"DES-PERATE HUSBANDS."
AAAA! BASE-BALL SEASON IS OVER!
AMEND

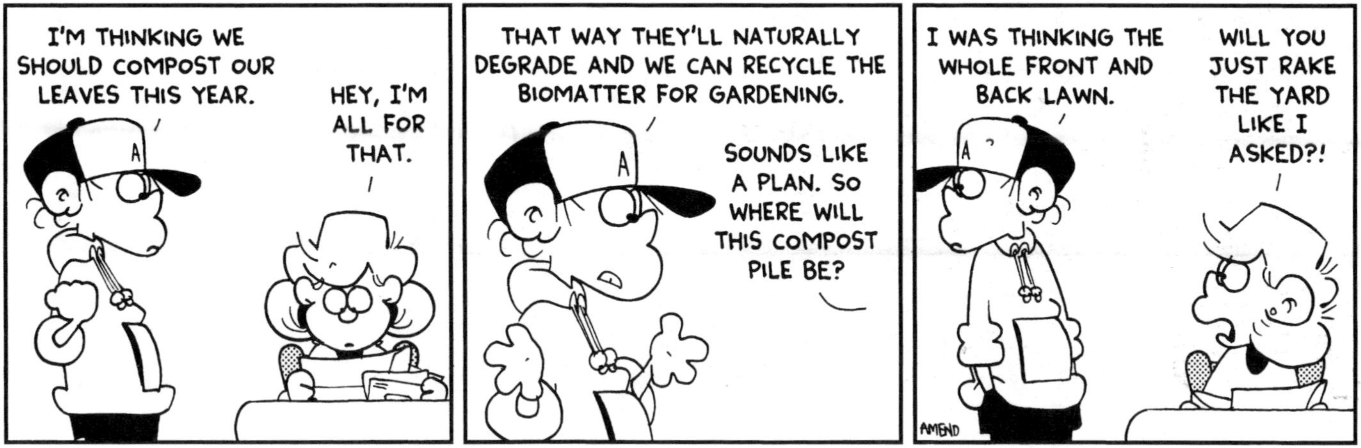
I'M THINKING WE SHOULD COMPOST OUR LEAVES THIS YEAR.
HEY, I'M ALL FOR THAT.
THAT WAY THEY'LL NATURALLY DEGRADE AND WE CAN RECYCLE THE BIOMATTER FOR GARDENING.
SOUNDS LIKE A PLAN. SO WHERE WILL THIS COMPOST PILE BE?
I WAS THINKING THE WHOLE FRONT AND BACK LAWN.
WILL YOU JUST RAKE THE YARD LIKE I ASKED?!
AMEND

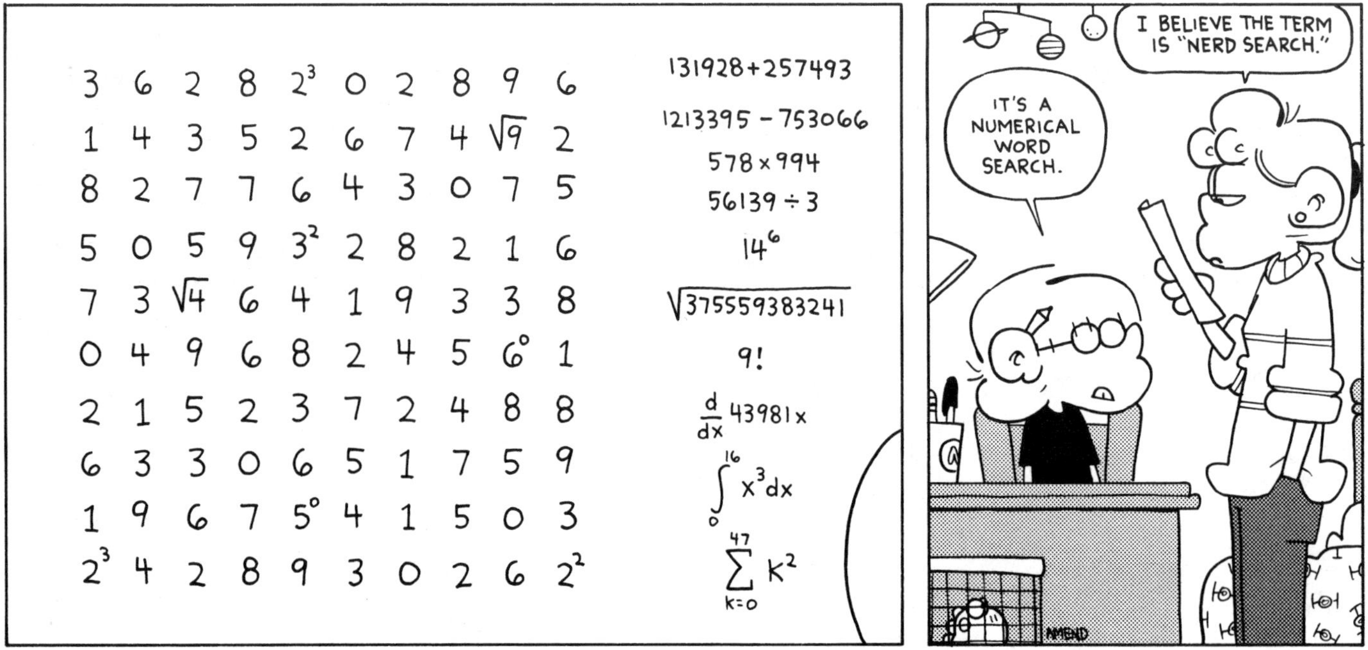
3 6 2 8 2^3 0 2 8 9 6
1 4 3 5 2 6 7 4 $\sqrt{9}$ 2
8 2 7 7 6 4 3 0 7 5
5 0 5 9 3^2 2 8 2 1 6
7 3 $\sqrt{4}$ 6 4 1 9 3 3 8
0 4 9 6 8 2 4 5 6^0 1
2 1 5 2 3 7 2 4 8 8
6 3 3 0 6 5 1 7 5 9
1 9 6 7 5^0 4 1 5 0 3
2^3 4 2 8 9 3 0 2 6 2^2
131928+257493
1213395 − 753066
578 × 994
56139 ÷ 3
14^6
$\sqrt{375559383241}$
9!
$\frac{d}{dx}$ 43981x
$\int_0^{16} x^3 dx$
$\sum_{k=0}^{47} k^2$
IT'S A NUMERICAL WORD SEARCH.
I BELIEVE THE TERM IS "NERD SEARCH."
AMEND

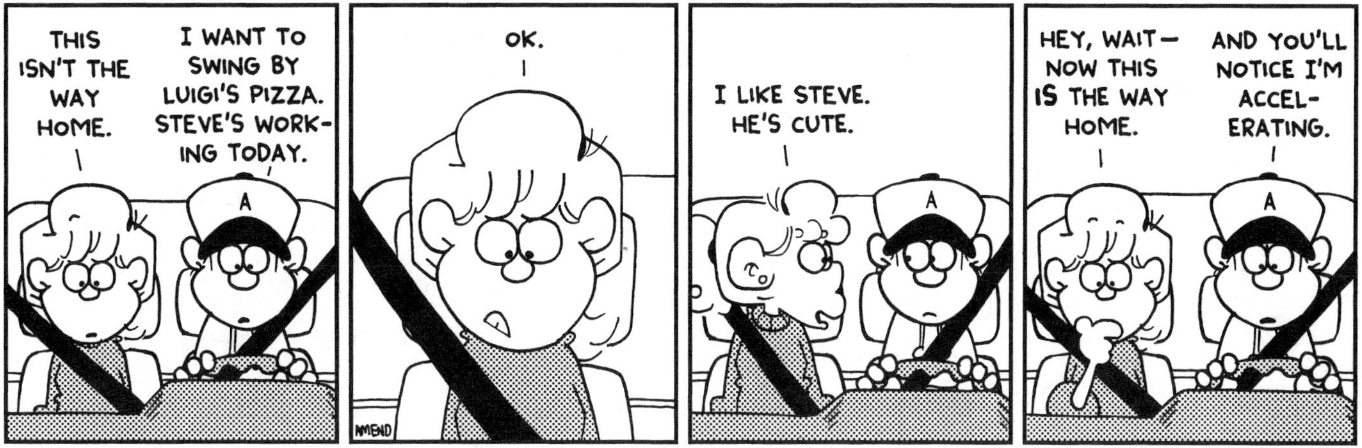
THIS ISN'T THE WAY HOME.
I WANT TO SWING BY LUIGI'S PIZZA. STEVE'S WORKING TODAY.
OK.
AMEND
I LIKE STEVE. HE'S CUTE.
HEY, WAIT— NOW THIS IS THE WAY HOME.
AND YOU'LL NOTICE I'M ACCELERATING.

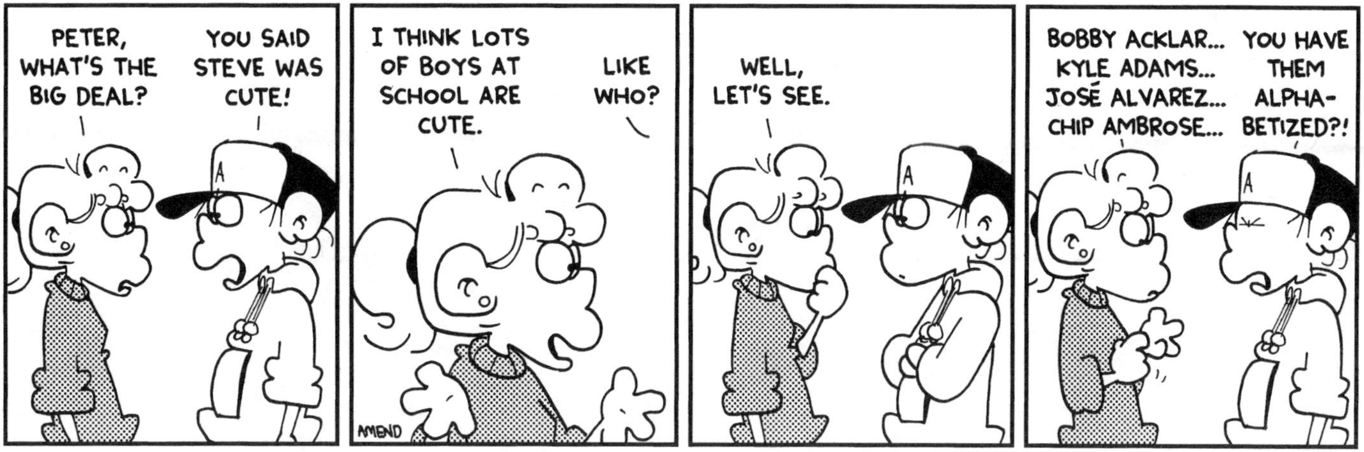
PETER, WHAT'S THE BIG DEAL?
YOU SAID STEVE WAS CUTE!
I THINK LOTS OF BOYS AT SCHOOL ARE CUTE.
LIKE WHO?
AMEND
WELL, LET'S SEE.
BOBBY ACKLAR... KYLE ADAMS... JOSÉ ALVAREZ... CHIP AMBROSE...
YOU HAVE THEM ALPHABETIZED?!

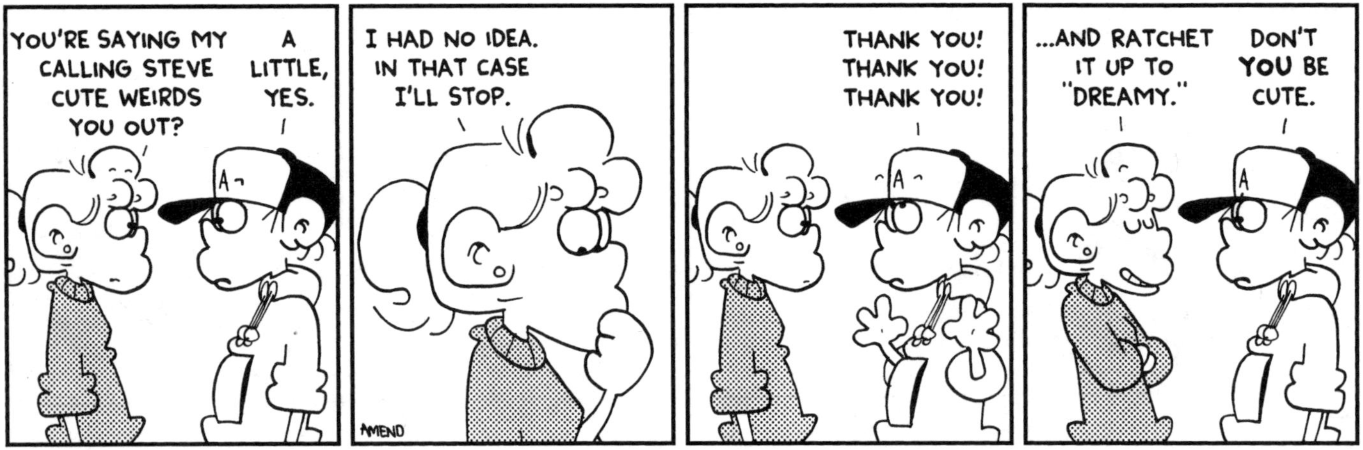
YOU'RE SAYING MY CALLING STEVE CUTE WEIRDS YOU OUT?
A LITTLE, YES.
I HAD NO IDEA. IN THAT CASE I'LL STOP.
AMEND
THANK YOU! THANK YOU! THANK YOU!
...AND RATCHET IT UP TO "DREAMY."
DON'T YOU BE CUTE.

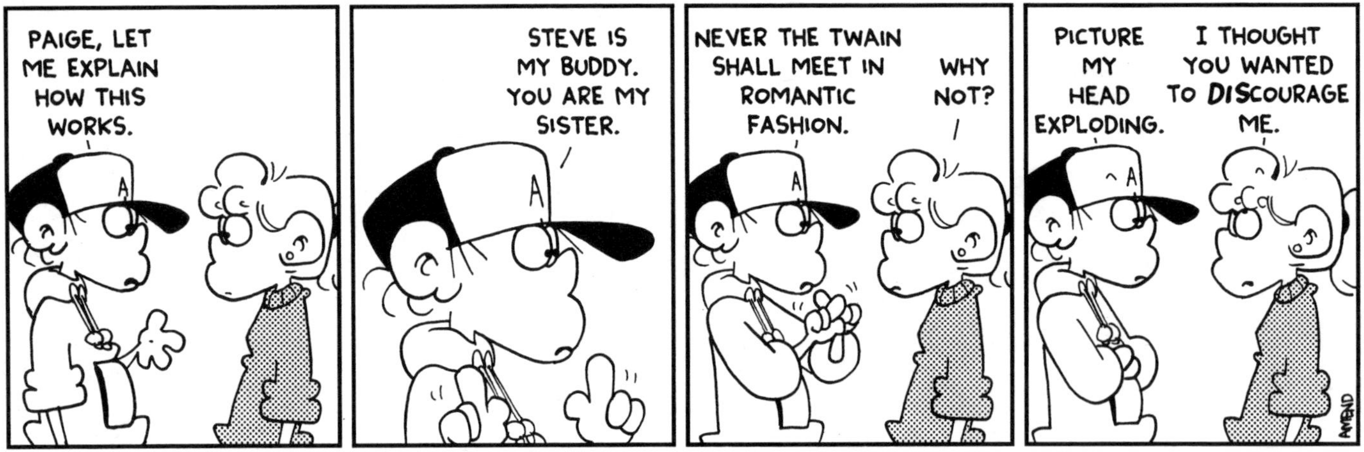
PAIGE, LET ME EXPLAIN HOW THIS WORKS.
STEVE IS MY BUDDY. YOU ARE MY SISTER.
NEVER THE TWAIN SHALL MEET IN ROMANTIC FASHION.
WHY NOT?
PICTURE MY HEAD EXPLODING.
I THOUGHT YOU WANTED TO DISCOURAGE ME.
AMEND

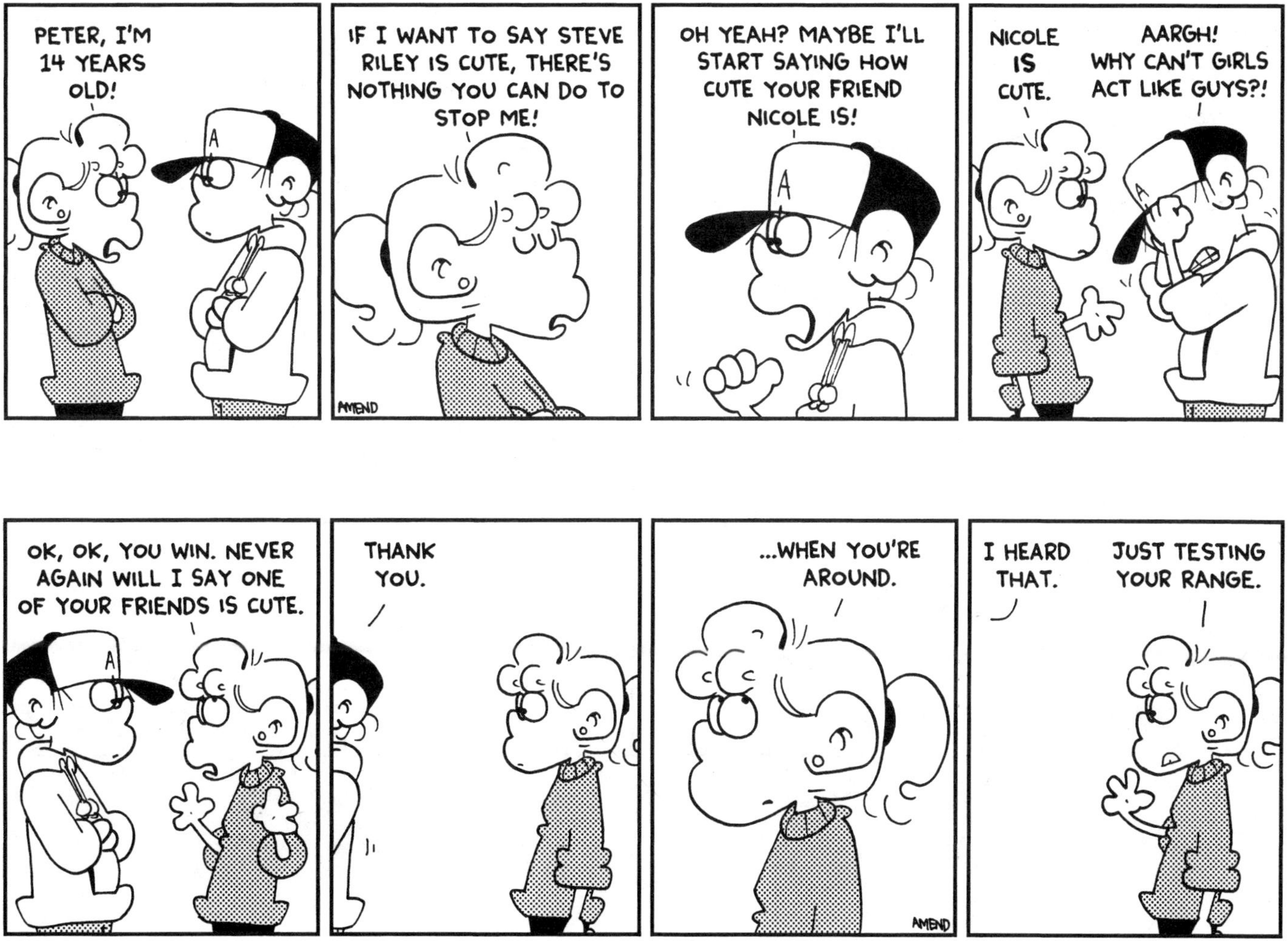
PETER, I'M 14 YEARS OLD!
IF I WANT TO SAY STEVE RILEY IS CUTE, THERE'S NOTHING YOU CAN DO TO STOP ME!
AMEND
OH YEAH? MAYBE I'LL START SAYING HOW CUTE YOUR FRIEND NICOLE IS!
NICOLE IS CUTE.
AARGH! WHY CAN'T GIRLS ACT LIKE GUYS?!
OK, OK, YOU WIN. NEVER AGAIN WILL I SAY ONE OF YOUR FRIENDS IS CUTE.
THANK YOU.
...WHEN YOU'RE AROUND.
AMEND
I HEARD THAT.
JUST TESTING YOUR RANGE.

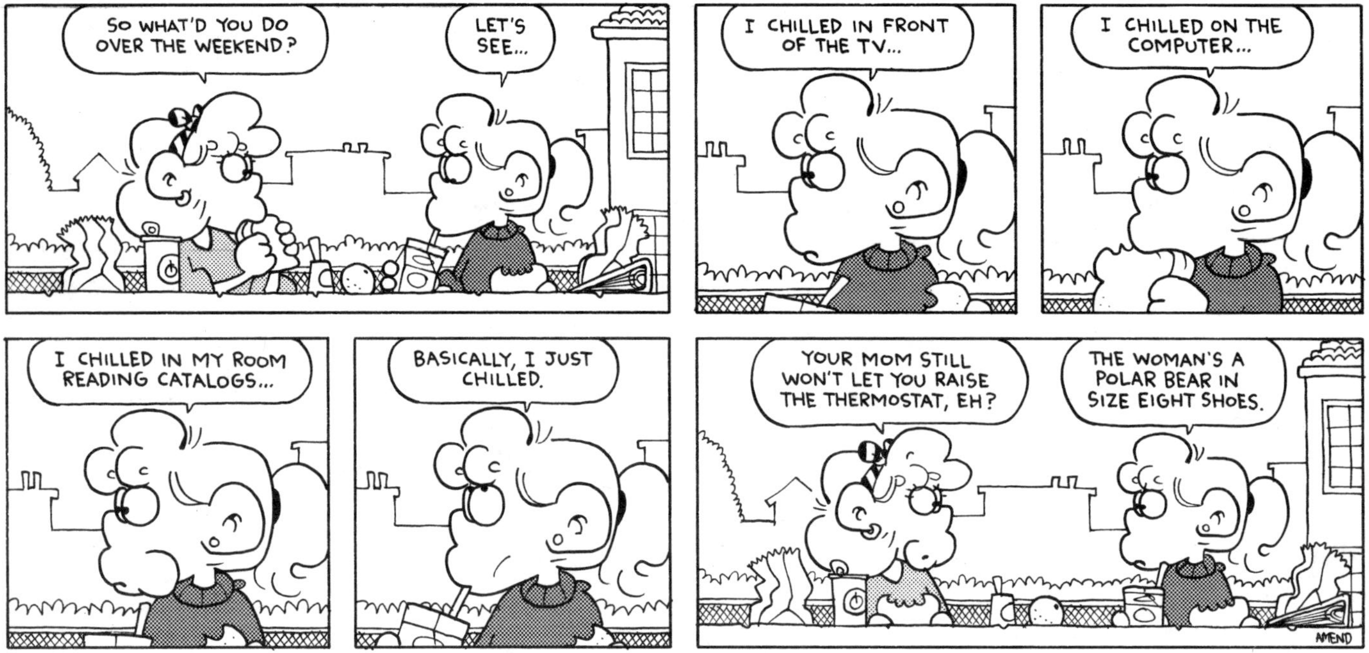
SO WHAT'D YOU DO OVER THE WEEKEND?
LET'S SEE...
I CHILLED IN FRONT OF THE TV...
I CHILLED ON THE COMPUTER...
I CHILLED IN MY ROOM READING CATALOGS...
BASICALLY, I JUST CHILLED.
YOUR MOM STILL WON'T LET YOU RAISE THE THERMOSTAT, EH?
THE WOMAN'S A POLAR BEAR IN SIZE EIGHT SHOES.
AMEND

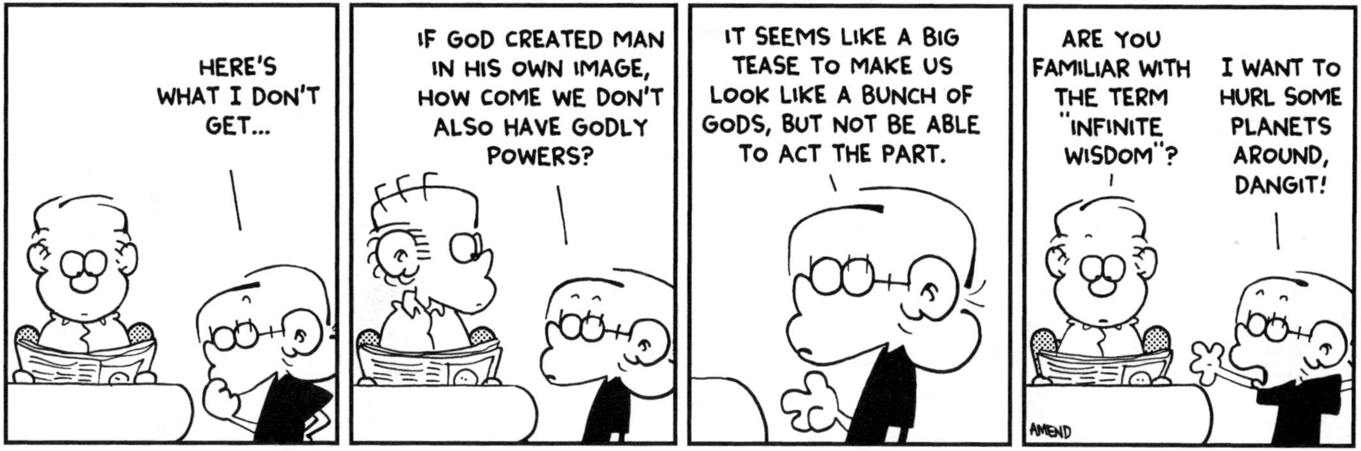
HERE'S WHAT I DON'T GET...
IF GOD CREATED MAN IN HIS OWN IMAGE, HOW COME WE DON'T ALSO HAVE GODLY POWERS?
IT SEEMS LIKE A BIG TEASE TO MAKE US LOOK LIKE A BUNCH OF GODS, BUT NOT BE ABLE TO ACT THE PART.
ARE YOU FAMILIAR WITH THE TERM "INFINITE WISDOM"?
I WANT TO HURL SOME PLANETS AROUND, DANGIT!
AMEND

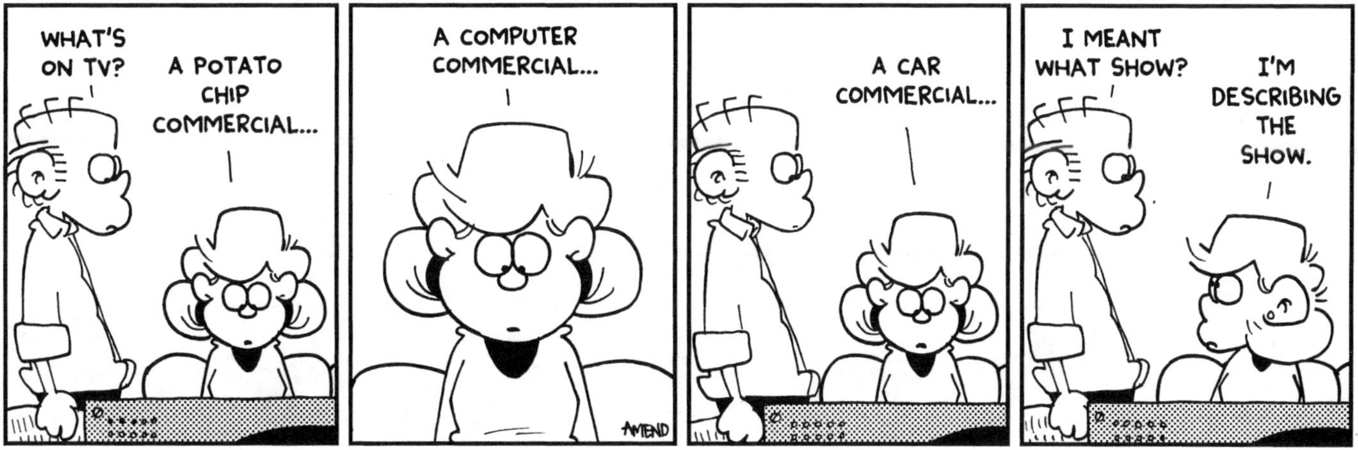
WHAT'S ON TV?
A POTATO CHIP COMMERCIAL...
A COMPUTER COMMERCIAL...
AMEND
A CAR COMMERCIAL...
I MEANT WHAT SHOW?
I'M DESCRIBING THE SHOW.

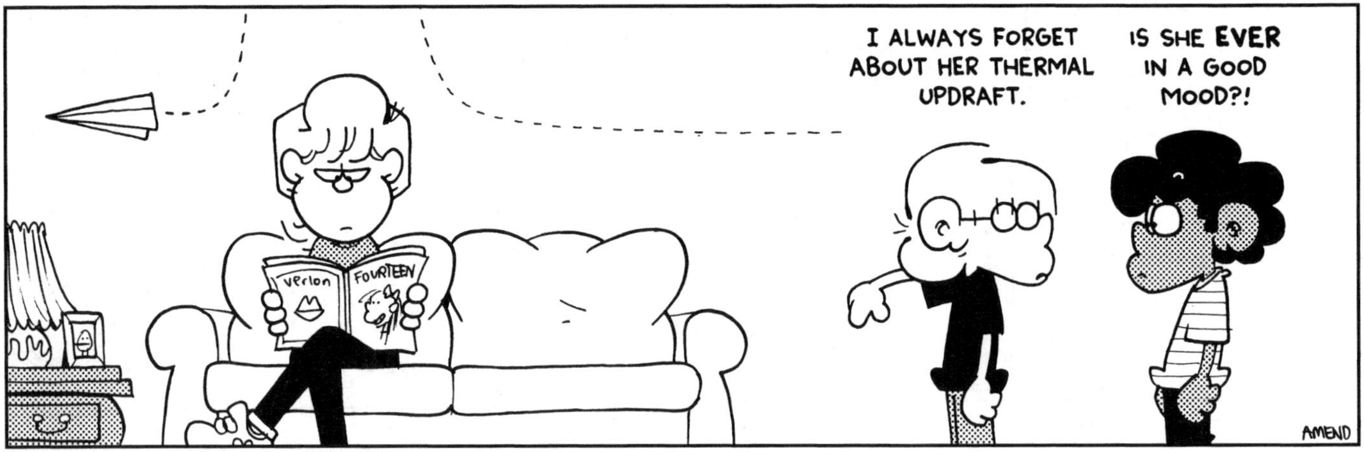
I ALWAYS FORGET ABOUT HER THERMAL UPDRAFT.
IS SHE **EVER** IN A GOOD MOOD?!
AMEND

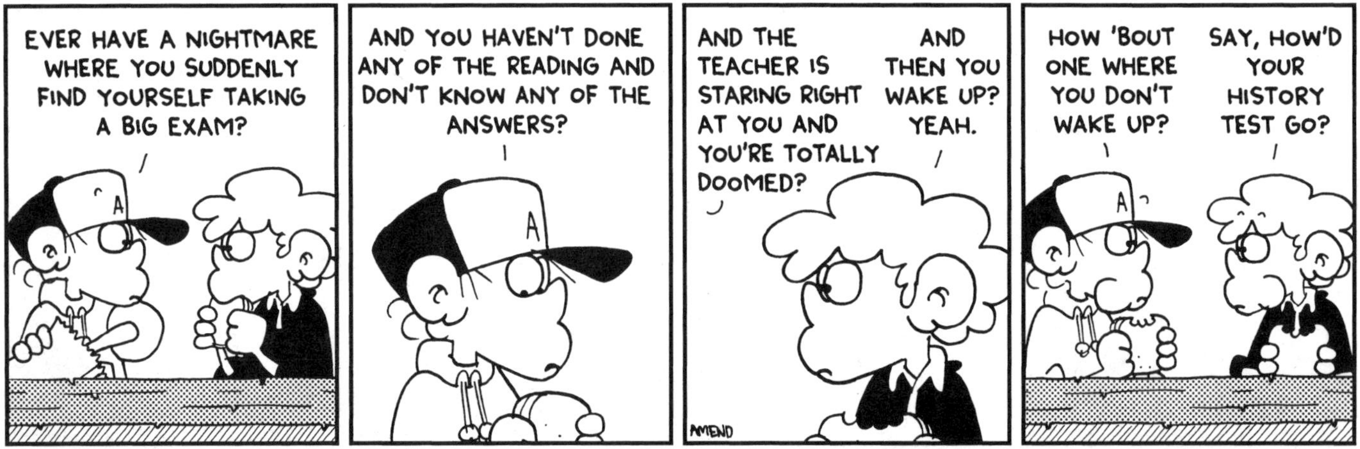
EVER HAVE A NIGHTMARE WHERE YOU SUDDENLY FIND YOURSELF TAKING A BIG EXAM?
AND YOU HAVEN'T DONE ANY OF THE READING AND DON'T KNOW ANY OF THE ANSWERS?
AND THE TEACHER IS STARING RIGHT AT YOU AND YOU'RE TOTALLY DOOMED?
AND THEN YOU WAKE UP? YEAH.
AMEND
HOW 'BOUT ONE WHERE YOU DON'T WAKE UP?
SAY, HOW'D YOUR HISTORY TEST GO?

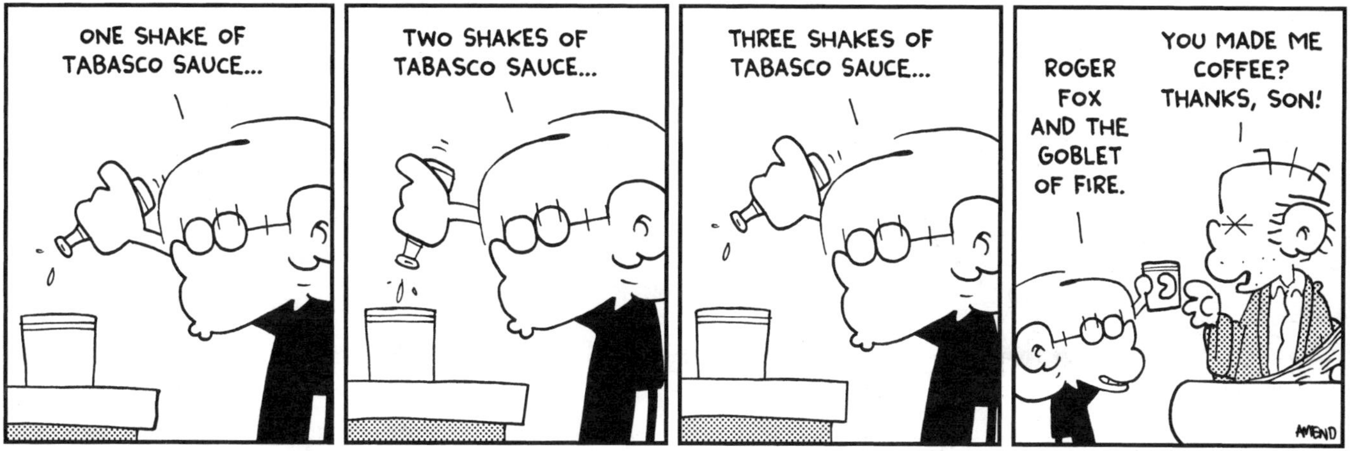
ONE SHAKE OF TABASCO SAUCE...
TWO SHAKES OF TABASCO SAUCE...
THREE SHAKES OF TABASCO SAUCE...
ROGER FOX AND THE GOBLET OF FIRE.
YOU MADE ME COFFEE? THANKS, SON!
AMEND

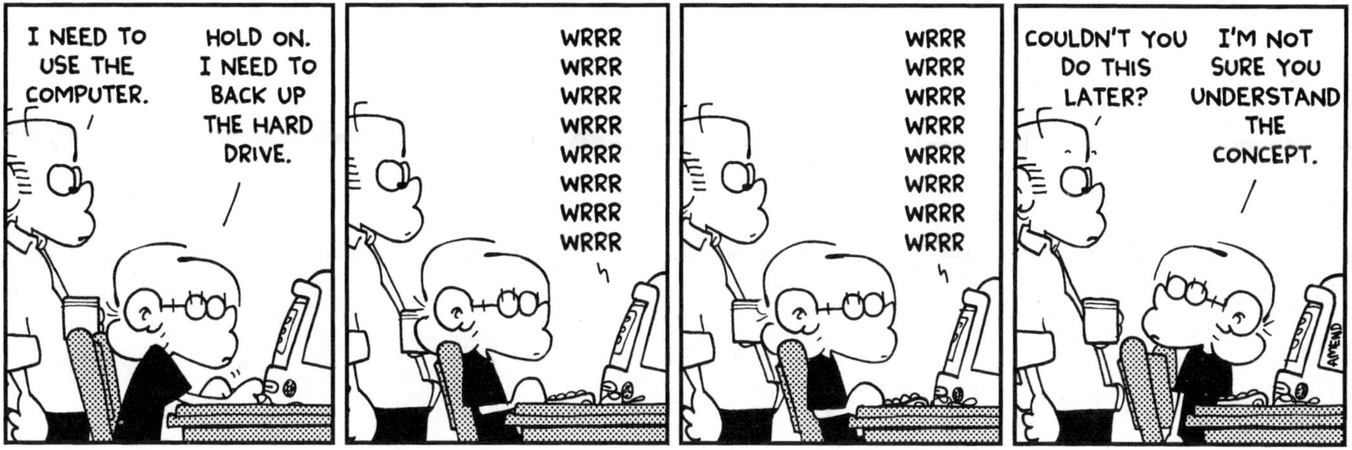
I NEED TO USE THE COMPUTER.
HOLD ON. I NEED TO BACK UP THE HARD DRIVE.
WRRR WRRR WRRR WRRR WRRR WRRR WRRR WRRR
WRRR WRRR WRRR WRRR WRRR WRRR WRRR WRRR
COULDN'T YOU DO THIS LATER?
I'M NOT SURE YOU UNDERSTAND THE CONCEPT.
AMEND

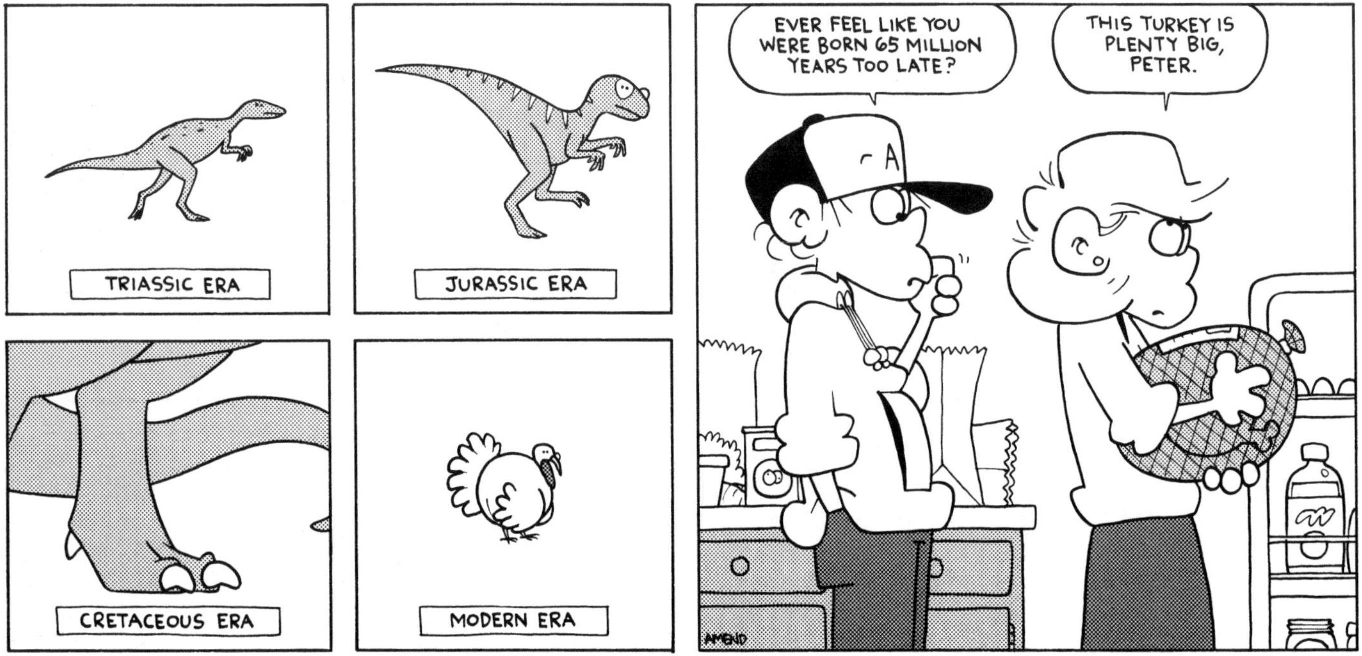
TRIASSIC ERA
JURASSIC ERA
CRETACEOUS ERA
MODERN ERA
EVER FEEL LIKE YOU WERE BORN 65 MILLION YEARS TOO LATE?
THIS TURKEY IS PLENTY BIG, PETER.
AMEND

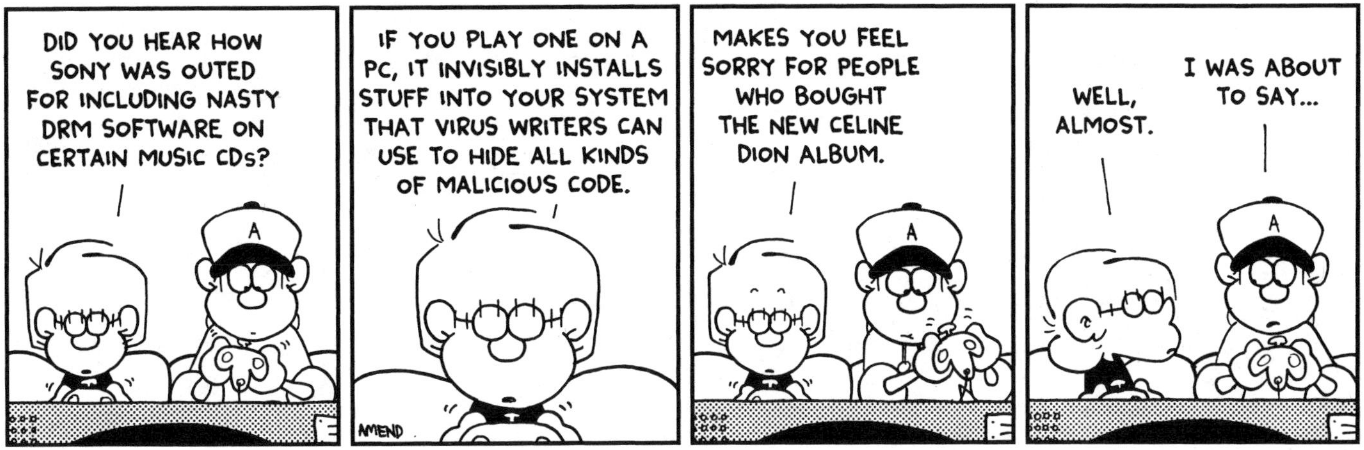
DID YOU HEAR HOW SONY WAS OUTED FOR INCLUDING NASTY DRM SOFTWARE ON CERTAIN MUSIC CDs?
IF YOU PLAY ONE ON A PC, IT INVISIBLY INSTALLS STUFF INTO YOUR SYSTEM THAT VIRUS WRITERS CAN USE TO HIDE ALL KINDS OF MALICIOUS CODE.
AMEND
MAKES YOU FEEL SORRY FOR PEOPLE WHO BOUGHT THE NEW CELINE DION ALBUM.
I WAS ABOUT TO SAY...
WELL, ALMOST.

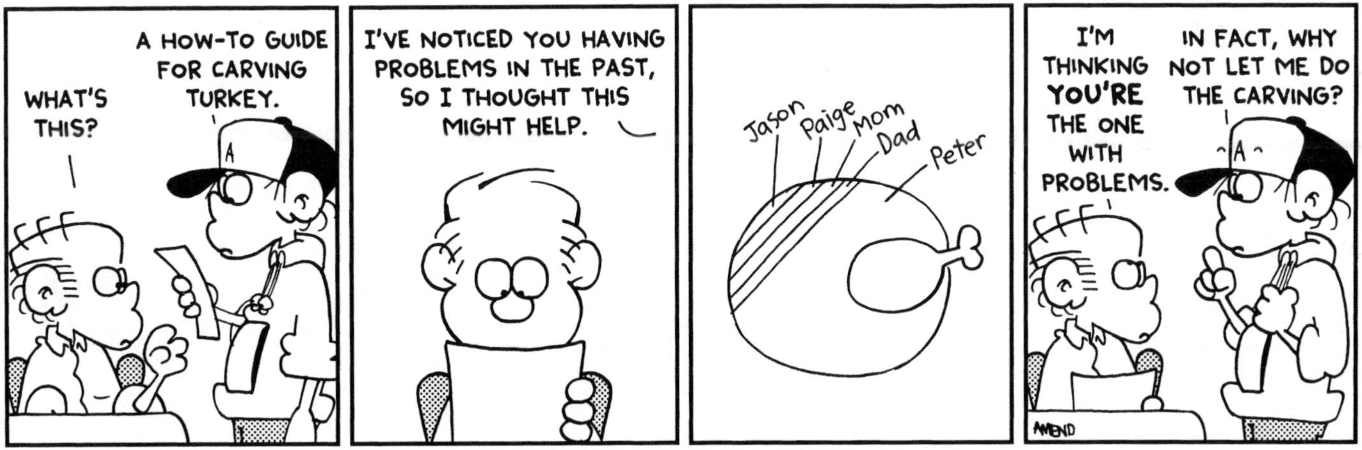
WHAT'S THIS?
A HOW-TO GUIDE FOR CARVING TURKEY.
I'VE NOTICED YOU HAVING PROBLEMS IN THE PAST, SO I THOUGHT THIS MIGHT HELP.
Jason
Paige
Mom
Dad
Peter
I'M THINKING **YOU'RE** THE ONE WITH PROBLEMS.
IN FACT, WHY NOT LET ME DO THE CARVING?
AMEND

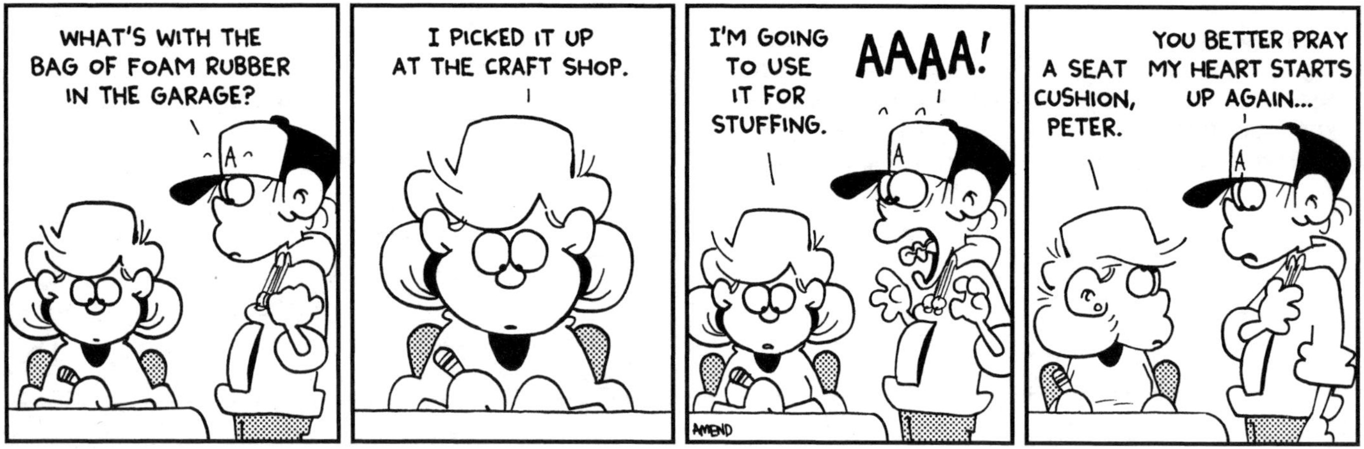
WHAT'S WITH THE BAG OF FOAM RUBBER IN THE GARAGE?
I PICKED IT UP AT THE CRAFT SHOP.
I'M GOING TO USE IT FOR STUFFING.
AAAA!
A SEAT CUSHION, PETER.
YOU BETTER PRAY MY HEART STARTS UP AGAIN...
AMEND

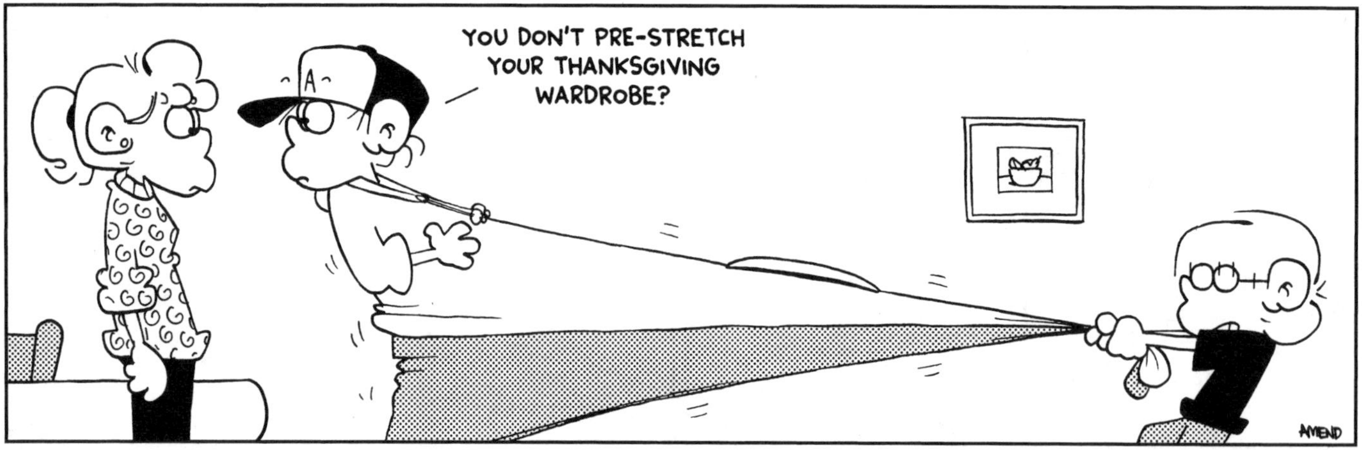
YOU DON'T PRE-STRETCH YOUR THANKSGIVING WARDROBE?
AMEND

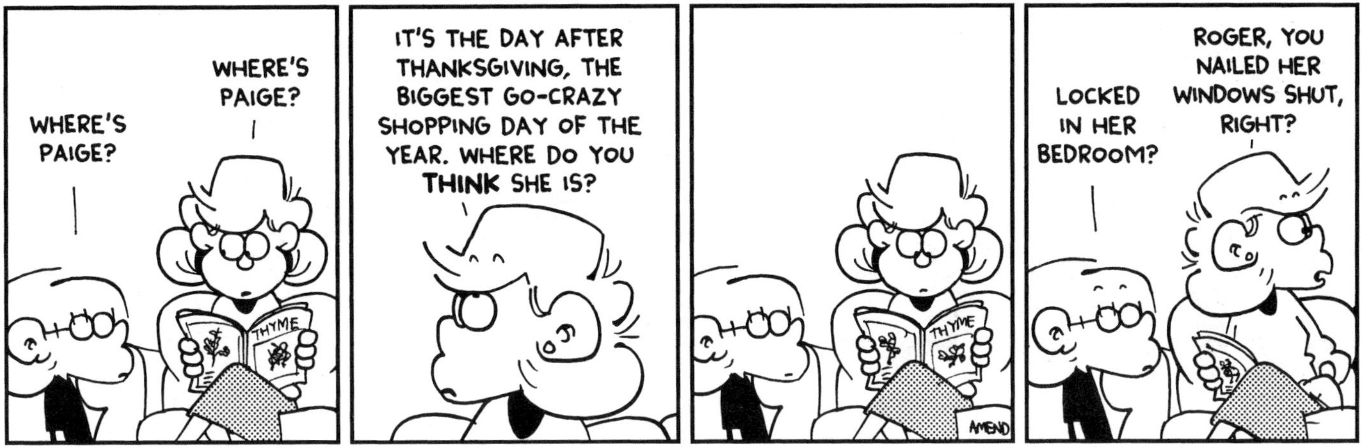
WHERE'S PAIGE?
WHERE'S PAIGE?
IT'S THE DAY AFTER THANKSGIVING, THE BIGGEST GO-CRAZY SHOPPING DAY OF THE YEAR. WHERE DO YOU **THINK** SHE IS?
THYME
AMEND
LOCKED IN HER BEDROOM?
ROGER, YOU NAILED HER WINDOWS SHUT, RIGHT?

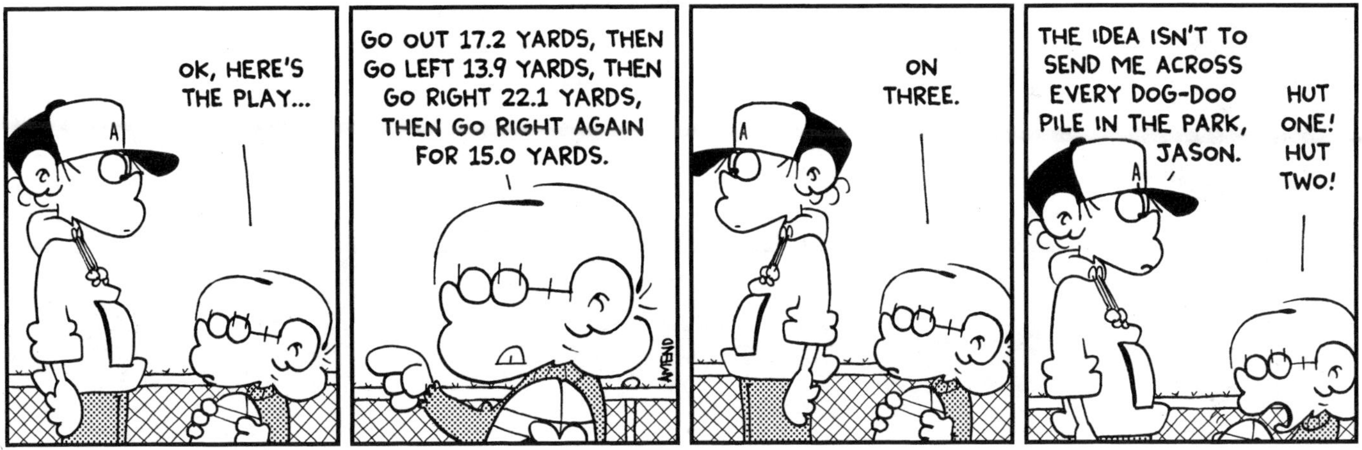
OK, HERE'S THE PLAY...
GO OUT 17.2 YARDS, THEN GO LEFT 13.9 YARDS, THEN GO RIGHT 22.1 YARDS, THEN GO RIGHT AGAIN FOR 15.0 YARDS.
AMEND
ON THREE.
THE IDEA ISN'T TO SEND ME ACROSS EVERY DOG-DOO PILE IN THE PARK, JASON.
HUT ONE! HUT TWO!

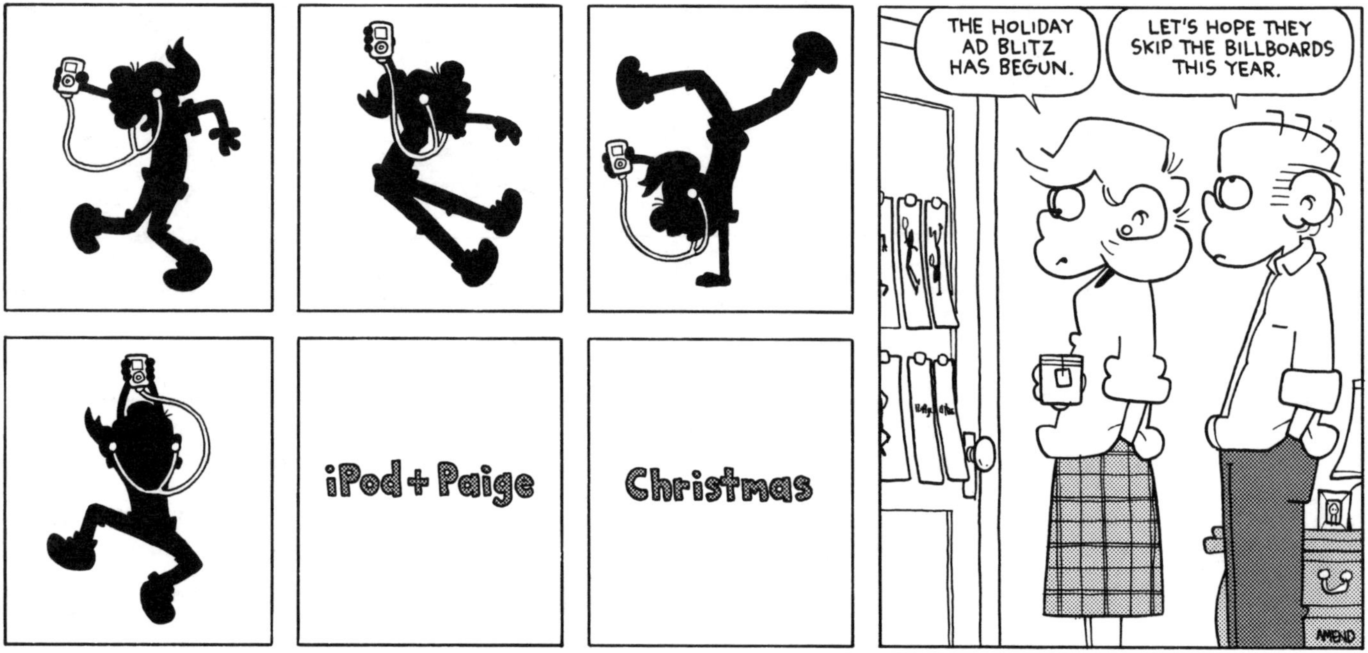
iPod + Paige
Christmas
THE HOLIDAY AD BLITZ HAS BEGUN.
LET'S HOPE THEY SKIP THE BILLBOARDS THIS YEAR.
AMEND

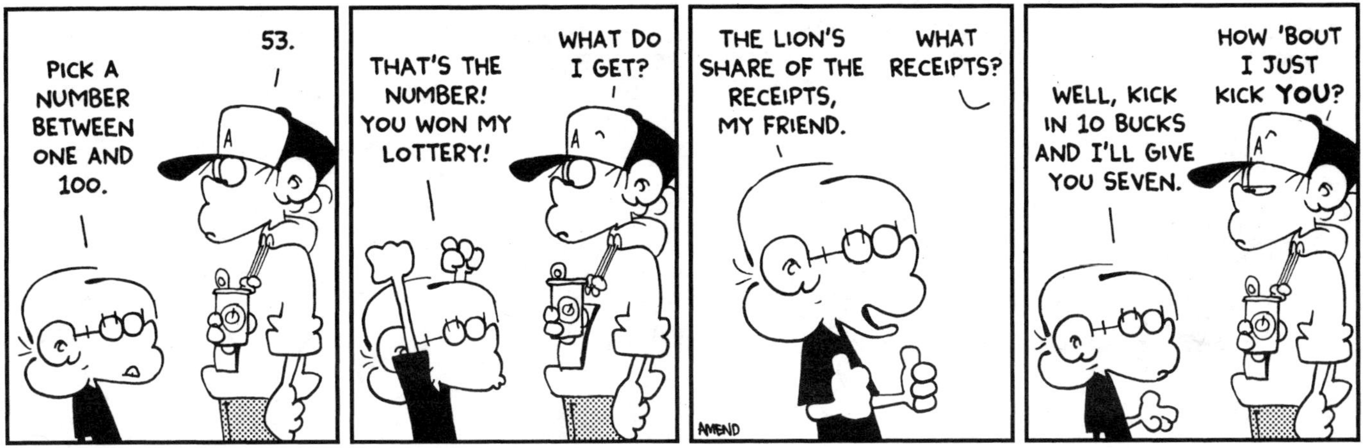
PICK A NUMBER BETWEEN ONE AND 100.
53.
THAT'S THE NUMBER! YOU WON MY LOTTERY!
WHAT DO I GET?
THE LION'S SHARE OF THE RECEIPTS, MY FRIEND.
WHAT RECEIPTS?
AMEND
WELL, KICK IN 10 BUCKS AND I'LL GIVE YOU SEVEN.
HOW 'BOUT I JUST KICK YOU?

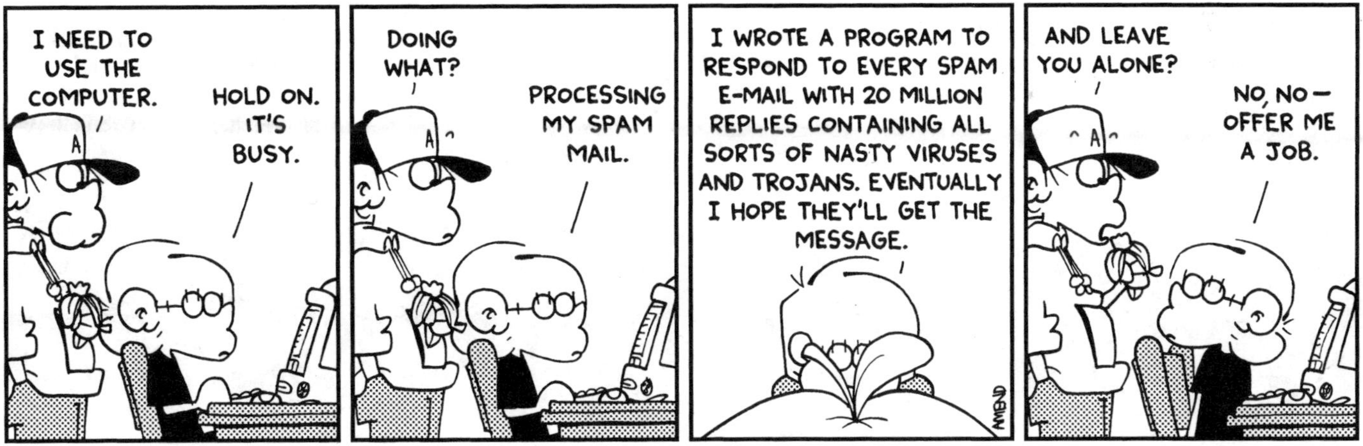
I NEED TO USE THE COMPUTER.
HOLD ON. IT'S BUSY.
DOING WHAT?
PROCESSING MY SPAM MAIL.
I WROTE A PROGRAM TO RESPOND TO EVERY SPAM E-MAIL WITH 20 MILLION REPLIES CONTAINING ALL SORTS OF NASTY VIRUSES AND TROJANS. EVENTUALLY I HOPE THEY'LL GET THE MESSAGE.
AMEND
AND LEAVE YOU ALONE?
NO, NO — OFFER ME A JOB.

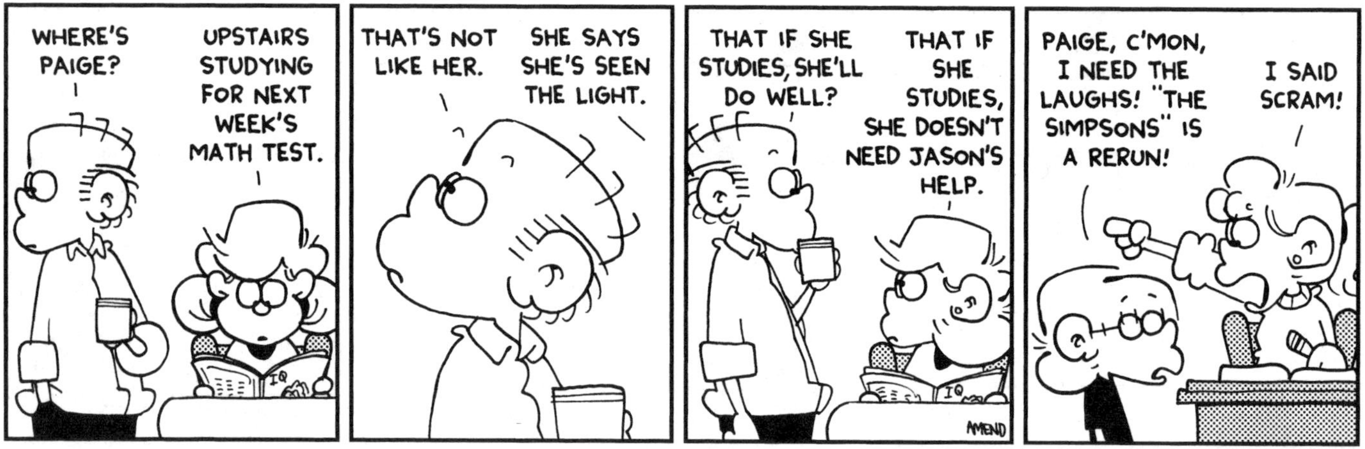
WHERE'S PAIGE?
UPSTAIRS STUDYING FOR NEXT WEEK'S MATH TEST.
THAT'S NOT LIKE HER.
SHE SAYS SHE'S SEEN THE LIGHT.
THAT IF SHE STUDIES, SHE'LL DO WELL?
THAT IF SHE STUDIES, SHE DOESN'T NEED JASON'S HELP.
AMEND
PAIGE, C'MON, I NEED THE LAUGHS! "THE SIMPSONS" IS A RERUN!
I SAID SCRAM!

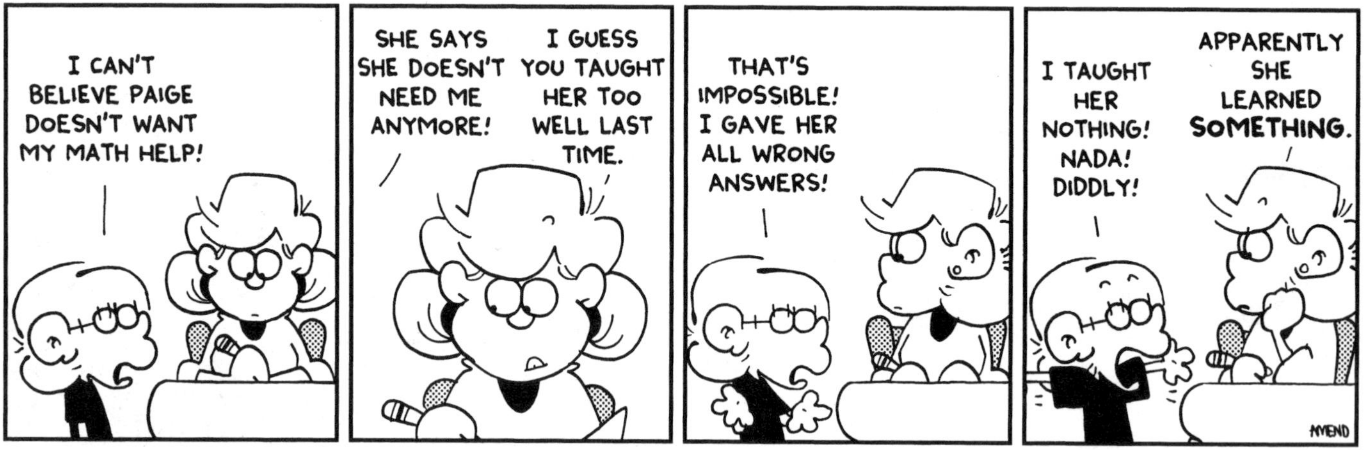
I CAN'T BELIEVE PAIGE DOESN'T WANT MY MATH HELP!
SHE SAYS SHE DOESN'T NEED ME ANYMORE!
I GUESS YOU TAUGHT HER TOO WELL LAST TIME.
THAT'S IMPOSSIBLE! I GAVE HER ALL WRONG ANSWERS!
I TAUGHT HER NOTHING! NADA! DIDDLY!
APPARENTLY SHE LEARNED SOMETHING.
AMEND

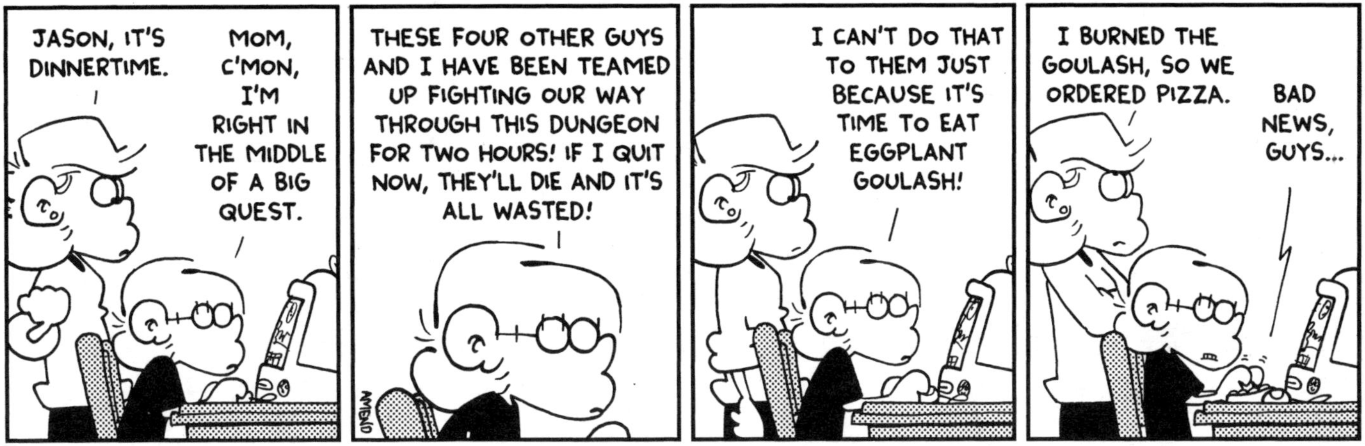
JASON, IT'S DINNERTIME.
MOM, C'MON, I'M RIGHT IN THE MIDDLE OF A BIG QUEST.
THESE FOUR OTHER GUYS AND I HAVE BEEN TEAMED UP FIGHTING OUR WAY THROUGH THIS DUNGEON FOR TWO HOURS! IF I QUIT NOW, THEY'LL DIE AND IT'S ALL WASTED!
AMEND
I CAN'T DO THAT TO THEM JUST BECAUSE IT'S TIME TO EAT EGGPLANT GOULASH!
I BURNED THE GOULASH, SO WE ORDERED PIZZA.
BAD NEWS, GUYS...

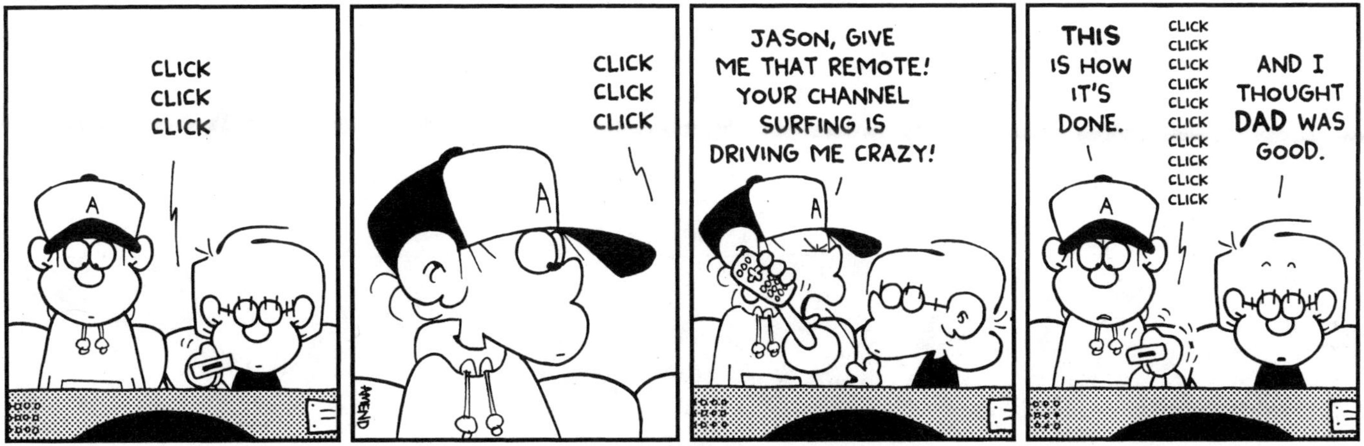
CLICK CLICK CLICK
CLICK CLICK CLICK
AMEND
JASON, GIVE ME THAT REMOTE! YOUR CHANNEL SURFING IS DRIVING ME CRAZY!
THIS IS HOW IT'S DONE.
CLICK CLICK CLICK CLICK CLICK CLICK CLICK CLICK CLICK CLICK
AND I THOUGHT **DAD** WAS GOOD.

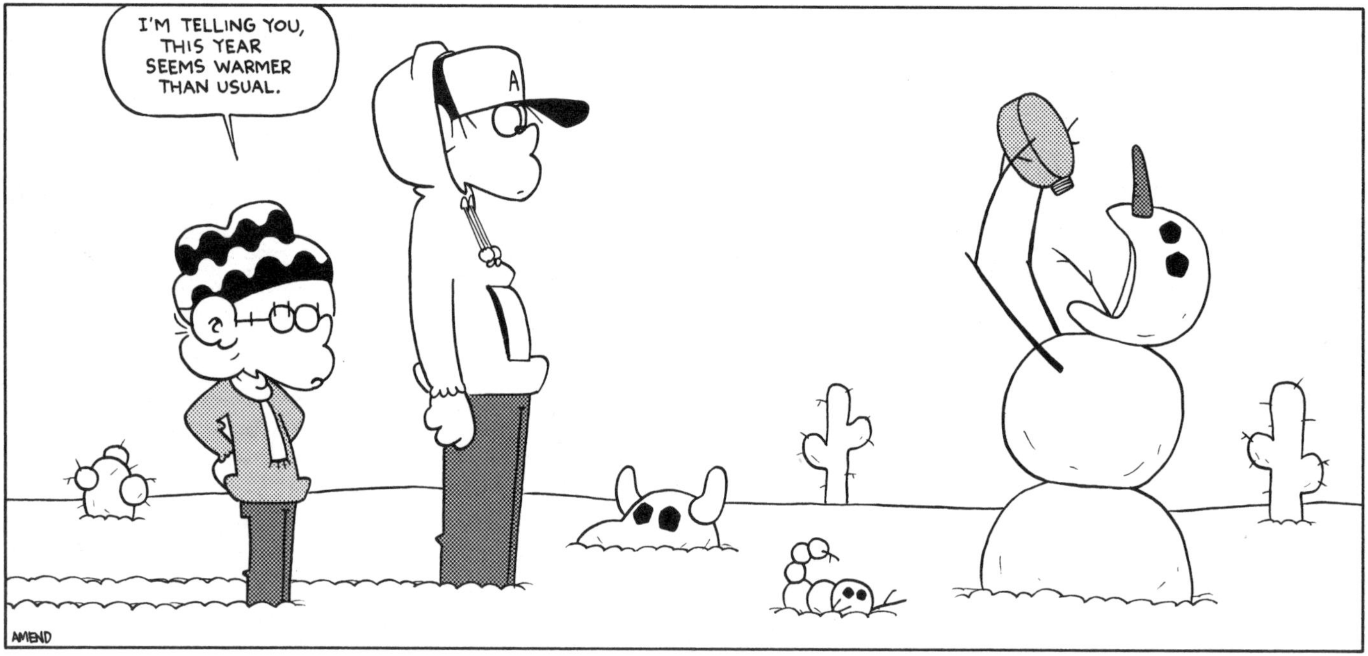
I'M TELLING YOU, THIS YEAR SEEMS WARMER THAN USUAL.
A
AMEND

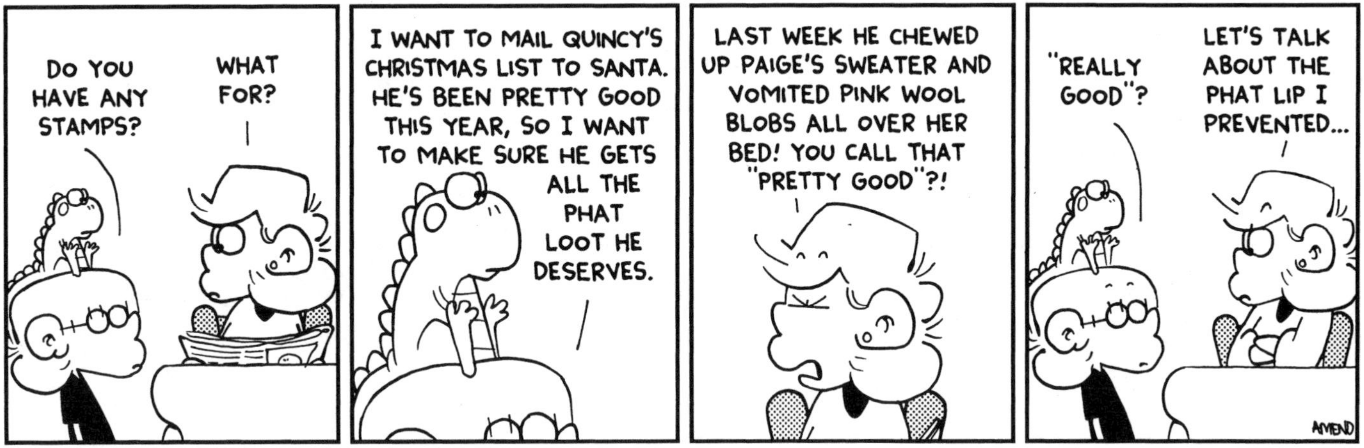
DO YOU HAVE ANY STAMPS?
WHAT FOR?
I WANT TO MAIL QUINCY'S CHRISTMAS LIST TO SANTA. HE'S BEEN PRETTY GOOD THIS YEAR, SO I WANT TO MAKE SURE HE GETS ALL THE PHAT LOOT HE DESERVES.
LAST WEEK HE CHEWED UP PAIGE'S SWEATER AND VOMITED PINK WOOL BLOBS ALL OVER HER BED! YOU CALL THAT "PRETTY GOOD"?!
"REALLY GOOD"?
LET'S TALK ABOUT THE PHAT LIP I PREVENTED...
AMEND

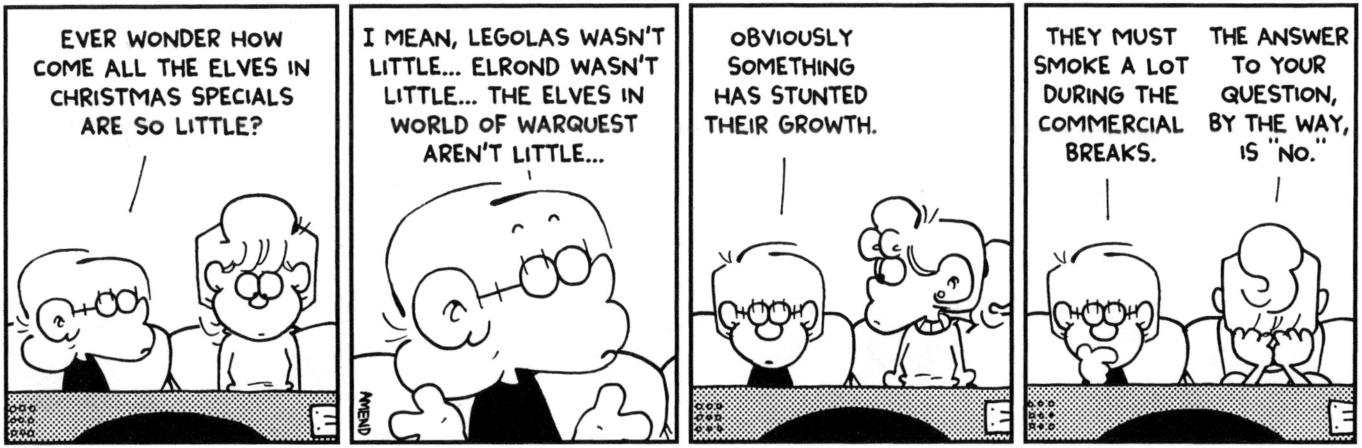
EVER WONDER HOW COME ALL THE ELVES IN CHRISTMAS SPECIALS ARE SO LITTLE?
I MEAN, LEGOLAS WASN'T LITTLE... ELROND WASN'T LITTLE... THE ELVES IN WORLD OF WARQUEST AREN'T LITTLE...
AMEND
OBVIOUSLY SOMETHING HAS STUNTED THEIR GROWTH.
THEY MUST SMOKE A LOT DURING THE COMMERCIAL BREAKS.
THE ANSWER TO YOUR QUESTION, BY THE WAY, IS "NO."

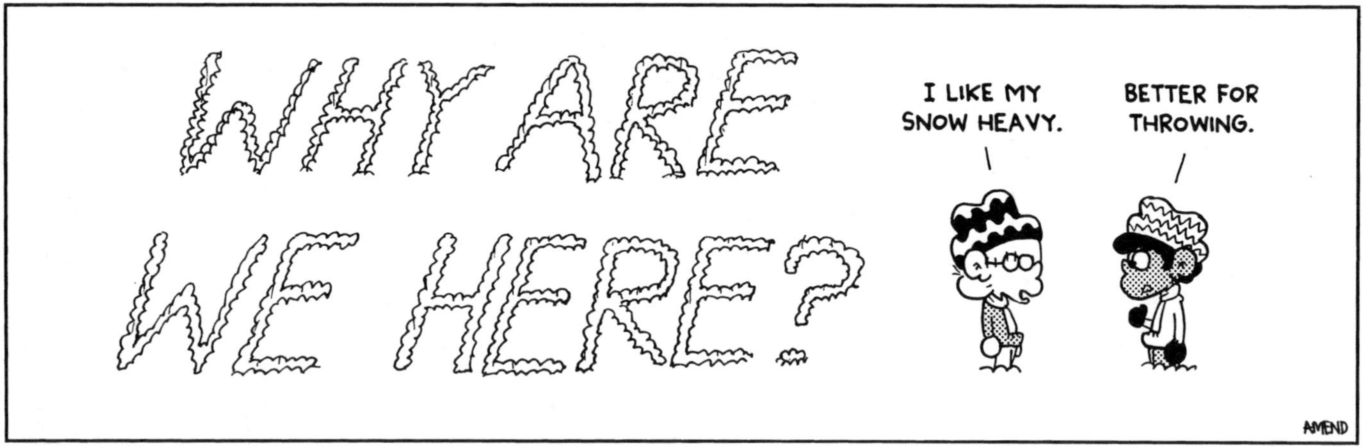
WHY ARE WE HERE?
I LIKE MY SNOW HEAVY.
BETTER FOR THROWING.
AMEND

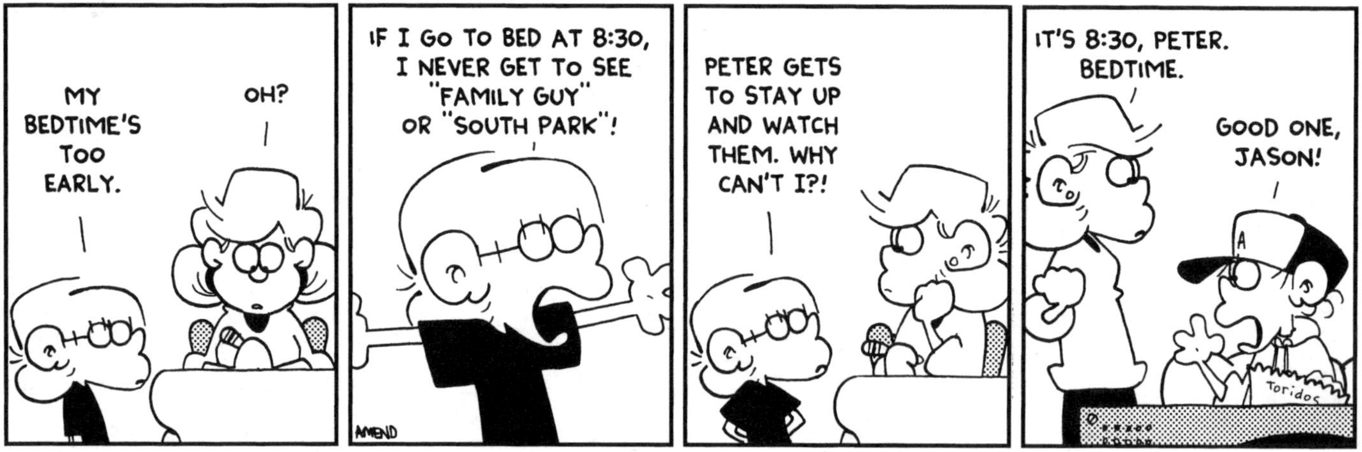
MY BEDTIME'S TOO EARLY.
OH?
IF I GO TO BED AT 8:30, I NEVER GET TO SEE "FAMILY GUY" OR "SOUTH PARK"!
AMEND
PETER GETS TO STAY UP AND WATCH THEM. WHY CAN'T I?!
IT'S 8:30, PETER. BEDTIME.
GOOD ONE, JASON!
Toridos

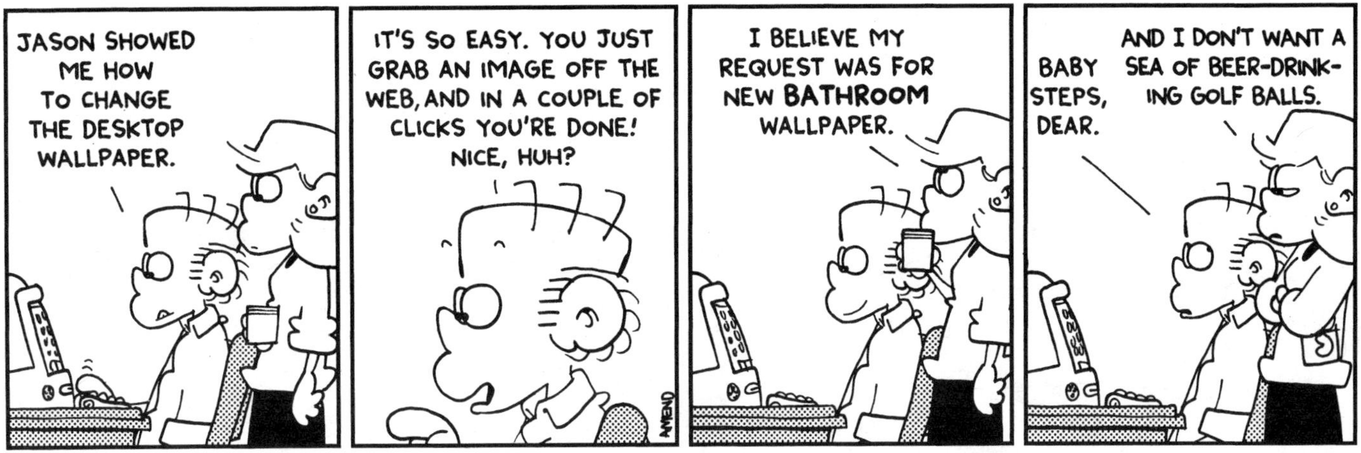
JASON SHOWED ME HOW TO CHANGE THE DESKTOP WALLPAPER.
IT'S SO EASY. YOU JUST GRAB AN IMAGE OFF THE WEB, AND IN A COUPLE OF CLICKS YOU'RE DONE! NICE, HUH?
I BELIEVE MY REQUEST WAS FOR NEW **BATHROOM** WALLPAPER.
BABY STEPS, DEAR.
AND I DON'T WANT A SEA OF BEER-DRINKING GOLF BALLS.
AMEND

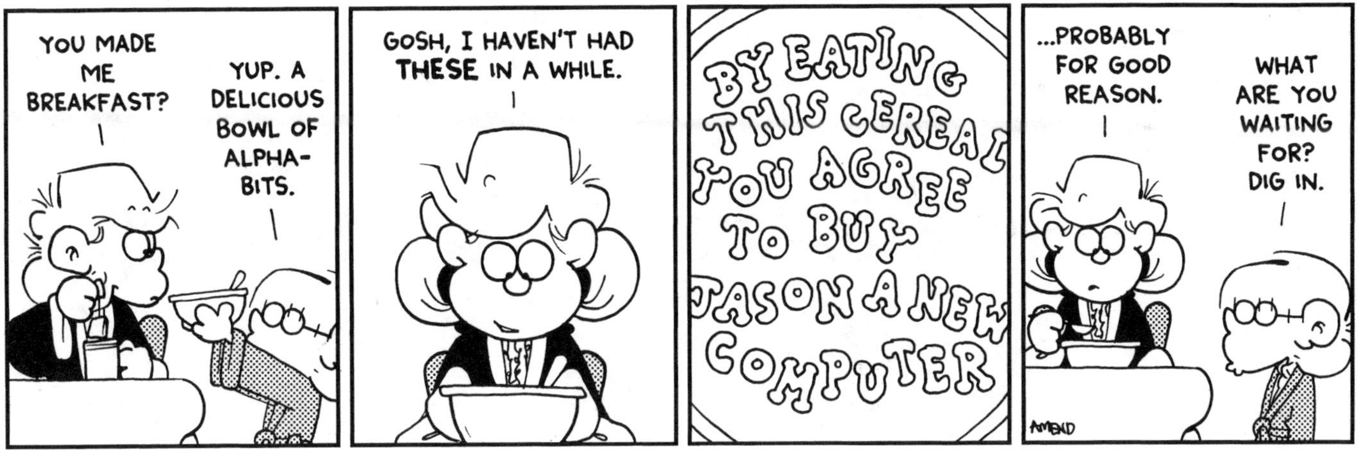
YOU MADE ME BREAKFAST?
YUP. A DELICIOUS BOWL OF ALPHA-BITS.
GOSH, I HAVEN'T HAD **THESE** IN A WHILE.
BY EATING THIS CEREAL YOU AGREE TO BUY JASON A NEW COMPUTER
...PROBABLY FOR GOOD REASON.
WHAT ARE YOU WAITING FOR? DIG IN.
AMEND

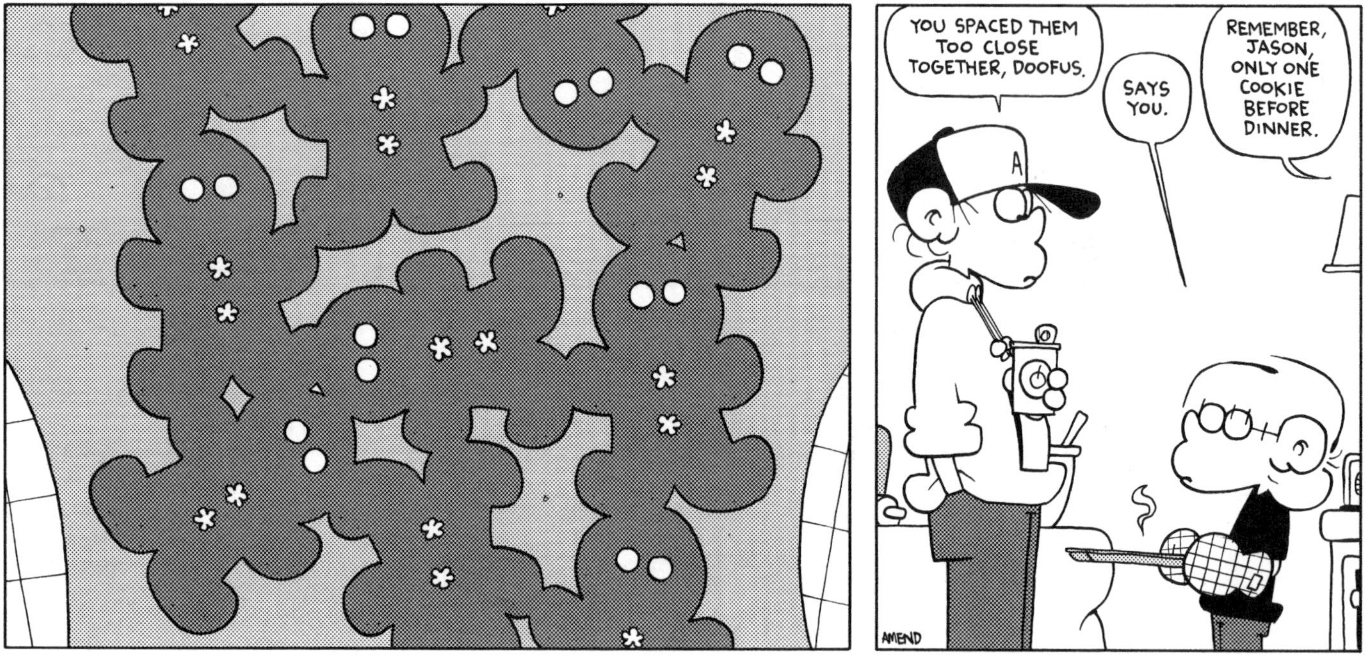
YOU SPACED THEM TOO CLOSE TOGETHER, DOOFUS.
SAYS YOU.
REMEMBER, JASON, ONLY ONE COOKIE BEFORE DINNER.
AMEND

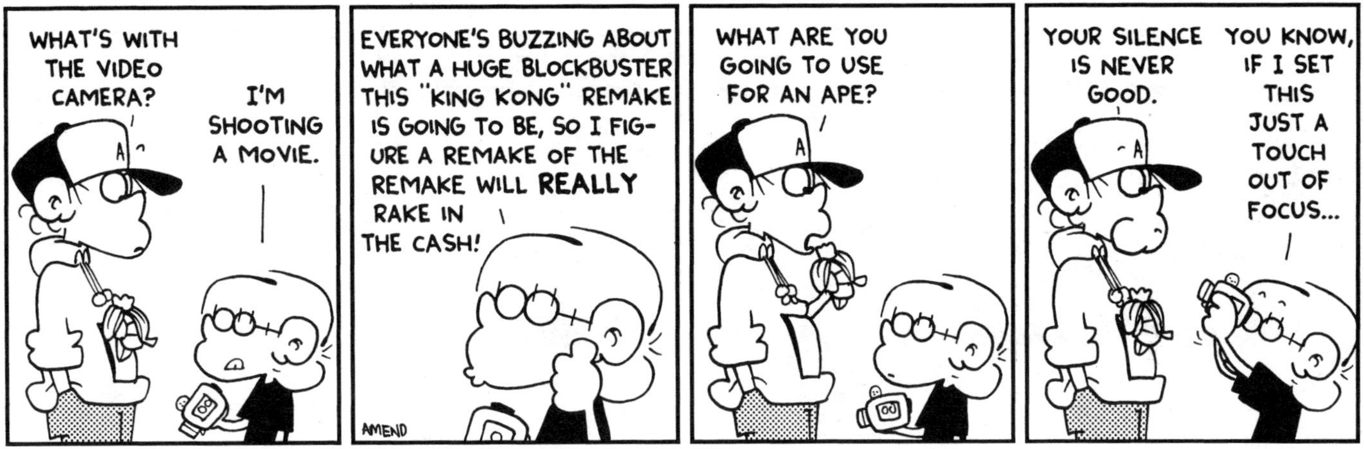
WHAT'S WITH THE VIDEO CAMERA?
I'M SHOOTING A MOVIE.
EVERYONE'S BUZZING ABOUT WHAT A HUGE BLOCKBUSTER THIS "KING KONG" REMAKE IS GOING TO BE, SO I FIGURE A REMAKE OF THE REMAKE WILL REALLY RAKE IN THE CASH!
AMEND
WHAT ARE YOU GOING TO USE FOR AN APE?
YOUR SILENCE IS NEVER GOOD.
YOU KNOW, IF I SET THIS JUST A TOUCH OUT OF FOCUS...

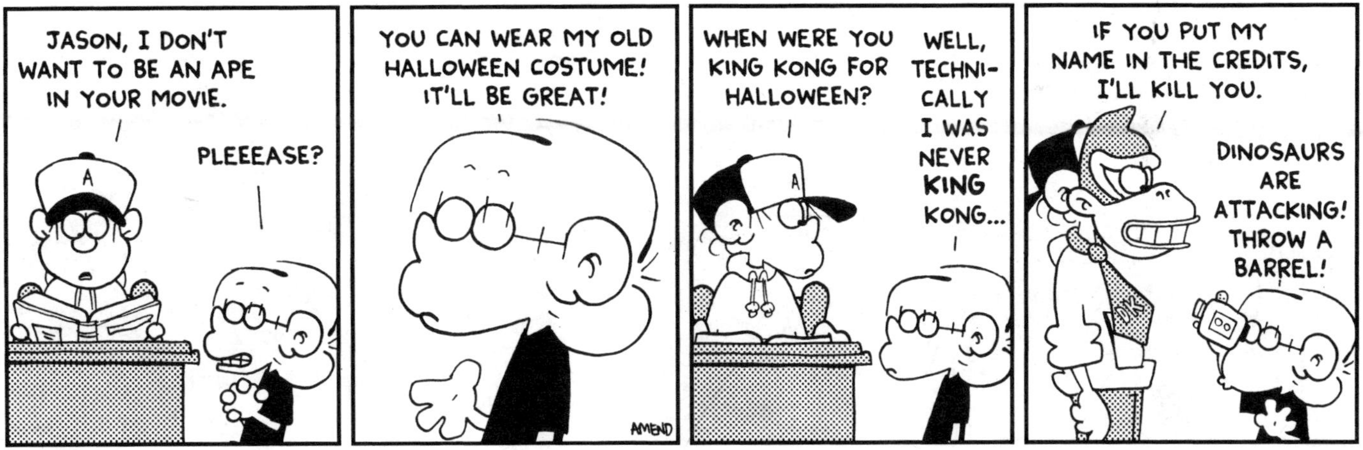
JASON, I DON'T WANT TO BE AN APE IN YOUR MOVIE.
PLEEEASE?
YOU CAN WEAR MY OLD HALLOWEEN COSTUME! IT'LL BE GREAT!
AMEND
WHEN WERE YOU KING KONG FOR HALLOWEEN?
WELL, TECHNICALLY I WAS NEVER KING KONG...
IF YOU PUT MY NAME IN THE CREDITS, I'LL KILL YOU.
DINOSAURS ARE ATTACKING! THROW A BARREL!
DK

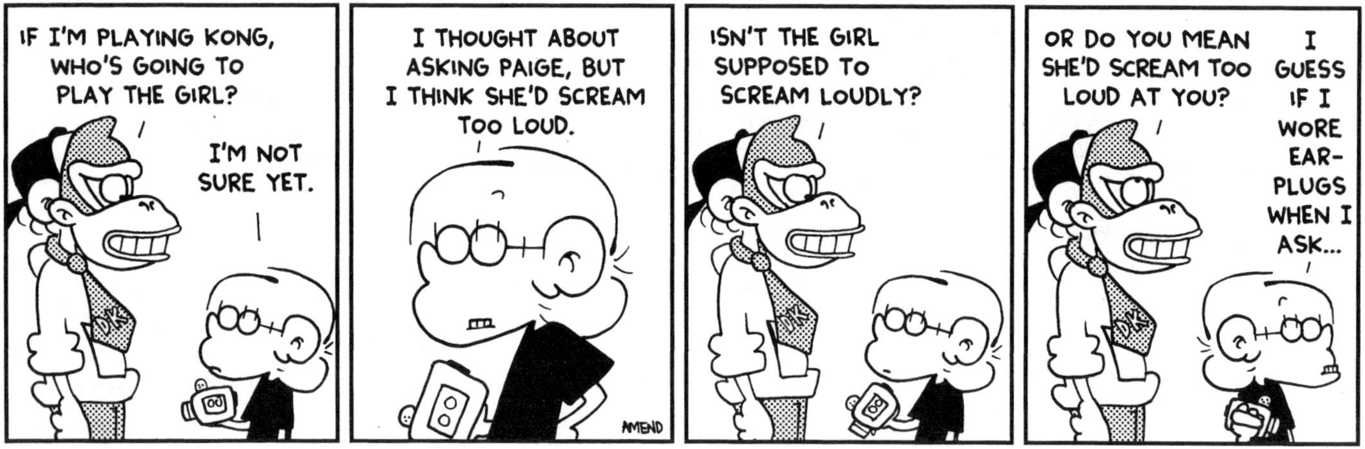
IF I'M PLAYING KONG, WHO'S GOING TO PLAY THE GIRL?
I'M NOT SURE YET.
I THOUGHT ABOUT ASKING PAIGE, BUT I THINK SHE'D SCREAM TOO LOUD.
AMEND
ISN'T THE GIRL SUPPOSED TO SCREAM LOUDLY?
OR DO YOU MEAN SHE'D SCREAM TOO LOUD AT YOU?
I GUESS IF I WORE EAR-PLUGS WHEN I ASK...

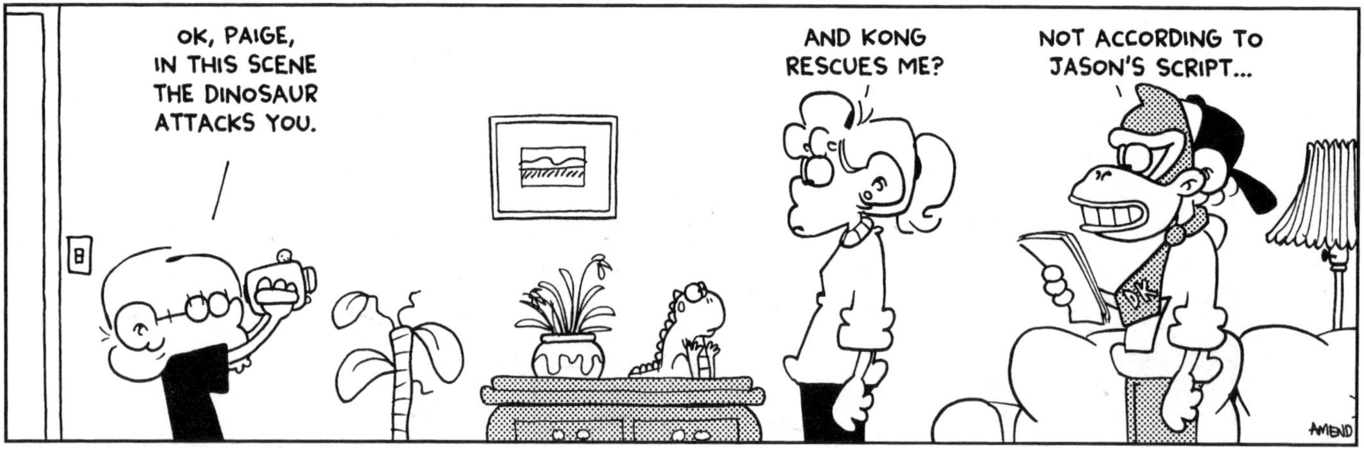
OK, PAIGE, IN THIS SCENE THE DINOSAUR ATTACKS YOU.
AND KONG RESCUES ME?
NOT ACCORDING TO JASON'S SCRIPT...
AMEND

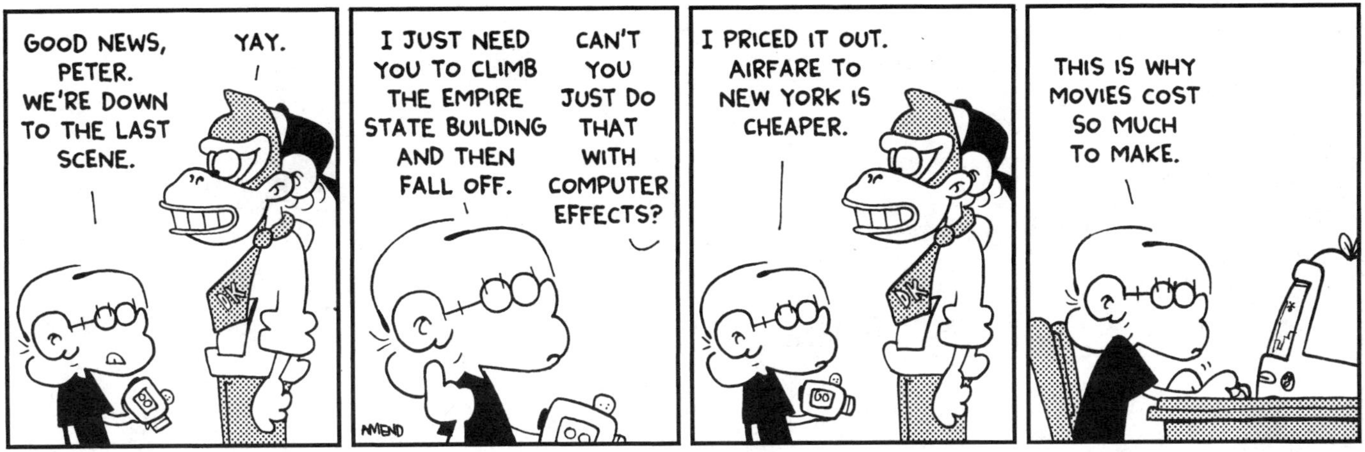
GOOD NEWS, PETER. WE'RE DOWN TO THE LAST SCENE.
YAY.
I JUST NEED YOU TO CLIMB THE EMPIRE STATE BUILDING AND THEN FALL OFF.
CAN'T YOU JUST DO THAT WITH COMPUTER EFFECTS?
AMEND
I PRICED IT OUT. AIRFARE TO NEW YORK IS CHEAPER.
THIS IS WHY MOVIES COST SO MUCH TO MAKE.

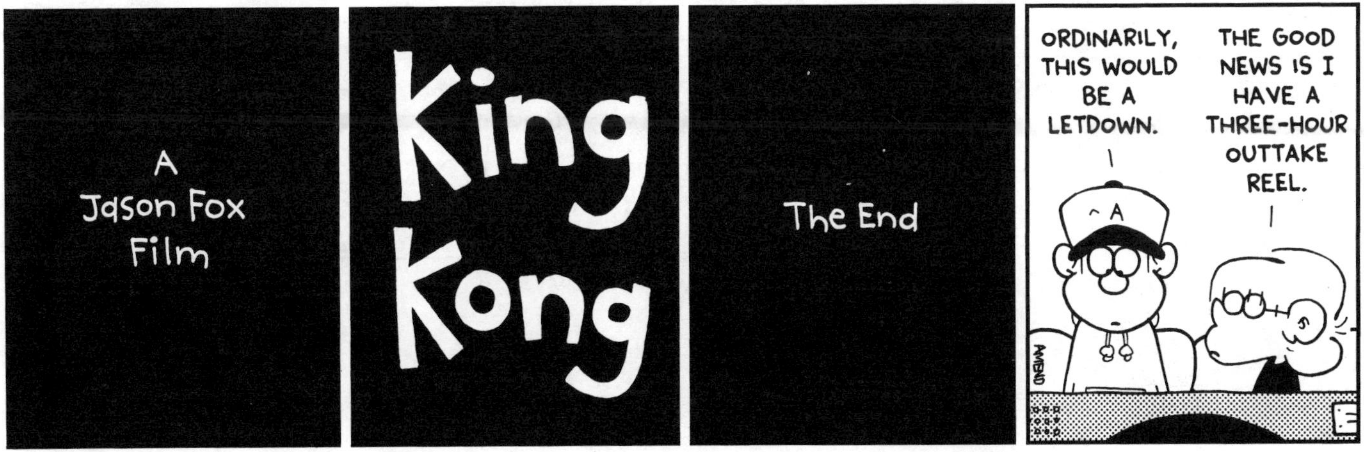
A Jason Fox Film
King Kong
The End
ORDINARILY, THIS WOULD BE A LETDOWN.
THE GOOD NEWS IS I HAVE A THREE-HOUR OUTTAKE REEL.
AMEND

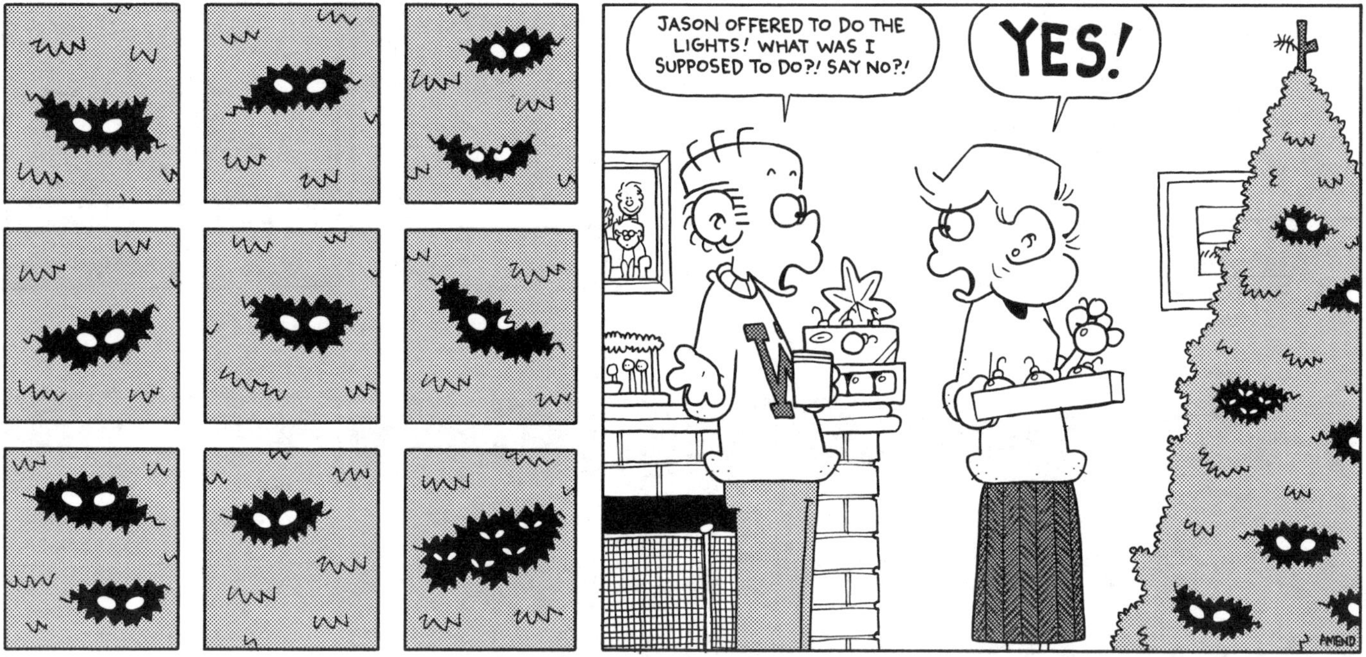
JASON OFFERED TO DO THE LIGHTS! WHAT WAS I SUPPOSED TO DO?! SAY NO?!
YES!
AMEND

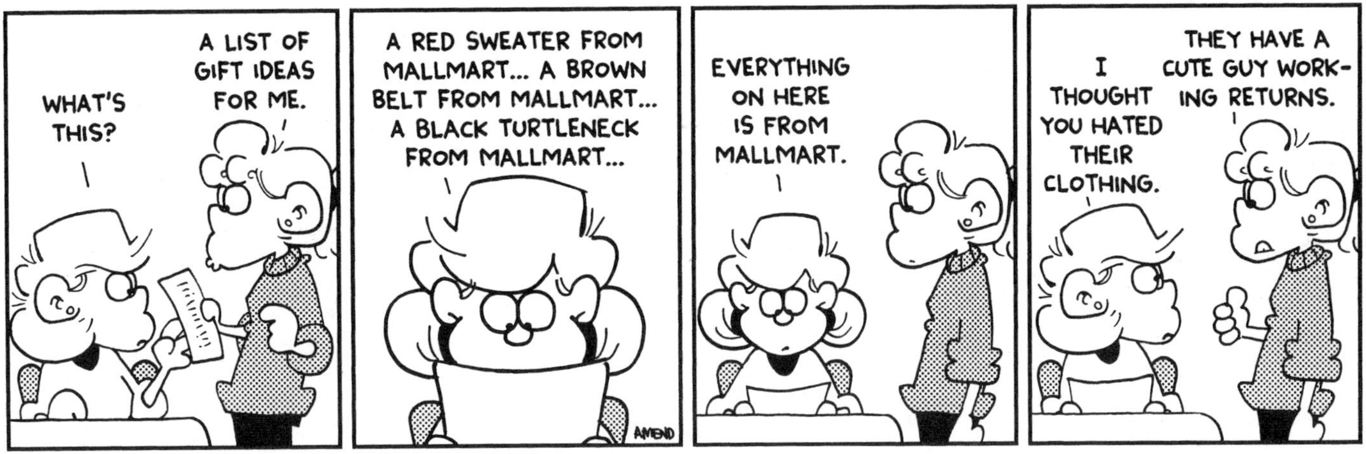
WHAT'S THIS?
A LIST OF GIFT IDEAS FOR ME.
A RED SWEATER FROM MALLMART... A BROWN BELT FROM MALLMART... A BLACK TURTLENECK FROM MALLMART...
AMEND
EVERYTHING ON HERE IS FROM MALLMART.
I THOUGHT YOU HATED THEIR CLOTHING.
THEY HAVE A CUTE GUY WORKING RETURNS.

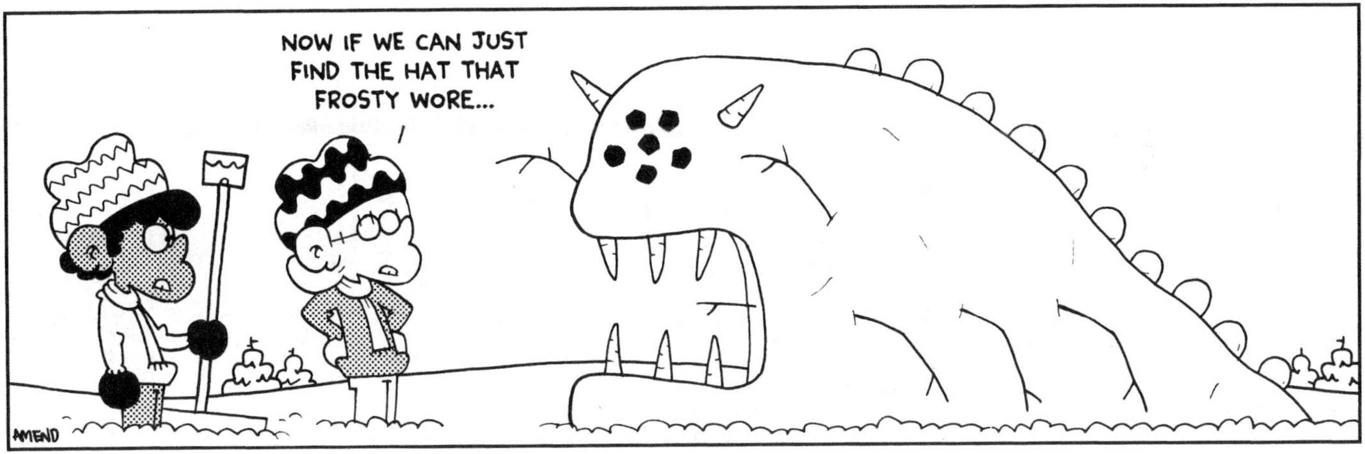
NOW IF WE CAN JUST FIND THE HAT THAT FROSTY WORE...
AMEND

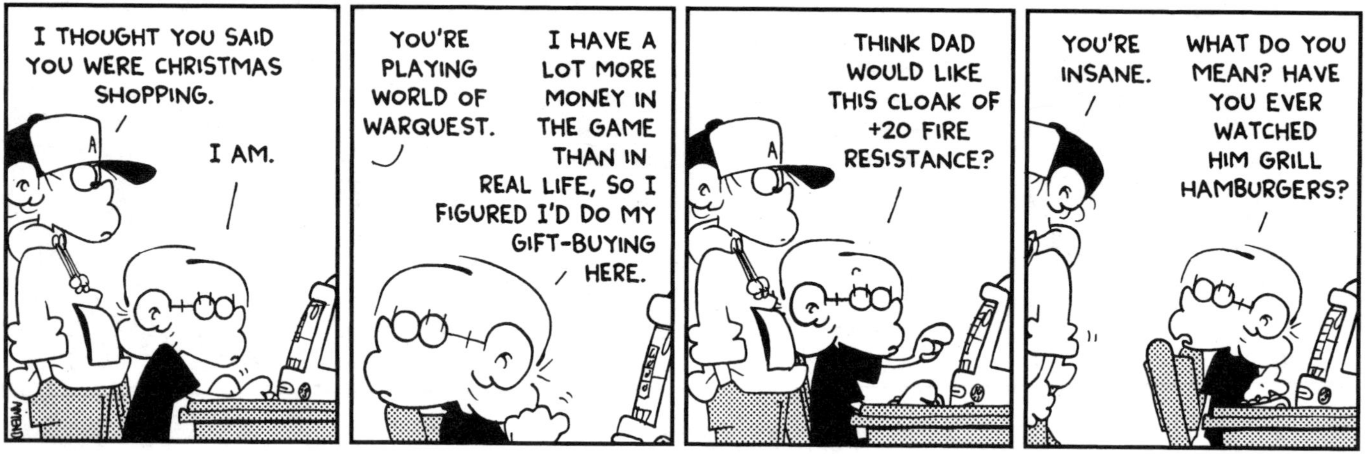
I THOUGHT YOU SAID YOU WERE CHRISTMAS SHOPPING.
I AM.
YOU'RE PLAYING WORLD OF WARQUEST.
I HAVE A LOT MORE MONEY IN THE GAME THAN IN REAL LIFE, SO I FIGURED I'D DO MY GIFT-BUYING HERE.
THINK DAD WOULD LIKE THIS CLOAK OF +20 FIRE RESISTANCE?
YOU'RE INSANE.
WHAT DO YOU MEAN? HAVE YOU EVER WATCHED HIM GRILL HAMBURGERS?

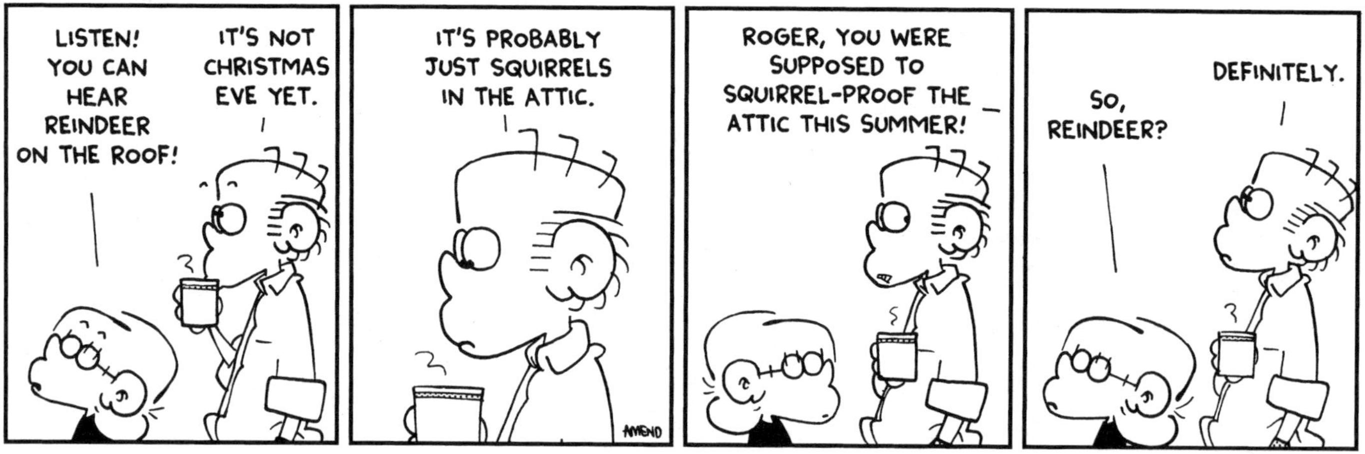
LISTEN! YOU CAN HEAR REINDEER ON THE ROOF!
IT'S NOT CHRISTMAS EVE YET.
IT'S PROBABLY JUST SQUIRRELS IN THE ATTIC.
AMEND
ROGER, YOU WERE SUPPOSED TO SQUIRREL-PROOF THE ATTIC THIS SUMMER!
SO, REINDEER?
DEFINITELY.

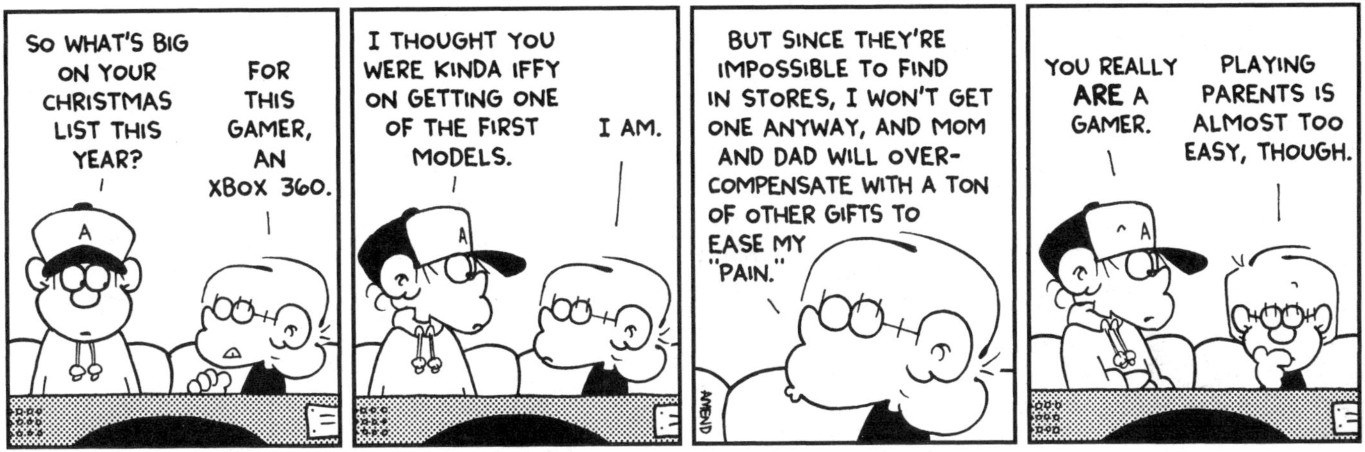
SO WHAT'S BIG ON YOUR CHRISTMAS LIST THIS YEAR?
FOR THIS GAMER, AN XBOX 360.
I THOUGHT YOU WERE KINDA IFFY ON GETTING ONE OF THE FIRST MODELS.
I AM.
BUT SINCE THEY'RE IMPOSSIBLE TO FIND IN STORES, I WON'T GET ONE ANYWAY, AND MOM AND DAD WILL OVER-COMPENSATE WITH A TON OF OTHER GIFTS TO EASE MY "PAIN."
AMEND
YOU REALLY ARE A GAMER.
PLAYING PARENTS IS ALMOST TOO EASY, THOUGH.

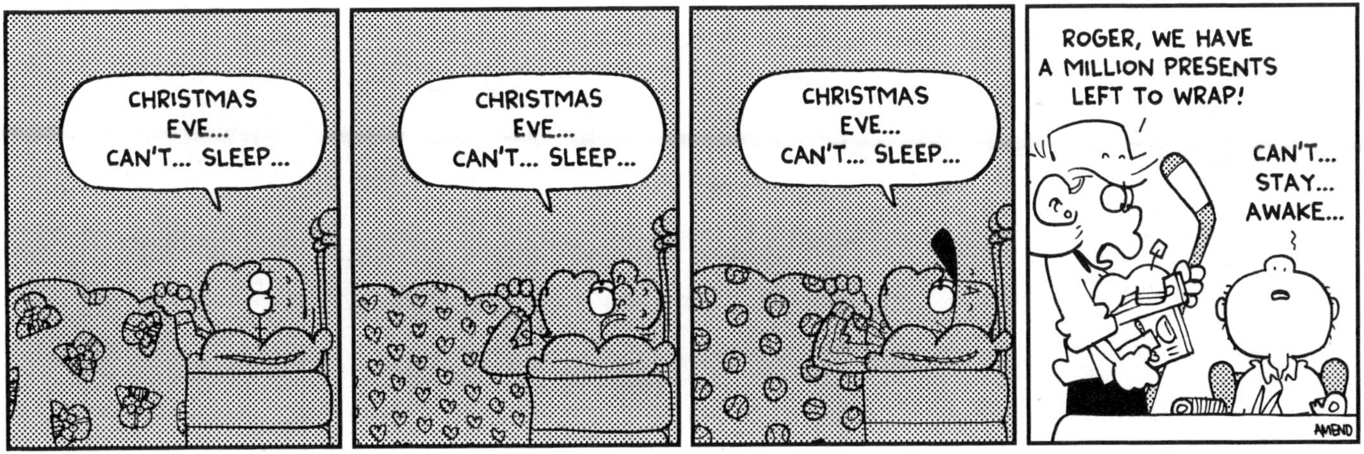
CHRISTMAS EVE... CAN'T... SLEEP...
CHRISTMAS EVE... CAN'T... SLEEP...
CHRISTMAS EVE... CAN'T... SLEEP...
ROGER, WE HAVE A MILLION PRESENTS LEFT TO WRAP!
CAN'T... STAY... AWAKE...
AMEND

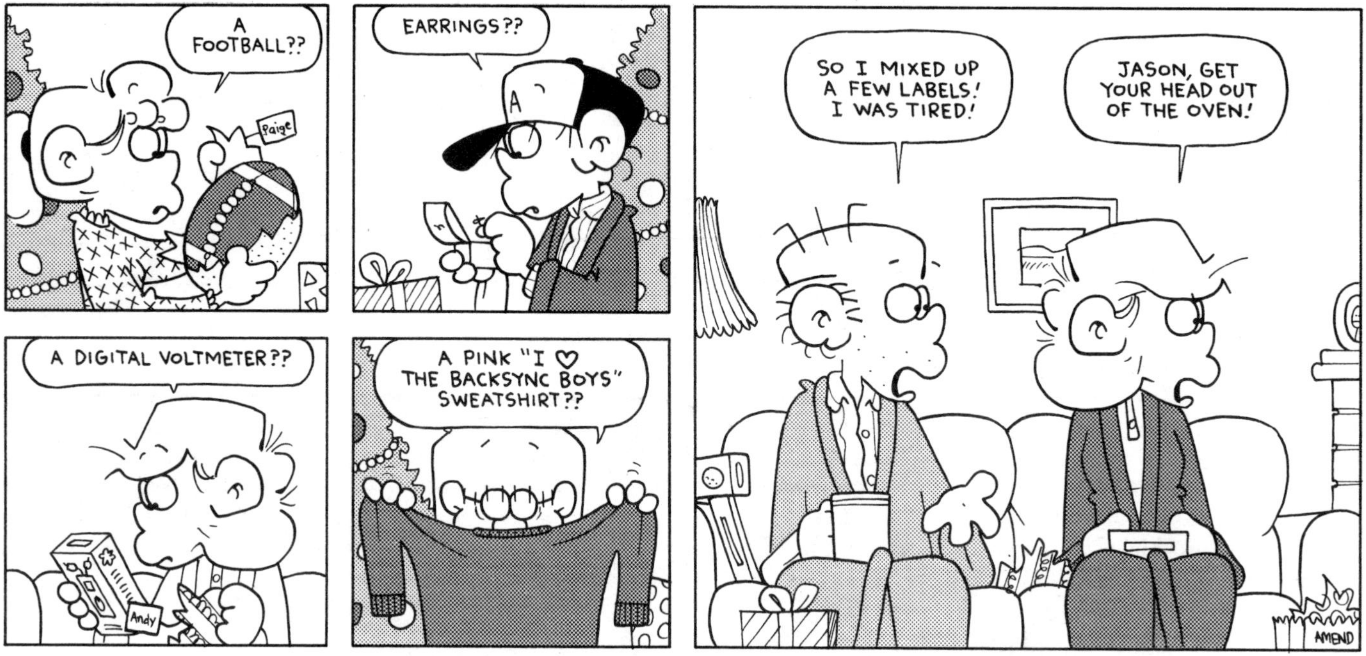
A FOOTBALL??
EARRINGS??
A DIGITAL VOLTMETER??
A PINK "I ♡ THE BACKSYNC BOYS" SWEATSHIRT??
SO I MIXED UP A FEW LABELS! I WAS TIRED!
JASON, GET YOUR HEAD OUT OF THE OVEN!
Paige
Andy
AMEND

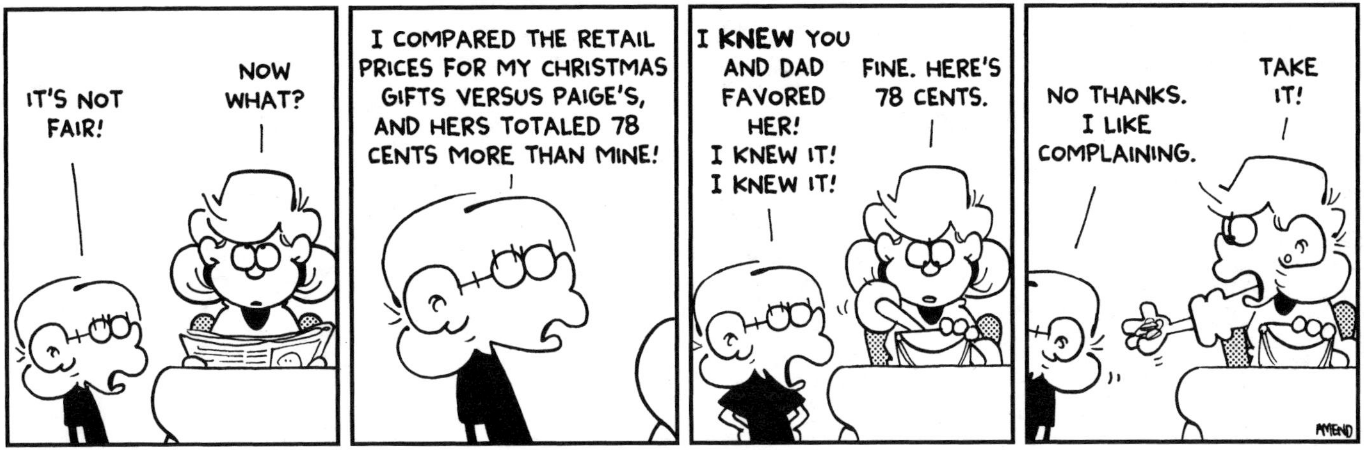
IT'S NOT FAIR!
NOW WHAT?
I COMPARED THE RETAIL PRICES FOR MY CHRISTMAS GIFTS VERSUS PAIGE'S, AND HERS TOTALED 78 CENTS MORE THAN MINE!
I **KNEW** YOU AND DAD FAVORED HER! I KNEW IT! I KNEW IT!
FINE. HERE'S 78 CENTS.
NO THANKS. I LIKE COMPLAINING.
TAKE IT!
AMEND

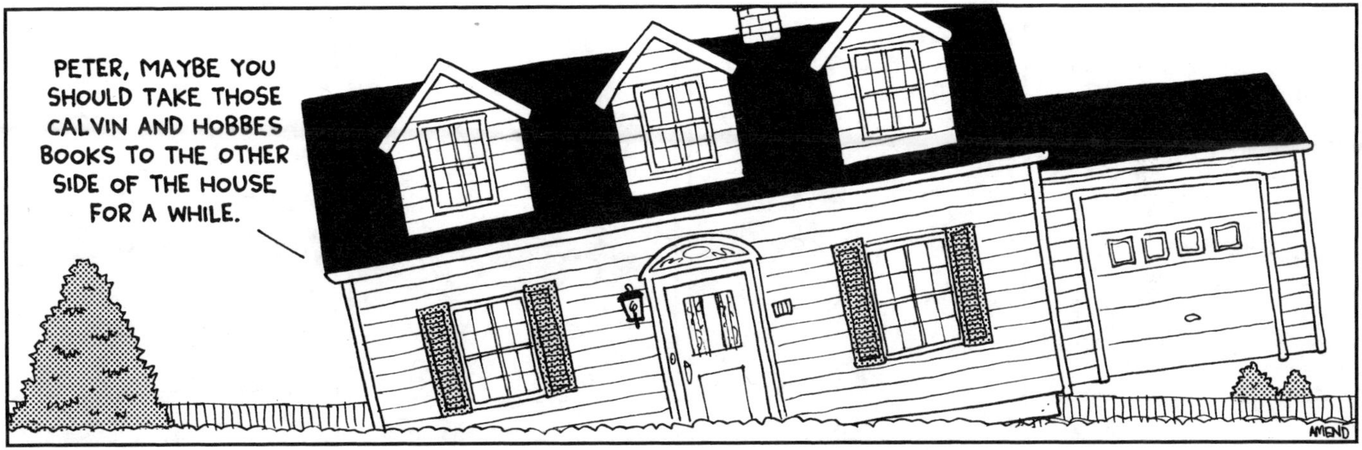
PETER, MAYBE YOU SHOULD TAKE THOSE CALVIN AND HOBBES BOOKS TO THE OTHER SIDE OF THE HOUSE FOR A WHILE.
AMEND

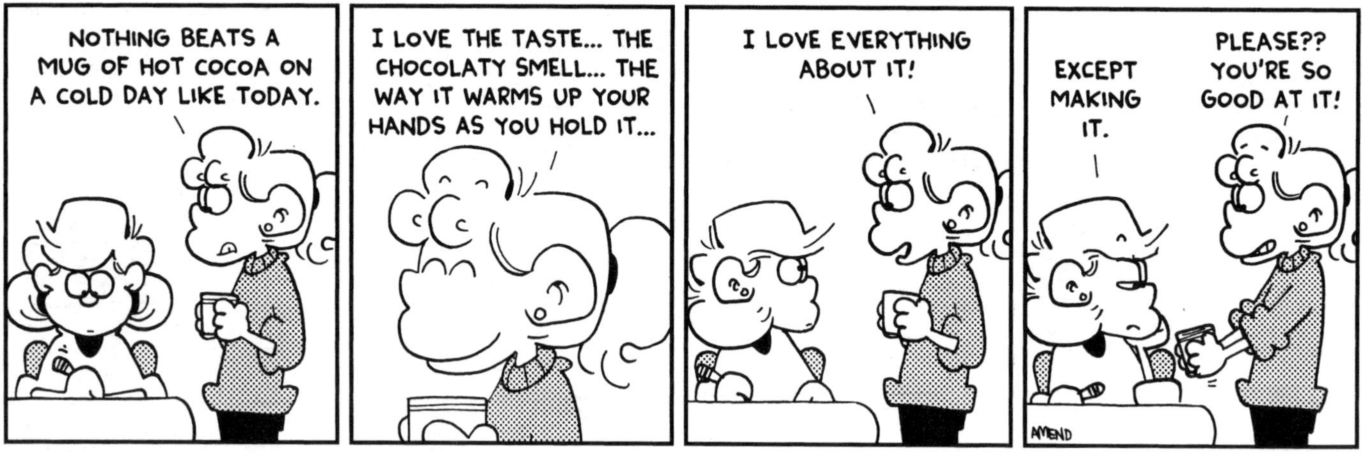
NOTHING BEATS A MUG OF HOT COCOA ON A COLD DAY LIKE TODAY.
I LOVE THE TASTE... THE CHOCOLATY SMELL... THE WAY IT WARMS UP YOUR HANDS AS YOU HOLD IT...
I LOVE EVERYTHING ABOUT IT!
EXCEPT MAKING IT.
PLEASE?? YOU'RE SO GOOD AT IT!
AMEND

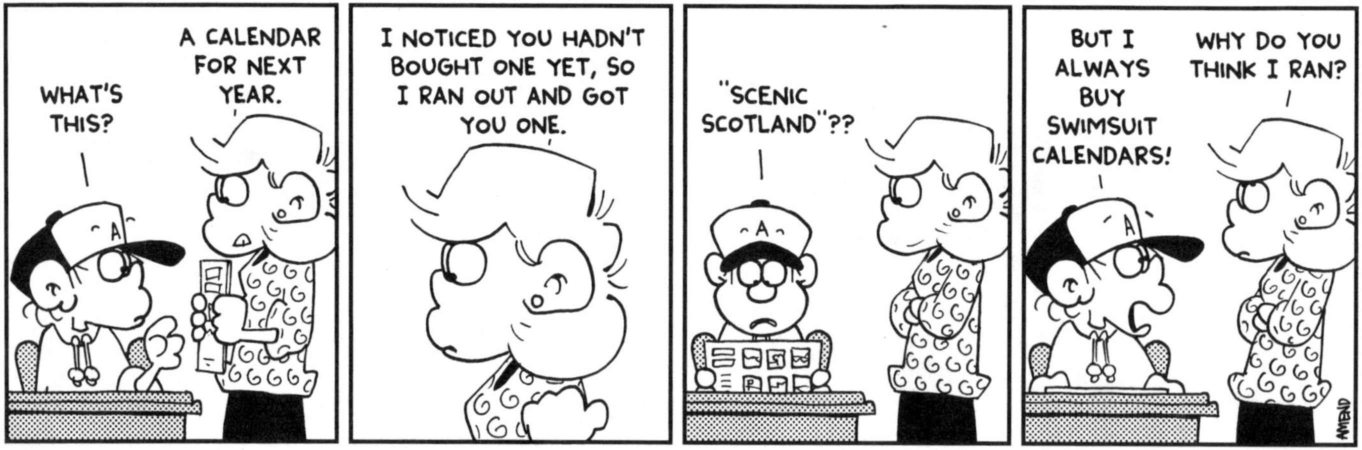
WHAT'S THIS?
A CALENDAR FOR NEXT YEAR.
I NOTICED YOU HADN'T BOUGHT ONE YET, SO I RAN OUT AND GOT YOU ONE.
"SCENIC SCOTLAND"??
BUT I ALWAYS BUY SWIMSUIT CALENDARS!
WHY DO YOU THINK I RAN?
AMEND

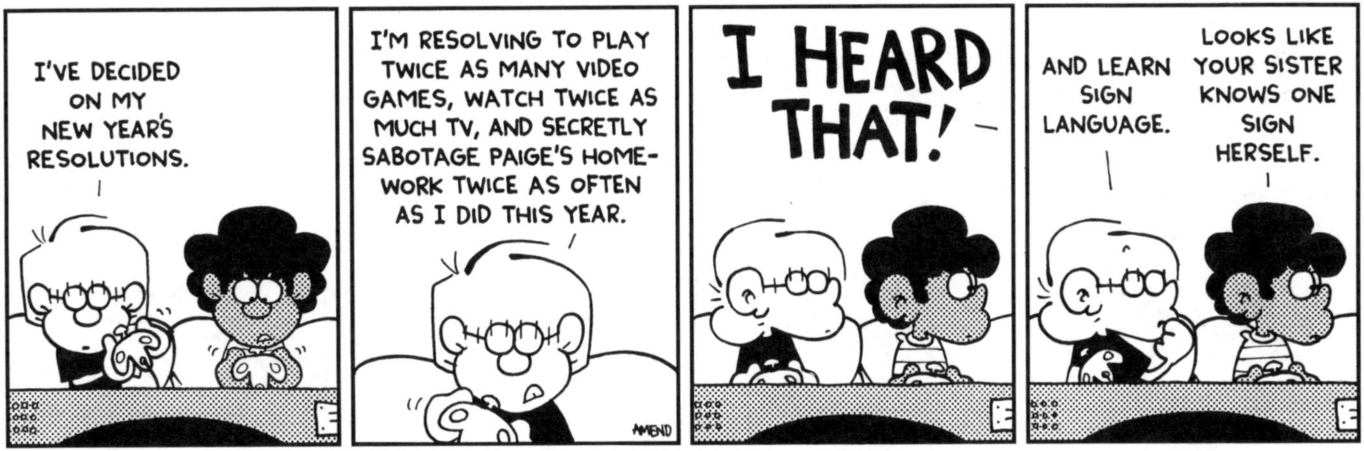
I'VE DECIDED ON MY NEW YEAR'S RESOLUTIONS.
I'M RESOLVING TO PLAY TWICE AS MANY VIDEO GAMES, WATCH TWICE AS MUCH TV, AND SECRETLY SABOTAGE PAIGE'S HOMEWORK TWICE AS OFTEN AS I DID THIS YEAR.
I HEARD THAT!
AND LEARN SIGN LANGUAGE.
LOOKS LIKE YOUR SISTER KNOWS ONE SIGN HERSELF.
AMEND

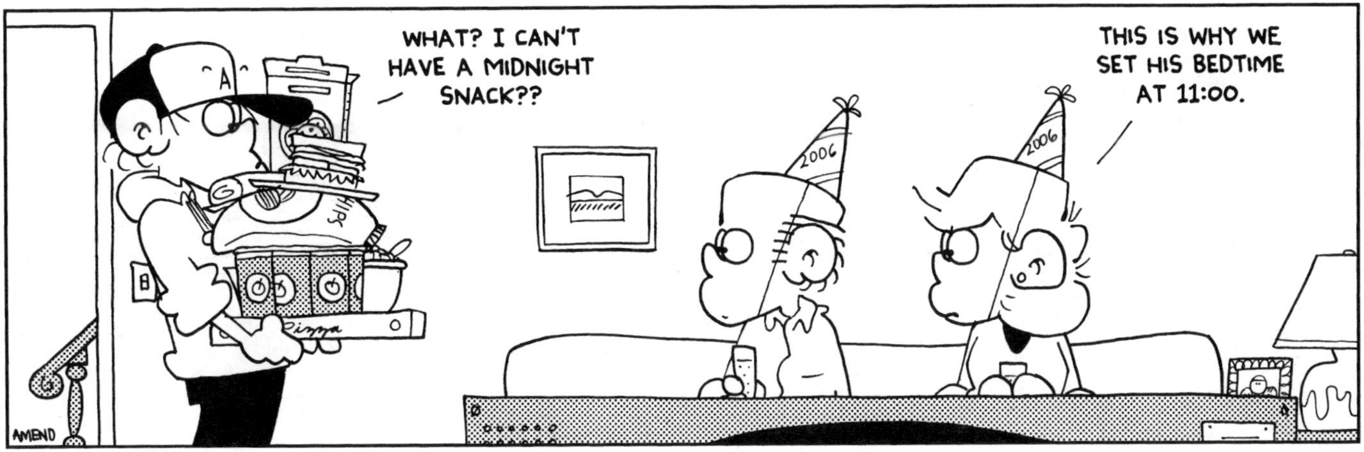
WHAT? I CAN'T HAVE A MIDNIGHT SNACK??
THIS IS WHY WE SET HIS BEDTIME AT 11:00.
2006
2006
AMEND

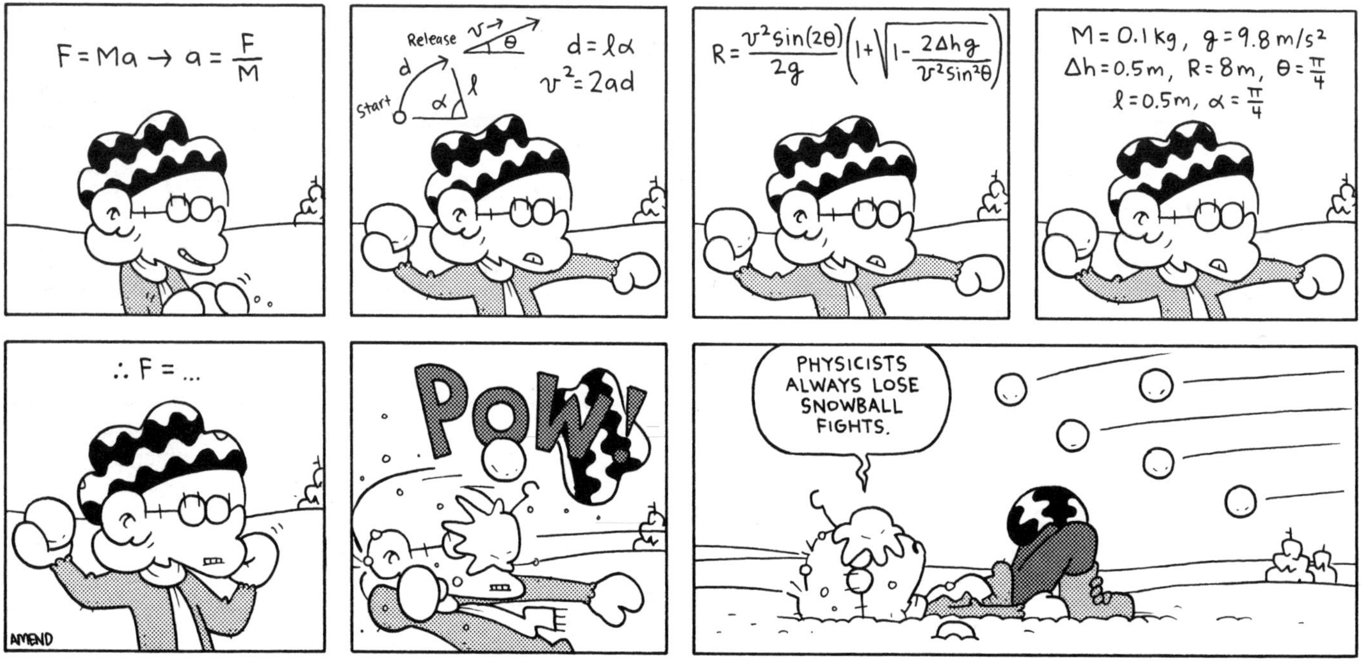
$F = Ma \rightarrow a = \frac{F}{M}$
Release
$v \rightarrow$
θ
d
Start
α
ℓ
$d = \ell\alpha$
$v^2 = 2ad$
$R = \frac{v^2 \sin(2\theta)}{2g}\left(1 + \sqrt{1 - \frac{2\Delta h g}{v^2 \sin^2\theta}}\right)$
$M = 0.1\,kg,\ g = 9.8\,m/s^2$
$\Delta h = 0.5\,m,\ R = 8\,m,\ \theta = \frac{\pi}{4}$
$\ell = 0.5\,m,\ \alpha = \frac{\pi}{4}$
$\therefore F = \ldots$
AMEND
POW!
PHYSICISTS ALWAYS LOSE SNOWBALL FIGHTS.

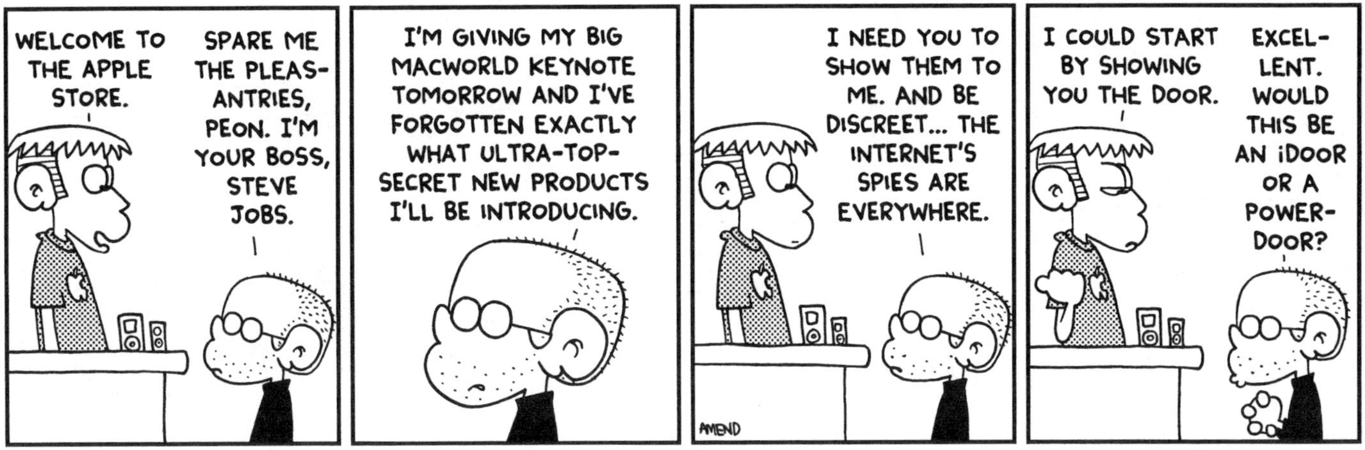
WELCOME TO THE APPLE STORE.
SPARE ME THE PLEASANTRIES, PEON. I'M YOUR BOSS, STEVE JOBS.
I'M GIVING MY BIG MACWORLD KEYNOTE TOMORROW AND I'VE FORGOTTEN EXACTLY WHAT ULTRA-TOP-SECRET NEW PRODUCTS I'LL BE INTRODUCING.
I NEED YOU TO SHOW THEM TO ME. AND BE DISCREET... THE INTERNET'S SPIES ARE EVERYWHERE.
AMEND
I COULD START BY SHOWING YOU THE DOOR.
EXCELLENT. WOULD THIS BE AN iDOOR OR A POWERDOOR?

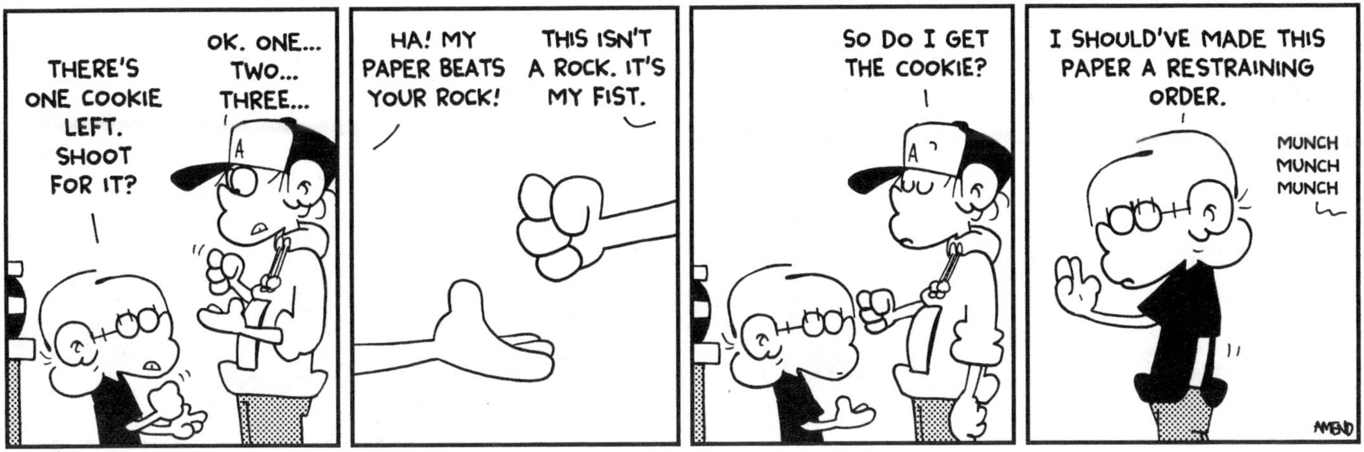
THERE'S ONE COOKIE LEFT. SHOOT FOR IT?
OK. ONE... TWO... THREE...
HA! MY PAPER BEATS YOUR ROCK!
THIS ISN'T A ROCK. IT'S MY FIST.
SO DO I GET THE COOKIE?
I SHOULD'VE MADE THIS PAPER A RESTRAINING ORDER.
MUNCH
MUNCH
MUNCH
AMEND

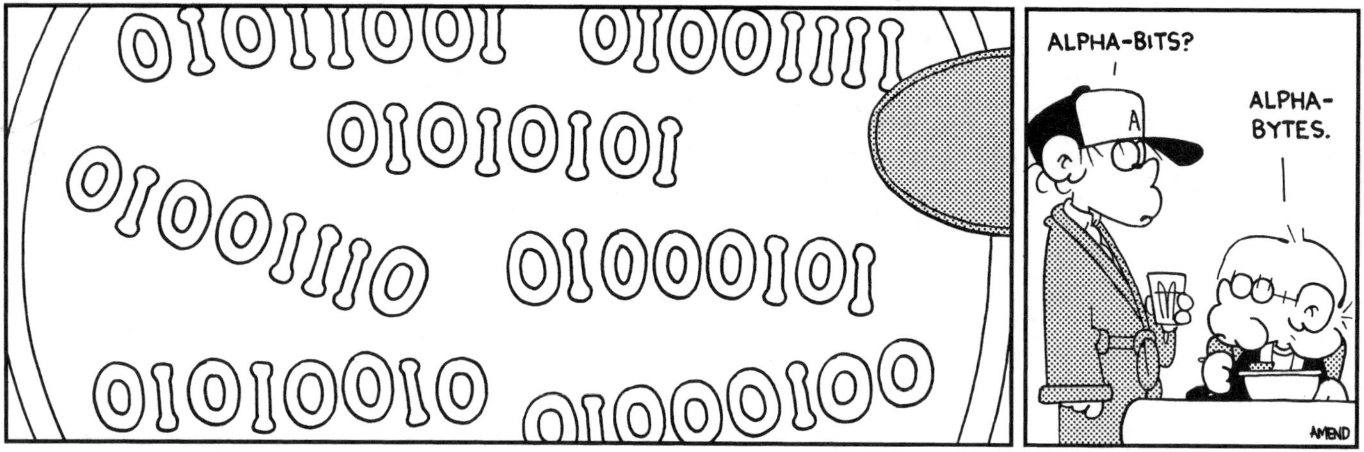

01011001 01001111
01010101
01001110 01000101
01010010 01000100
ALPHA-BITS?
ALPHA-BYTES.
AMEND

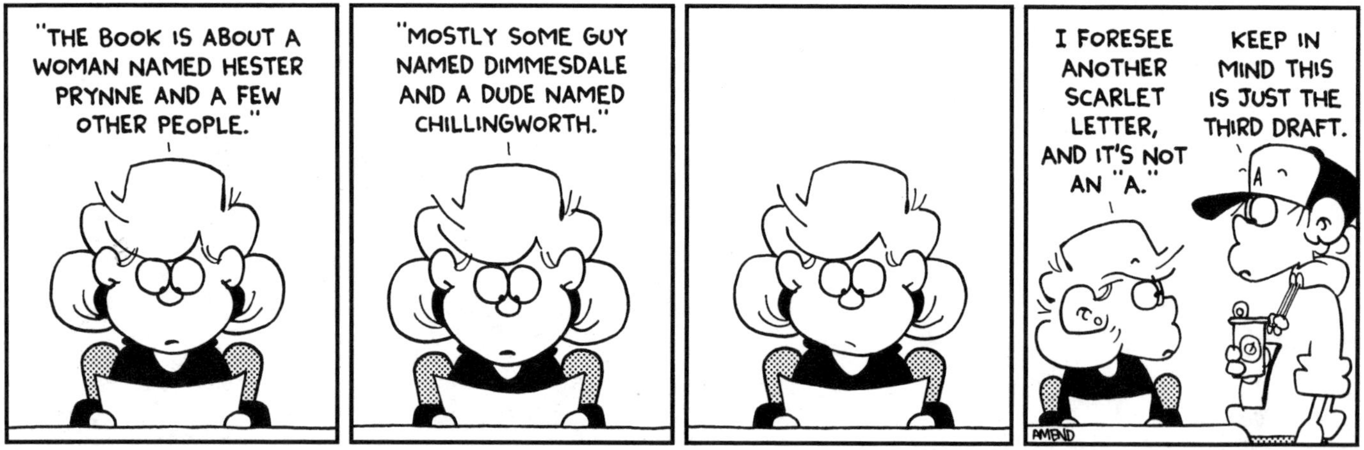

"THE BOOK IS ABOUT A WOMAN NAMED HESTER PRYNNE AND A FEW OTHER PEOPLE."
"MOSTLY SOME GUY NAMED DIMMESDALE AND A DUDE NAMED CHILLINGWORTH."
I FORESEE ANOTHER SCARLET LETTER, AND IT'S NOT AN "A."
KEEP IN MIND THIS IS JUST THE THIRD DRAFT.
AMEND

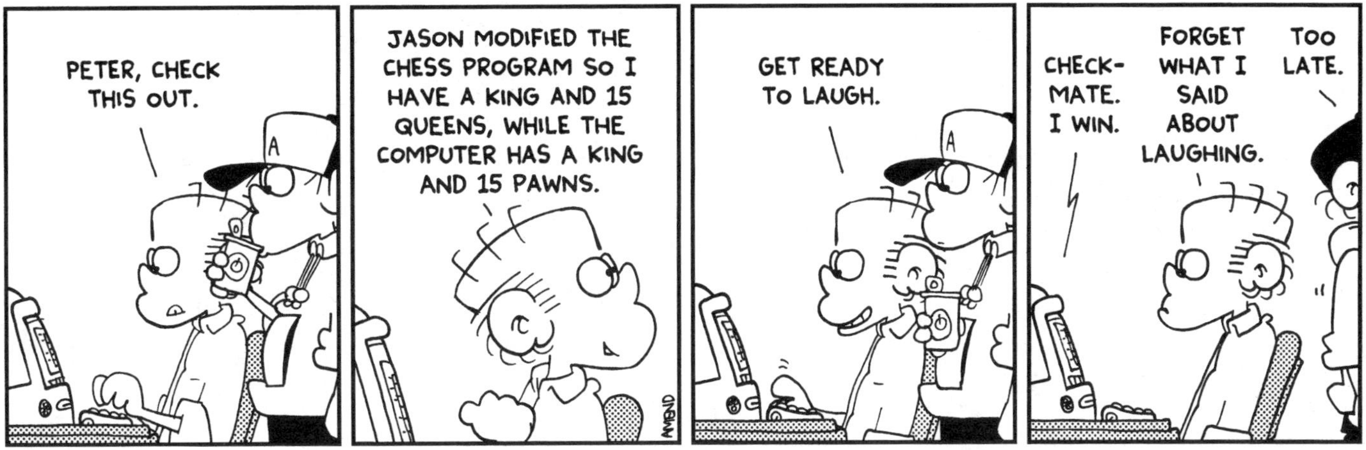
PETER, CHECK THIS OUT.
JASON MODIFIED THE CHESS PROGRAM SO I HAVE A KING AND 15 QUEENS, WHILE THE COMPUTER HAS A KING AND 15 PAWNS.
AMEND
GET READY TO LAUGH.
CHECK-MATE. I WIN.
FORGET WHAT I SAID ABOUT LAUGHING.
TOO LATE.

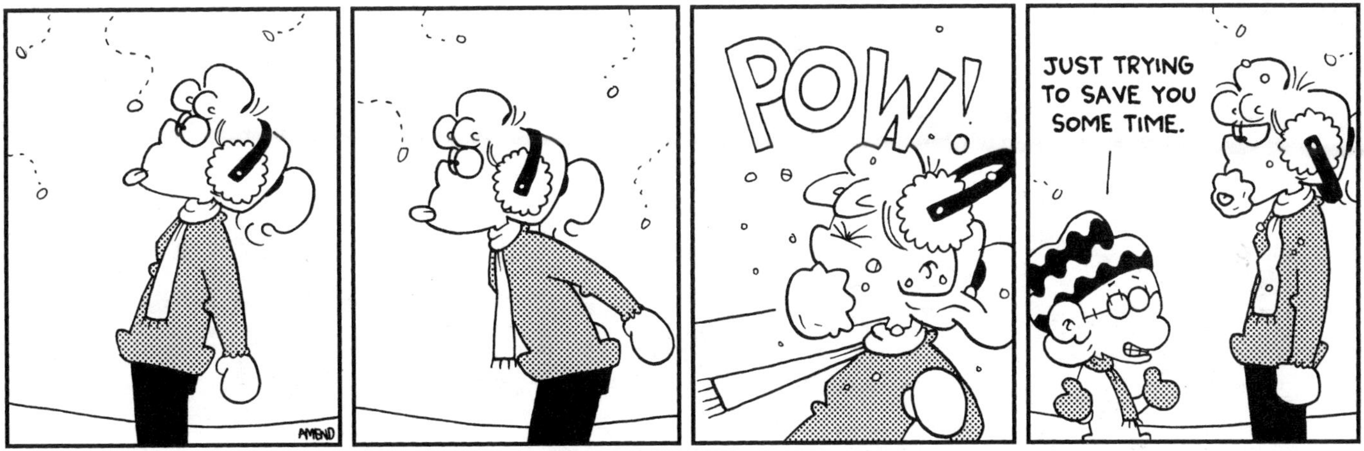
AMEND
POW!
JUST TRYING TO SAVE YOU SOME TIME.

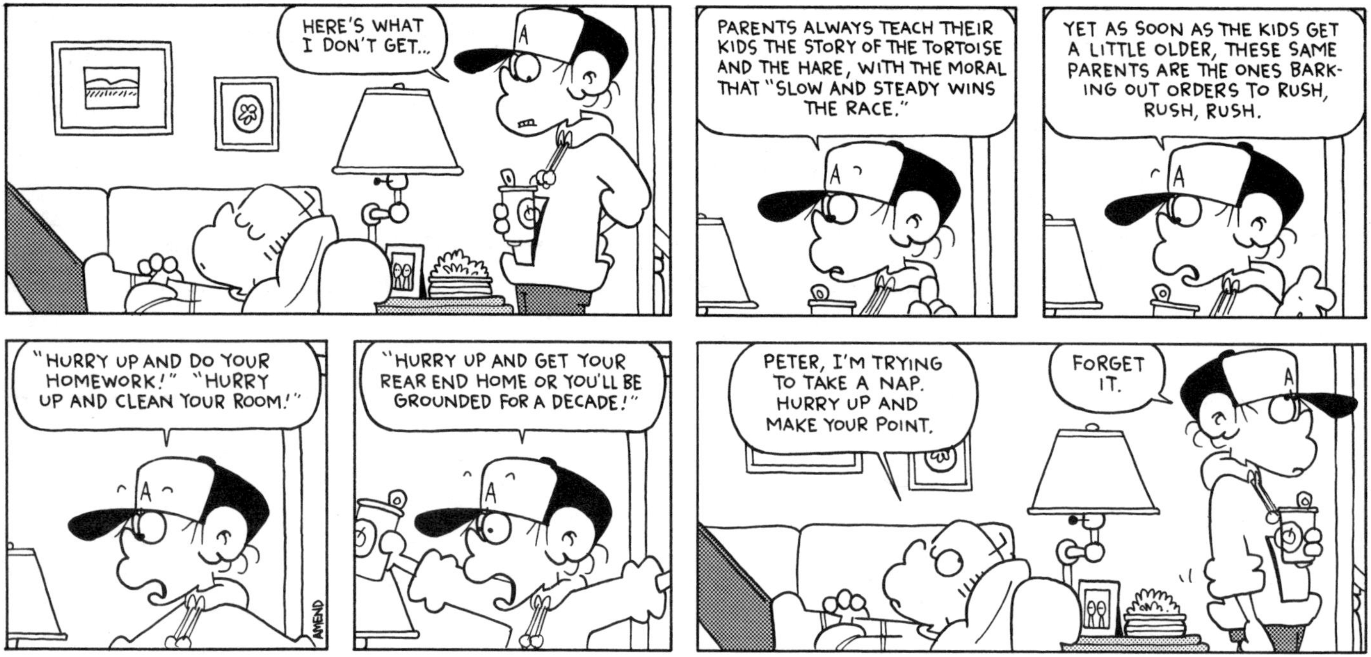
HERE'S WHAT I DON'T GET...
PARENTS ALWAYS TEACH THEIR KIDS THE STORY OF THE TORTOISE AND THE HARE, WITH THE MORAL THAT "SLOW AND STEADY WINS THE RACE."
YET AS SOON AS THE KIDS GET A LITTLE OLDER, THESE SAME PARENTS ARE THE ONES BARKING OUT ORDERS TO RUSH, RUSH, RUSH.
"HURRY UP AND DO YOUR HOMEWORK!" "HURRY UP AND CLEAN YOUR ROOM!"
AMEND
"HURRY UP AND GET YOUR REAR END HOME OR YOU'LL BE GROUNDED FOR A DECADE!"
PETER, I'M TRYING TO TAKE A NAP. HURRY UP AND MAKE YOUR POINT.
FORGET IT.

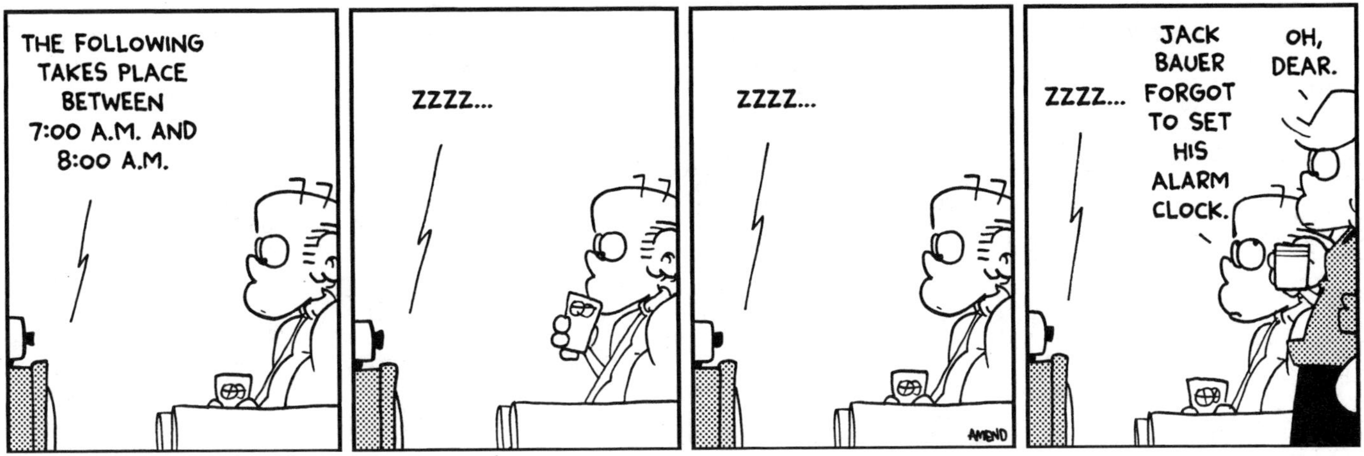
THE FOLLOWING TAKES PLACE BETWEEN 7:00 A.M. AND 8:00 A.M.
ZZZZ...
ZZZZ...
AMEND
ZZZZ...
JACK BAUER FORGOT TO SET HIS ALARM CLOCK.
OH, DEAR.

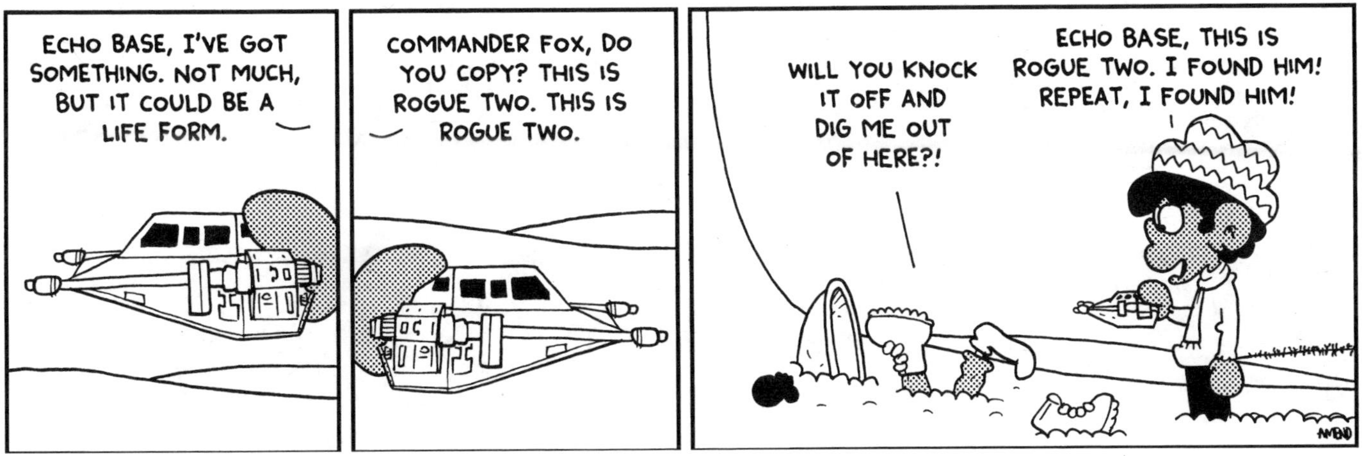
ECHO BASE, I'VE GOT SOMETHING. NOT MUCH, BUT IT COULD BE A LIFE FORM.
COMMANDER FOX, DO YOU COPY? THIS IS ROGUE TWO. THIS IS ROGUE TWO.
WILL YOU KNOCK IT OFF AND DIG ME OUT OF HERE?!
ECHO BASE, THIS IS ROGUE TWO. I FOUND HIM! REPEAT, I FOUND HIM!
AMEND

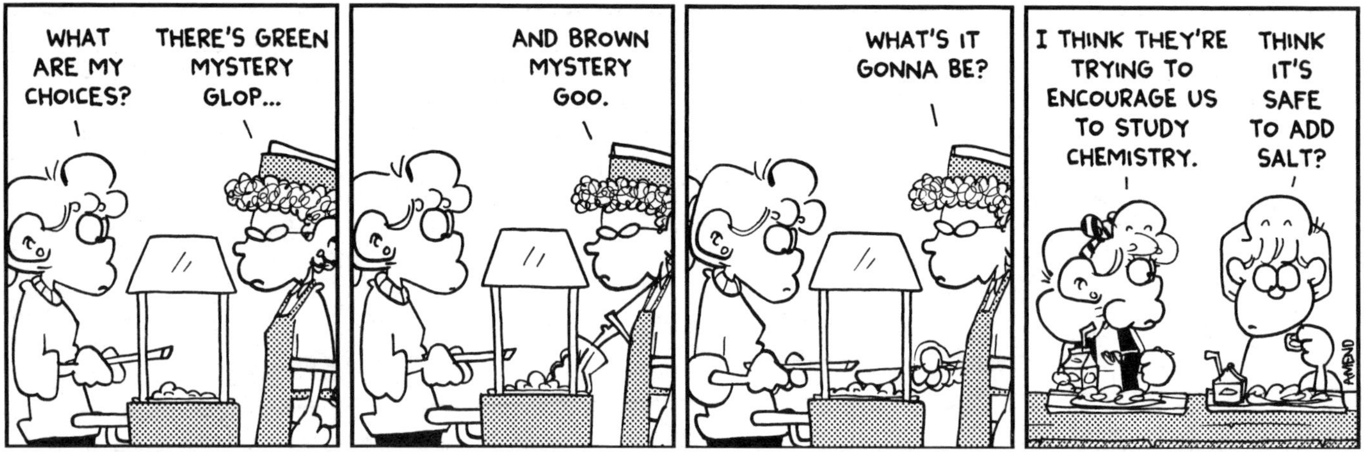
WHAT ARE MY CHOICES?
THERE'S GREEN MYSTERY GLOP...
AND BROWN MYSTERY GOO.
WHAT'S IT GONNA BE?
I THINK THEY'RE TRYING TO ENCOURAGE US TO STUDY CHEMISTRY.
THINK IT'S SAFE TO ADD SALT?
AMEND

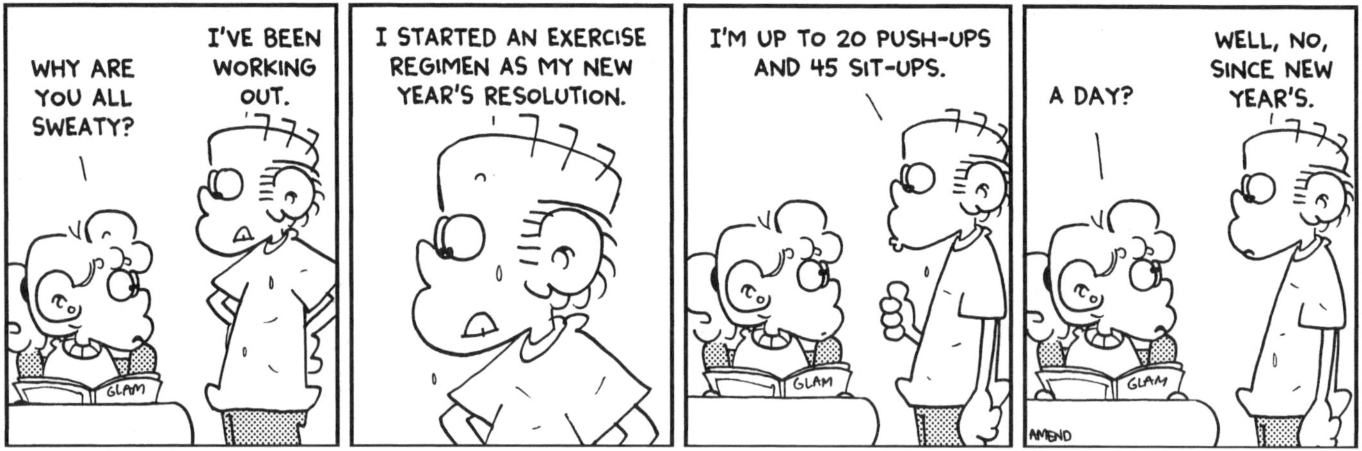
WHY ARE YOU ALL SWEATY?
I'VE BEEN WORKING OUT.
GLAM
I STARTED AN EXERCISE REGIMEN AS MY NEW YEAR'S RESOLUTION.
I'M UP TO 20 PUSH-UPS AND 45 SIT-UPS.
GLAM
A DAY?
WELL, NO, SINCE NEW YEAR'S.
GLAM
AMEND

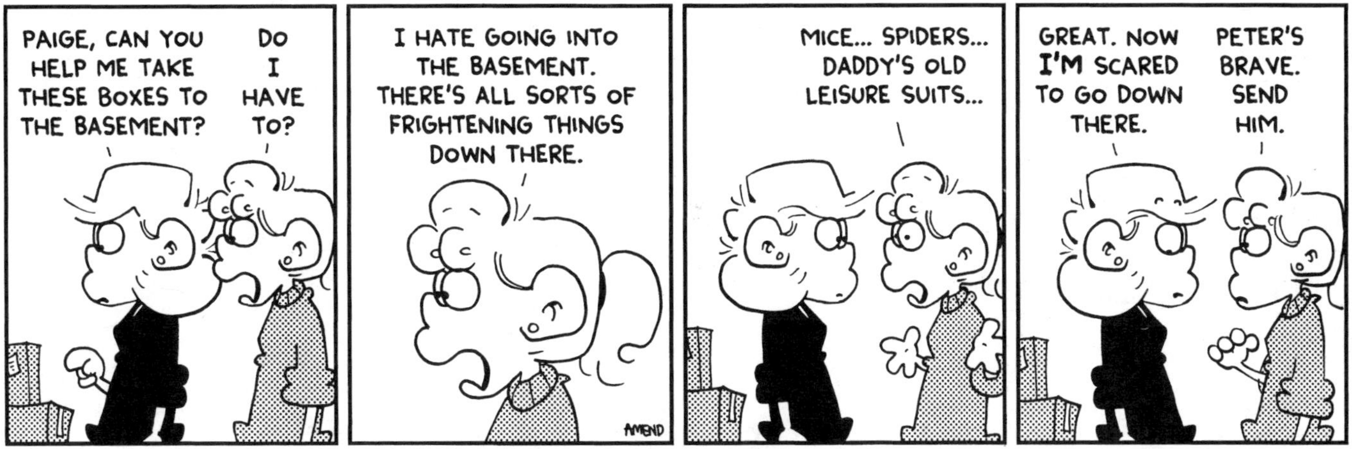
PAIGE, CAN YOU HELP ME TAKE THESE BOXES TO THE BASEMENT?
DO I HAVE TO?
I HATE GOING INTO THE BASEMENT. THERE'S ALL SORTS OF FRIGHTENING THINGS DOWN THERE.
MICE... SPIDERS... DADDY'S OLD LEISURE SUITS...
GREAT. NOW I'M SCARED TO GO DOWN THERE.
PETER'S BRAVE. SEND HIM.
AMEND

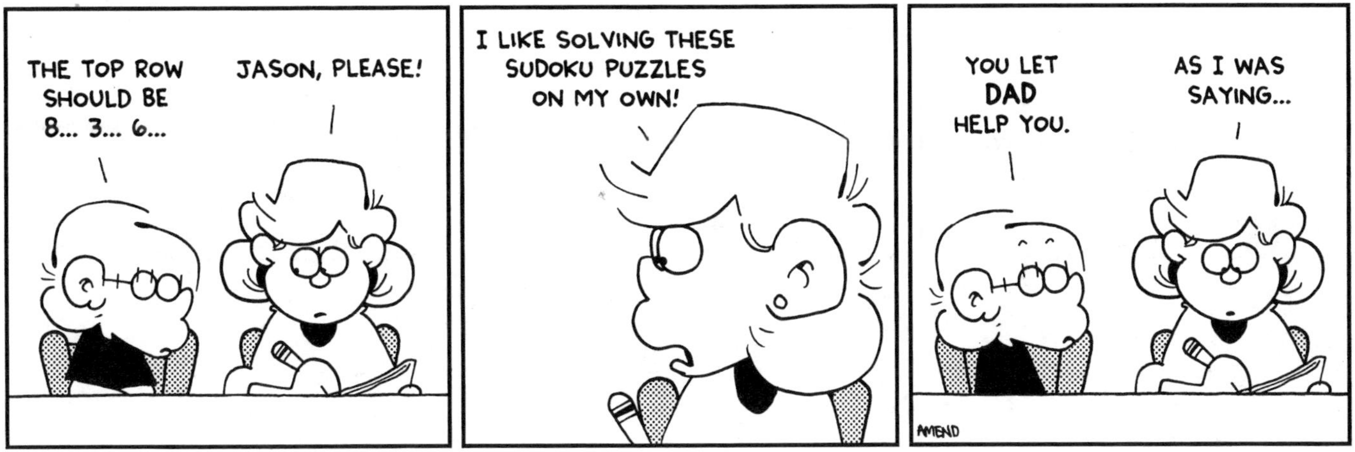
THE TOP ROW SHOULD BE 8... 3... 6...
JASON, PLEASE!
I LIKE SOLVING THESE SUDOKU PUZZLES ON MY OWN!
YOU LET DAD HELP YOU.
AS I WAS SAYING...
AMEND

WOULD YOU SAY THIS GLASS IS HALF-FULL OR HALF-EMPTY?
HALF-EMPTY.
WOULD YOU SAY THIS GLASS IS HALF-FULL OR HALF-EMPTY?
HALF-FULL.
WOULD YOU SAY THIS GLASS IS HALF-FULL OR HALF-EMPTY?
HALF-EMPTY.
WOULD YOU SAY THIS GLASS IS HALF-FULL OR HALF-EMPTY?
HALF-FULL.
HA HA! YOU'RE ALL WRONG! THE GLASS IS FIVE-TWELFTHS FULL AND SEVEN-TWELFTHS EMPTY! SUCKERRRS!
AMEND
WHEN DO WE GET TO GIVE A PSYCHOLOGICAL TEST TO **HIM**?
YOU REALLY THINK A TEST IS NECESSARY?

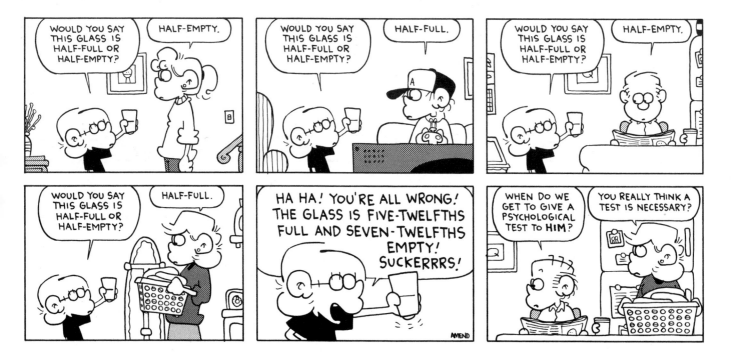

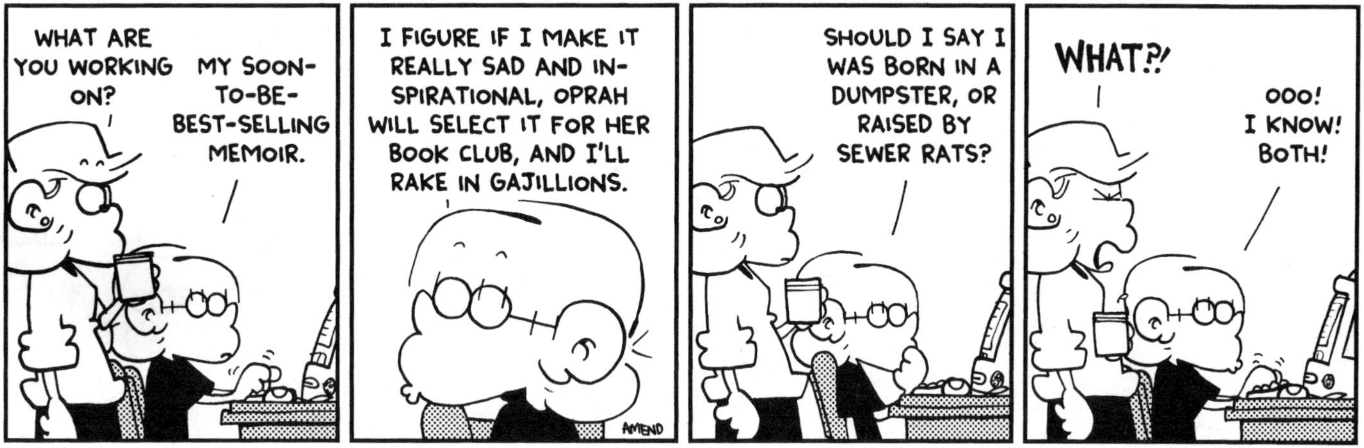
WHAT ARE YOU WORKING ON?
MY SOON-TO-BE-BEST-SELLING MEMOIR.
I FIGURE IF I MAKE IT REALLY SAD AND INSPIRATIONAL, OPRAH WILL SELECT IT FOR HER BOOK CLUB, AND I'LL RAKE IN GAJILLIONS.
AMEND
SHOULD I SAY I WAS BORN IN A DUMPSTER, OR RAISED BY SEWER RATS?
WHAT?!
OOO! I KNOW! BOTH!

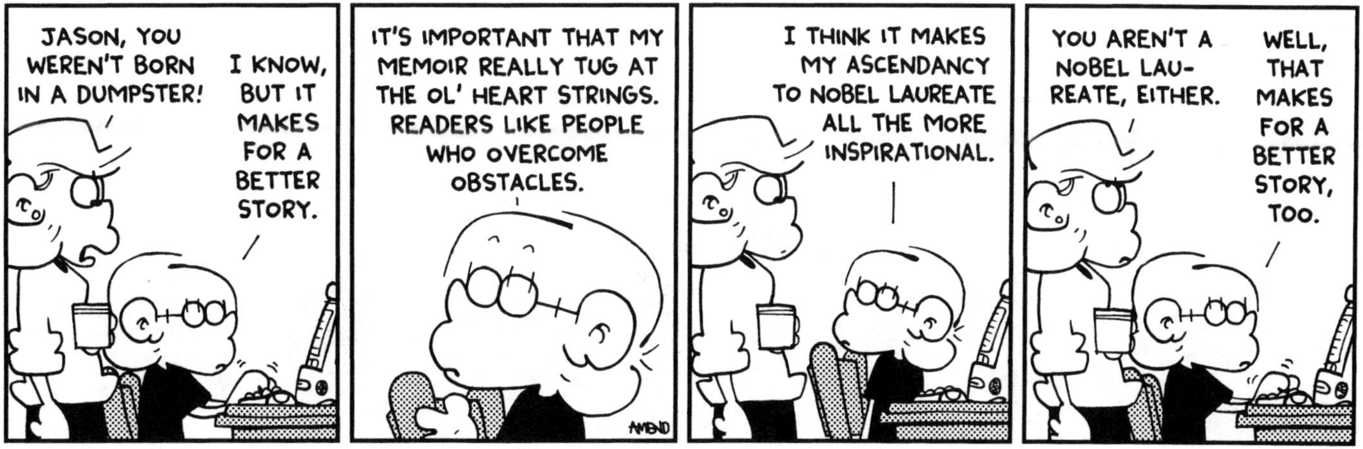
JASON, YOU WEREN'T BORN IN A DUMPSTER!
I KNOW, BUT IT MAKES FOR A BETTER STORY.
IT'S IMPORTANT THAT MY MEMOIR REALLY TUG AT THE OL' HEART STRINGS. READERS LIKE PEOPLE WHO OVERCOME OBSTACLES.
AMEND
I THINK IT MAKES MY ASCENDANCY TO NOBEL LAUREATE ALL THE MORE INSPIRATIONAL.
YOU AREN'T A NOBEL LAUREATE, EITHER.
WELL, THAT MAKES FOR A BETTER STORY, TOO.

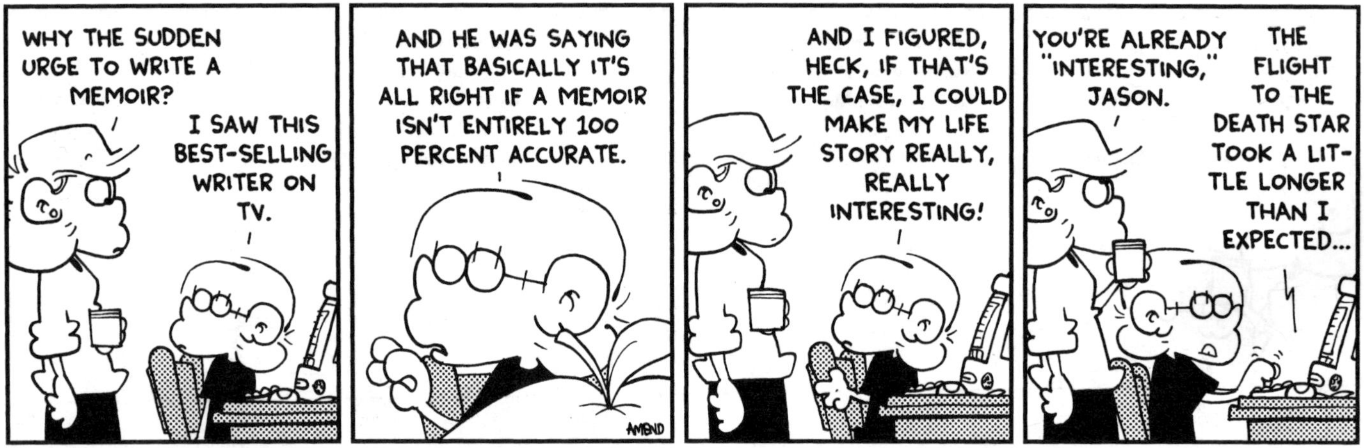
WHY THE SUDDEN URGE TO WRITE A MEMOIR?
I SAW THIS BEST-SELLING WRITER ON TV.
AND HE WAS SAYING THAT BASICALLY IT'S ALL RIGHT IF A MEMOIR ISN'T ENTIRELY 100 PERCENT ACCURATE.
AMEND
AND I FIGURED, HECK, IF THAT'S THE CASE, I COULD MAKE MY LIFE STORY REALLY, REALLY INTERESTING!
YOU'RE ALREADY "INTERESTING," JASON.
THE FLIGHT TO THE DEATH STAR TOOK A LITTLE LONGER THAN I EXPECTED...

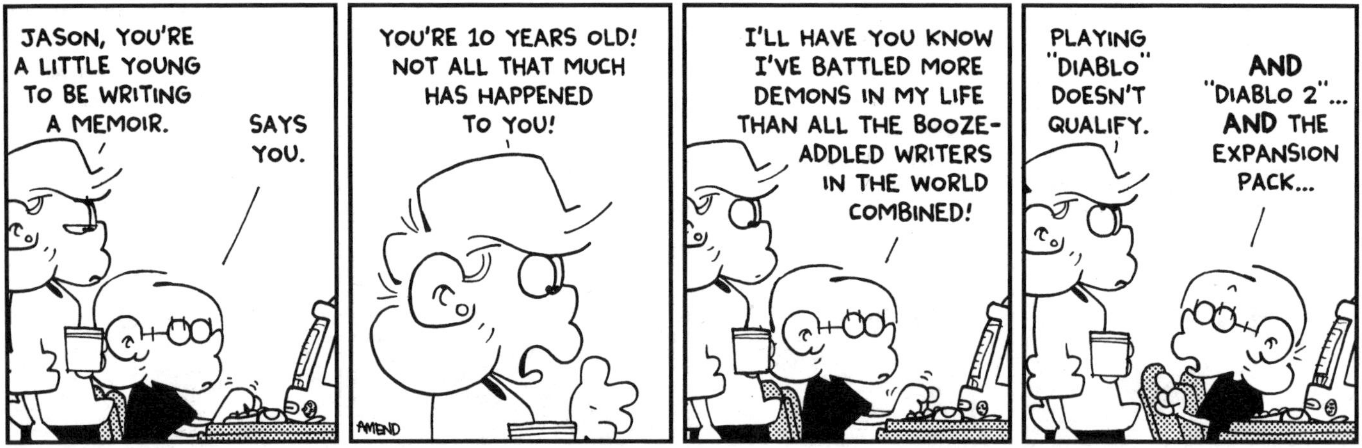
JASON, YOU'RE A LITTLE YOUNG TO BE WRITING A MEMOIR.
SAYS YOU.
YOU'RE 10 YEARS OLD! NOT ALL THAT MUCH HAS HAPPENED TO YOU!
AMEND
I'LL HAVE YOU KNOW I'VE BATTLED MORE DEMONS IN MY LIFE THAN ALL THE BOOZE-ADDLED WRITERS IN THE WORLD COMBINED!
PLAYING "DIABLO" DOESN'T QUALIFY.
AND "DIABLO 2"... AND THE EXPANSION PACK...

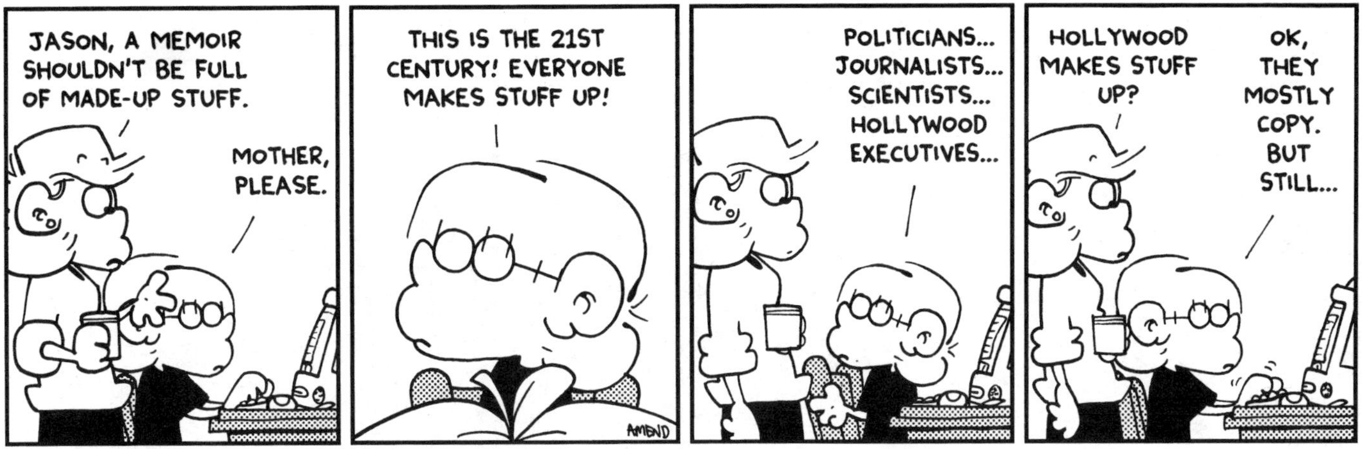
JASON, A MEMOIR SHOULDN'T BE FULL OF MADE-UP STUFF.
MOTHER, PLEASE.
THIS IS THE 21ST CENTURY! EVERYONE MAKES STUFF UP!
POLITICIANS... JOURNALISTS... SCIENTISTS... HOLLYWOOD EXECUTIVES...
HOLLYWOOD MAKES STUFF UP?
OK, THEY MOSTLY COPY. BUT STILL...
AMEND

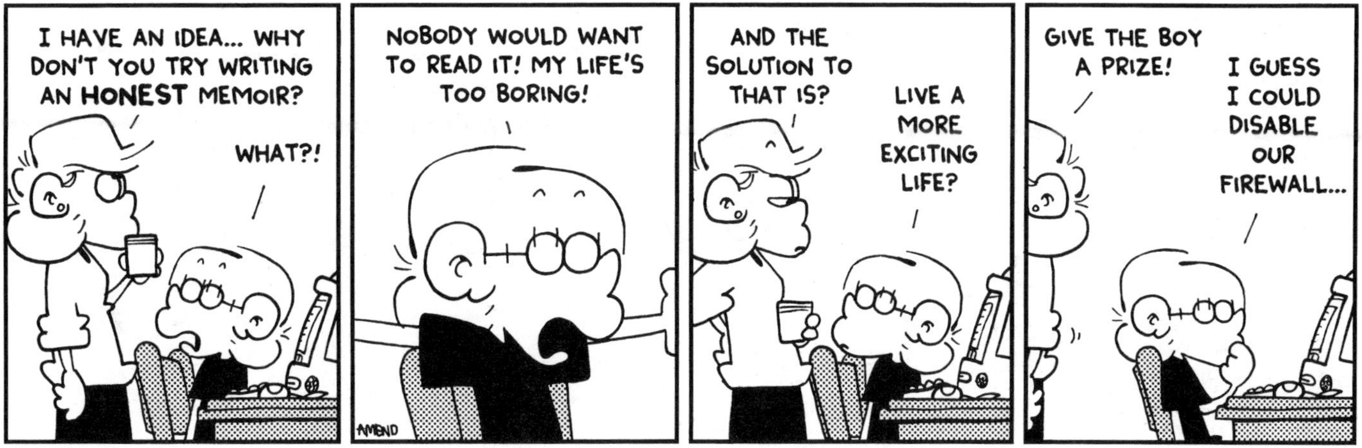
I HAVE AN IDEA... WHY DON'T YOU TRY WRITING AN HONEST MEMOIR?
WHAT?!
NOBODY WOULD WANT TO READ IT! MY LIFE'S TOO BORING!
AMEND
AND THE SOLUTION TO THAT IS?
LIVE A MORE EXCITING LIFE?
GIVE THE BOY A PRIZE!
I GUESS I COULD DISABLE OUR FIREWALL...

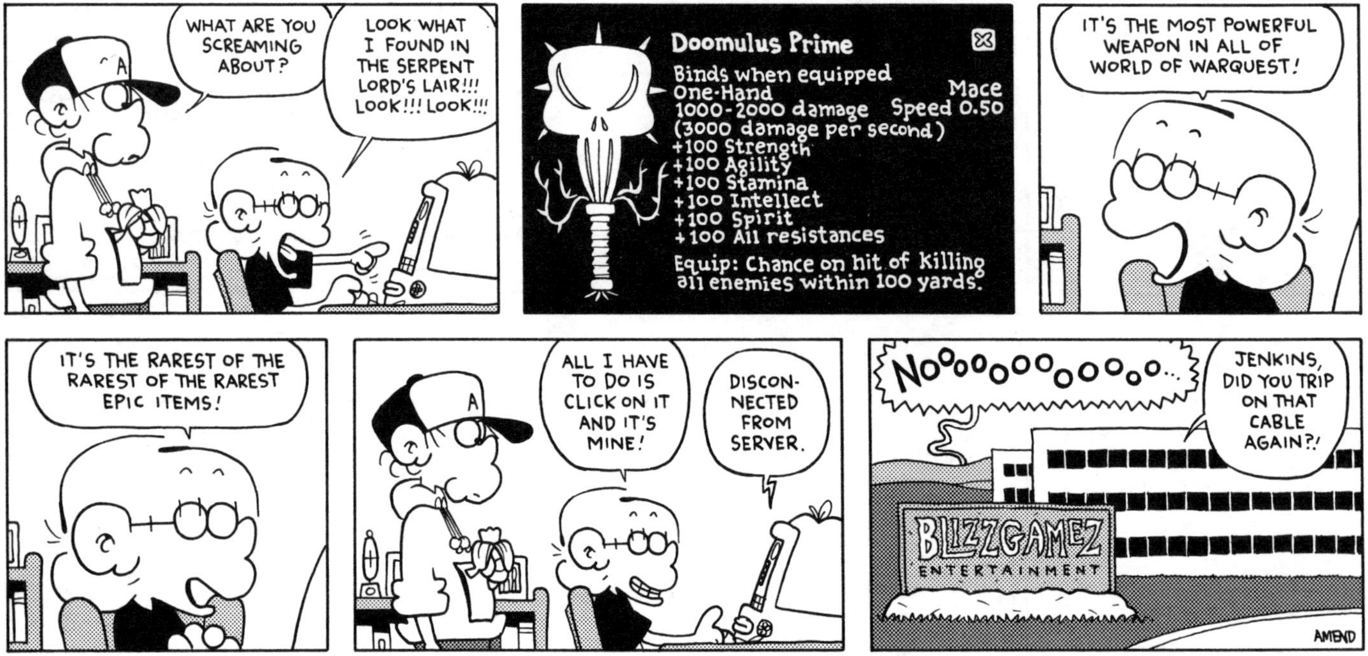
WHAT ARE YOU SCREAMING ABOUT?
LOOK WHAT I FOUND IN THE SERPENT LORD'S LAIR!!! LOOK!!! LOOK!!!
Doomulus Prime
Binds when equipped
One-Hand Mace
1000-2000 damage Speed 0.50
(3000 damage per second)
+100 Strength
+100 Agility
+100 Stamina
+100 Intellect
+100 Spirit
+100 All resistances
Equip: Chance on hit of killing all enemies within 100 yards.
IT'S THE MOST POWERFUL WEAPON IN ALL OF WORLD OF WARQUEST!
IT'S THE RAREST OF THE RAREST OF THE RAREST EPIC ITEMS!
ALL I HAVE TO DO IS CLICK ON IT AND IT'S MINE!
DISCON-NECTED FROM SERVER.
NOoooooooooo...
JENKINS, DID YOU TRIP ON THAT CABLE AGAIN?!
BLIZZGAMEZ ENTERTAINMENT
AMEND

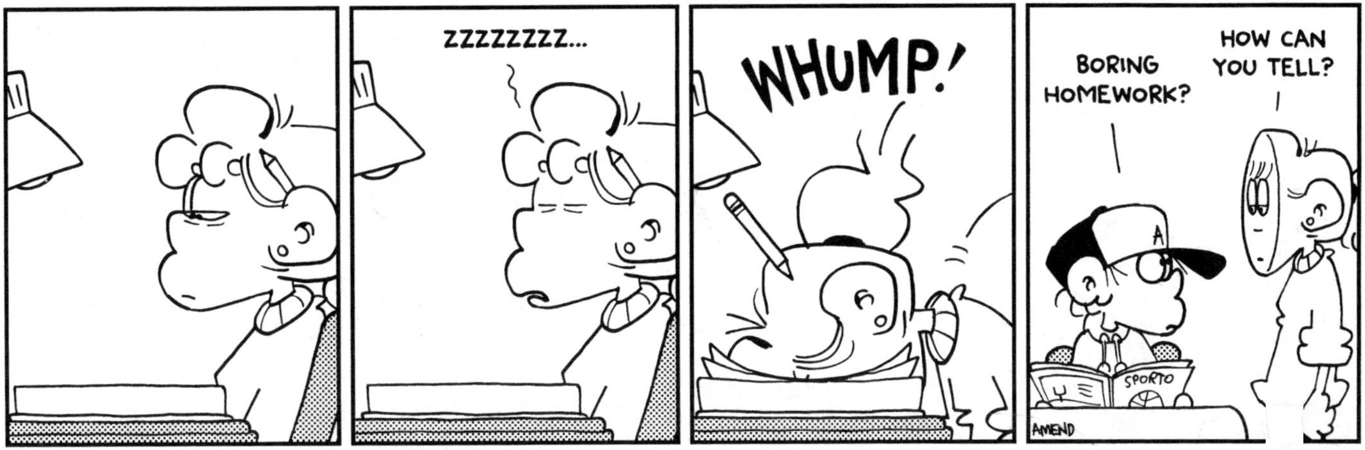
ZZZZZZZZ...
WHUMP!
BORING HOMEWORK?
HOW CAN YOU TELL?
SPORTO
AMEND

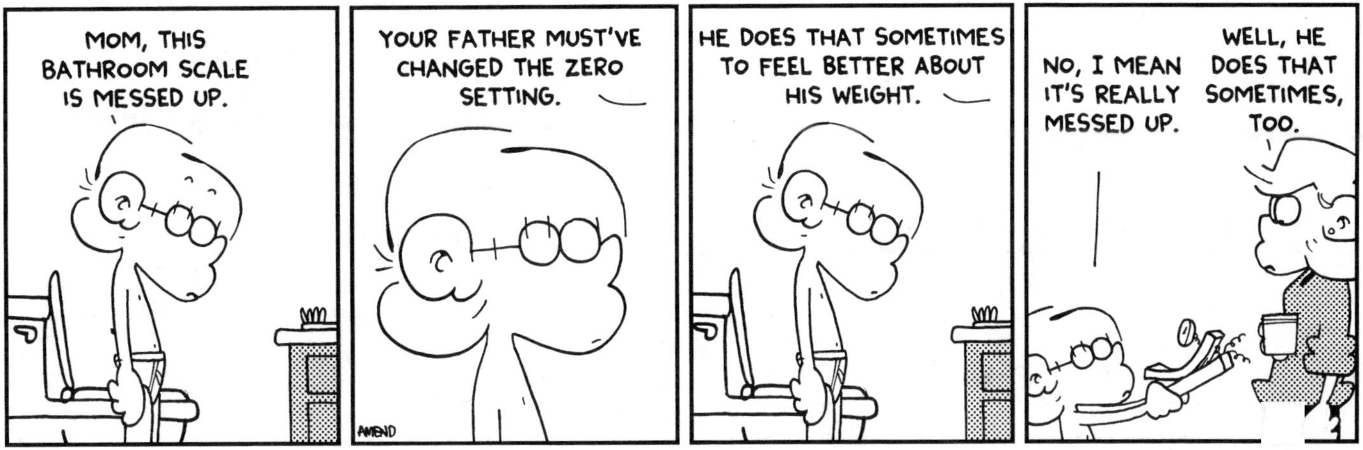
MOM, THIS BATHROOM SCALE IS MESSED UP.
YOUR FATHER MUST'VE CHANGED THE ZERO SETTING.
AMEND
HE DOES THAT SOMETIMES TO FEEL BETTER ABOUT HIS WEIGHT.
NO, I MEAN IT'S REALLY MESSED UP.
WELL, HE DOES THAT SOMETIMES, TOO.

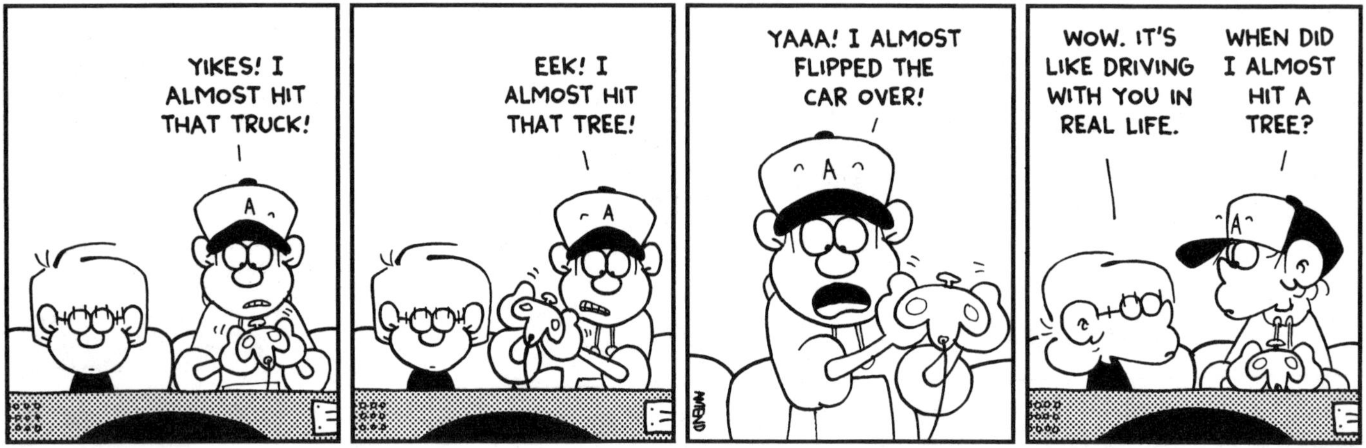
YIKES! I ALMOST HIT THAT TRUCK!
EEK! I ALMOST HIT THAT TREE!
YAAA! I ALMOST FLIPPED THE CAR OVER!
WOW. IT'S LIKE DRIVING WITH YOU IN REAL LIFE.
WHEN DID I ALMOST HIT A TREE?

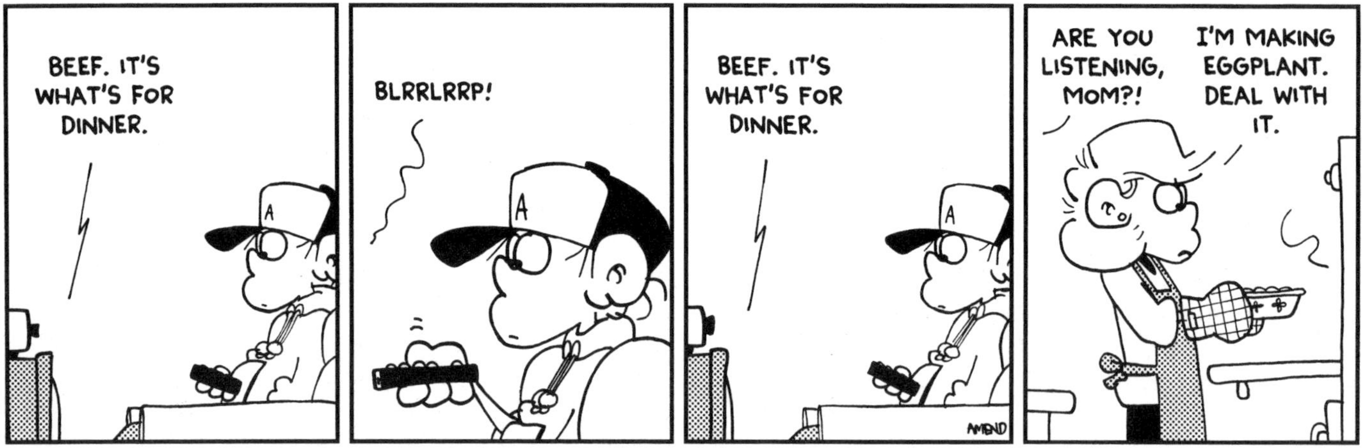
BEEF. IT'S WHAT'S FOR DINNER.
BLRRLRRP!
BEEF. IT'S WHAT'S FOR DINNER.
ARE YOU LISTENING, MOM?!
I'M MAKING EGGPLANT. DEAL WITH IT.

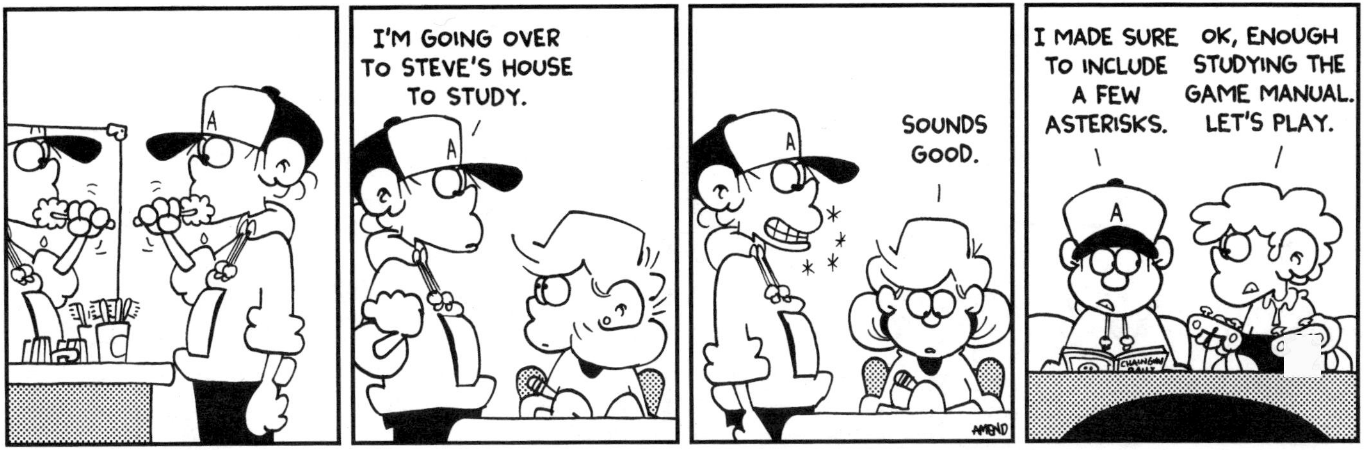
I'M GOING OVER TO STEVE'S HOUSE TO STUDY.
SOUNDS GOOD.
AMEND
I MADE SURE TO INCLUDE A FEW ASTERISKS.
OK, ENOUGH STUDYING THE GAME MANUAL. LET'S PLAY.

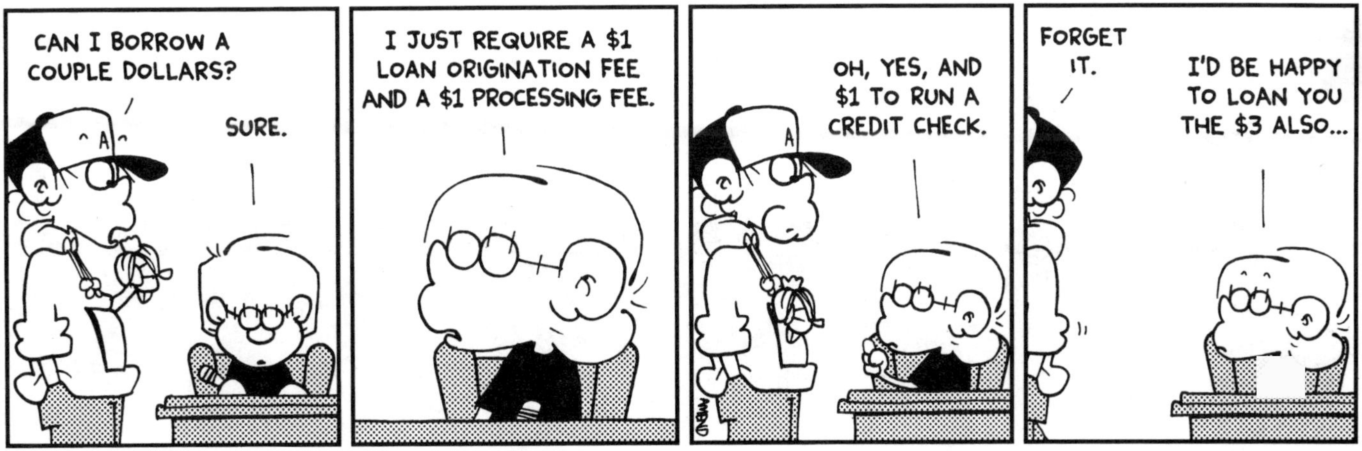
CAN I BORROW A COUPLE DOLLARS?
SURE.
I JUST REQUIRE A $1 LOAN ORIGINATION FEE AND A $1 PROCESSING FEE.
AMEND
OH, YES, AND $1 TO RUN A CREDIT CHECK.
FORGET IT.
I'D BE HAPPY TO LOAN YOU THE $3 ALSO...

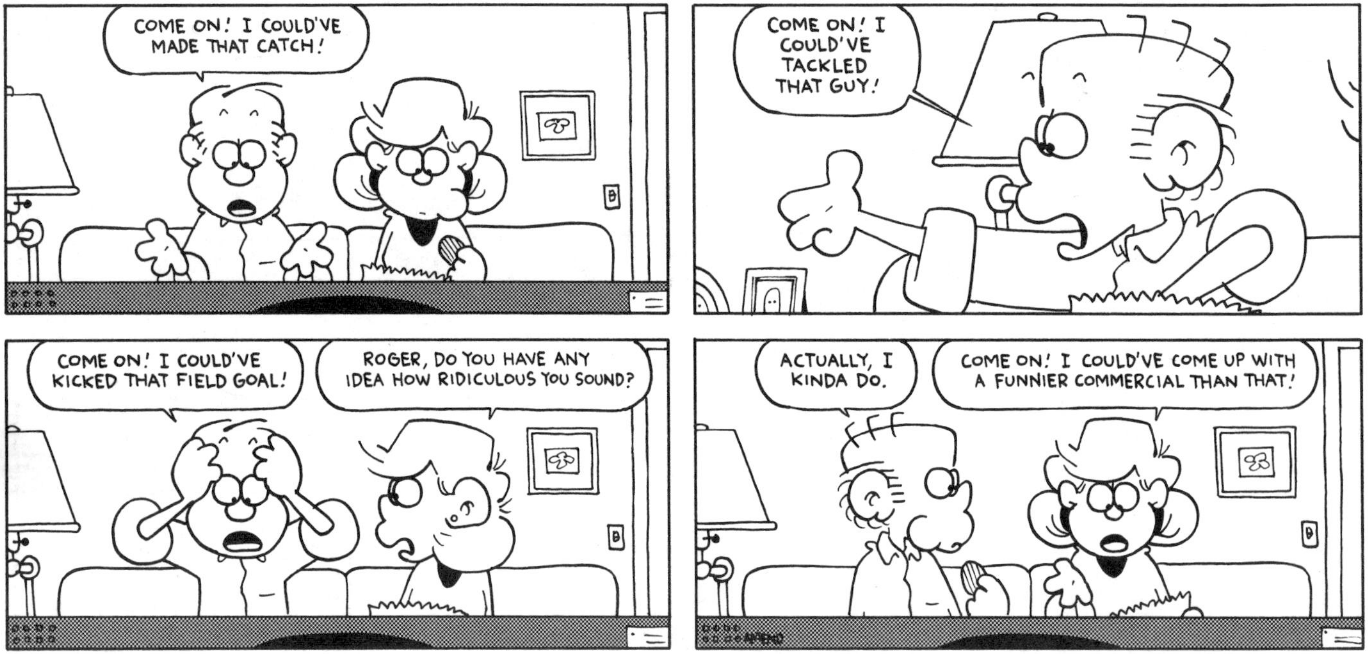
COME ON! I COULD'VE MADE THAT CATCH!
COME ON! I COULD'VE TACKLED THAT GUY!
COME ON! I COULD'VE KICKED THAT FIELD GOAL!
ROGER, DO YOU HAVE ANY IDEA HOW RIDICULOUS YOU SOUND?
ACTUALLY, I KINDA DO.
COME ON! I COULD'VE COME UP WITH A FUNNIER COMMERCIAL THAN THAT!

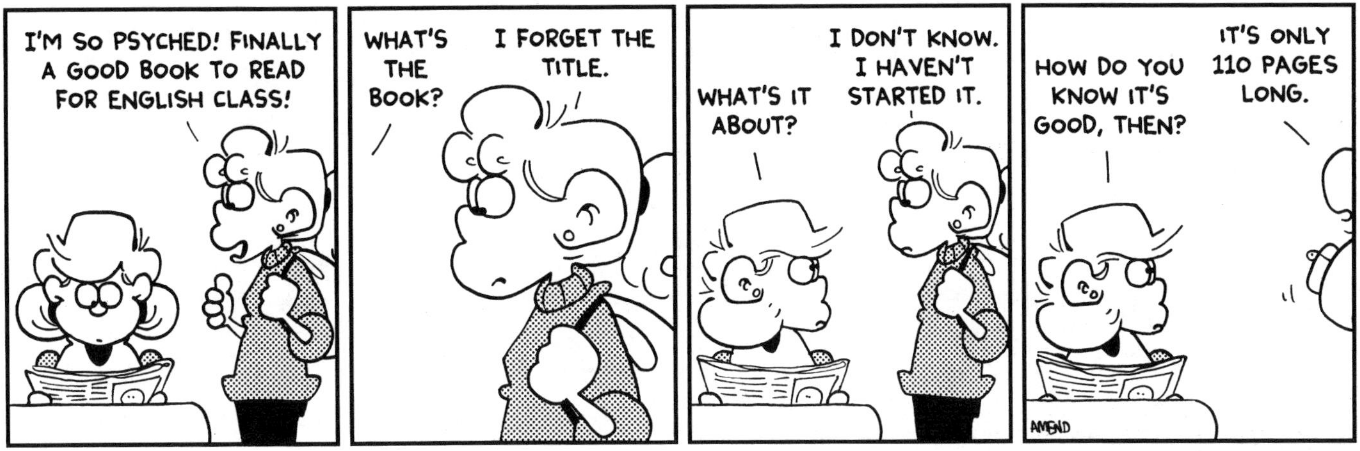
I'M SO PSYCHED! FINALLY A GOOD BOOK TO READ FOR ENGLISH CLASS!
WHAT'S THE BOOK?
I FORGET THE TITLE.
WHAT'S IT ABOUT?
I DON'T KNOW. I HAVEN'T STARTED IT.
HOW DO YOU KNOW IT'S GOOD, THEN?
IT'S ONLY 110 PAGES LONG.
AMEND

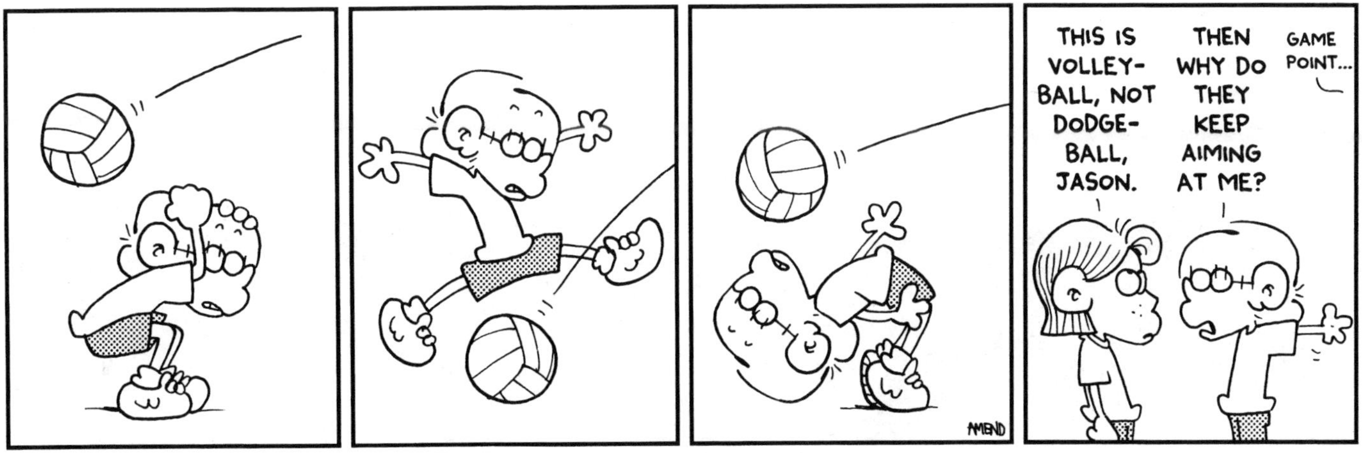
AMEND
THIS IS VOLLEY-BALL, NOT DODGE-BALL, JASON.
THEN WHY DO THEY KEEP AIMING AT ME?
GAME POINT...

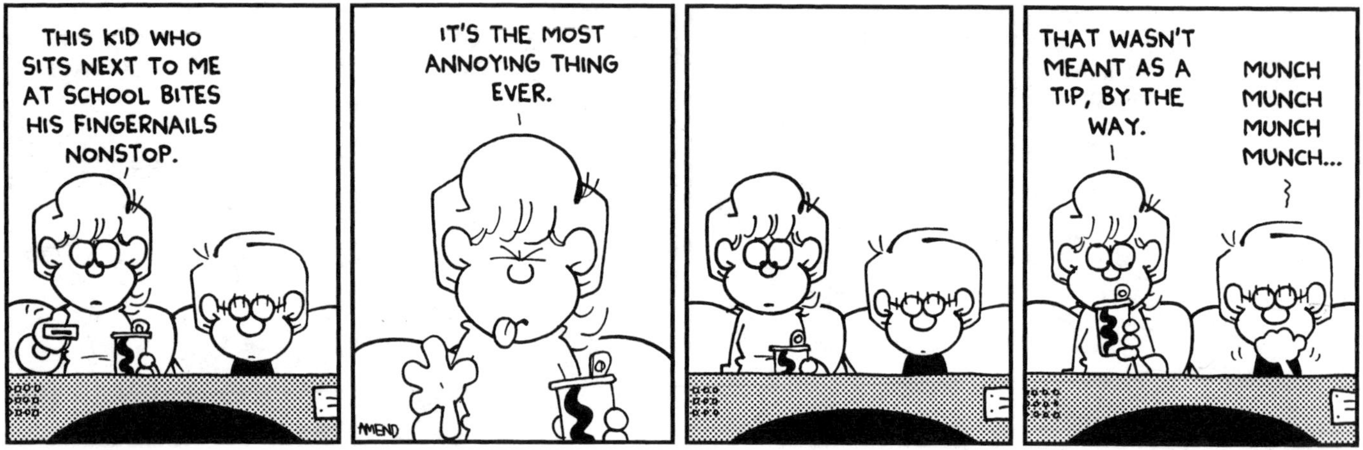
THIS KID WHO SITS NEXT TO ME AT SCHOOL BITES HIS FINGERNAILS NONSTOP.
IT'S THE MOST ANNOYING THING EVER.
AMEND
THAT WASN'T MEANT AS A TIP, BY THE WAY.
MUNCH MUNCH MUNCH MUNCH...

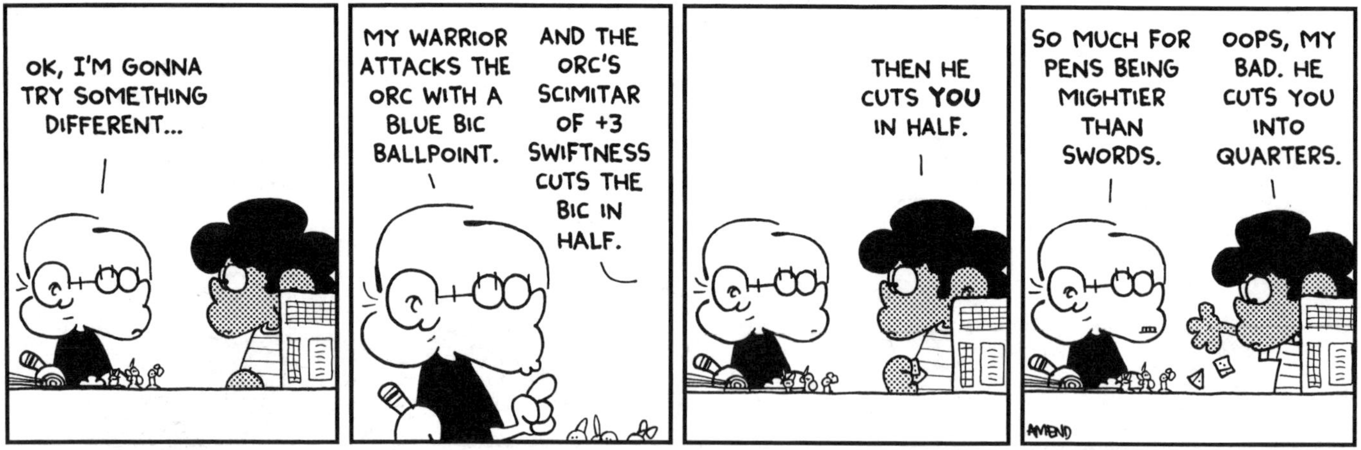
OK, I'M GONNA TRY SOMETHING DIFFERENT...
MY WARRIOR ATTACKS THE ORC WITH A BLUE BIC BALLPOINT.
AND THE ORC'S SCIMITAR OF +3 SWIFTNESS CUTS THE BIC IN HALF.
THEN HE CUTS **YOU** IN HALF.
SO MUCH FOR PENS BEING MIGHTIER THAN SWORDS.
OOPS, MY BAD. HE CUTS YOU INTO QUARTERS.
AMEND

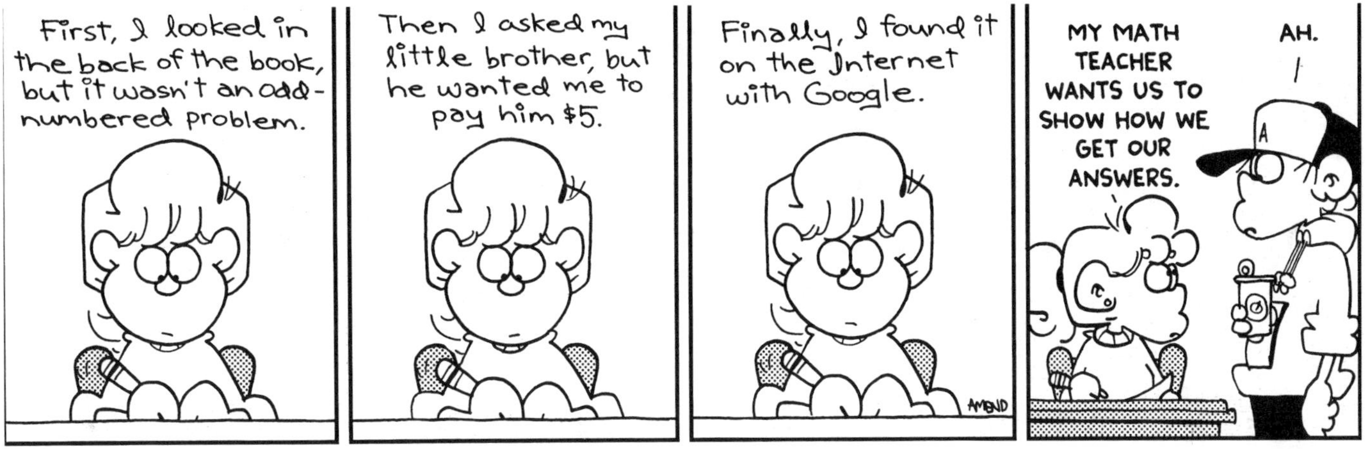
First, I looked in the back of the book, but it wasn't an odd-numbered problem.
Then I asked my little brother, but he wanted me to pay him $5.
Finally, I found it on the Internet with Google.
MY MATH TEACHER WANTS US TO SHOW HOW WE GET OUR ANSWERS.
AH.
AMEND

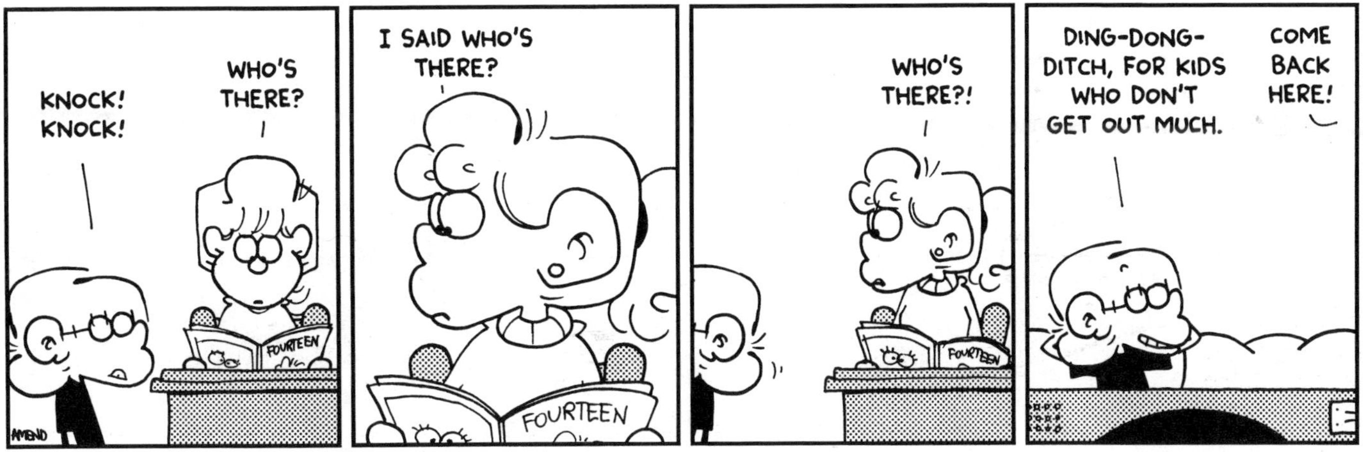
KNOCK! KNOCK!
WHO'S THERE?
FOURTEEN
AMEND
I SAID WHO'S THERE?
FOURTEEN
WHO'S THERE?!
FOURTEEN
DING-DONG-DITCH, FOR KIDS WHO DON'T GET OUT MUCH.
COME BACK HERE!

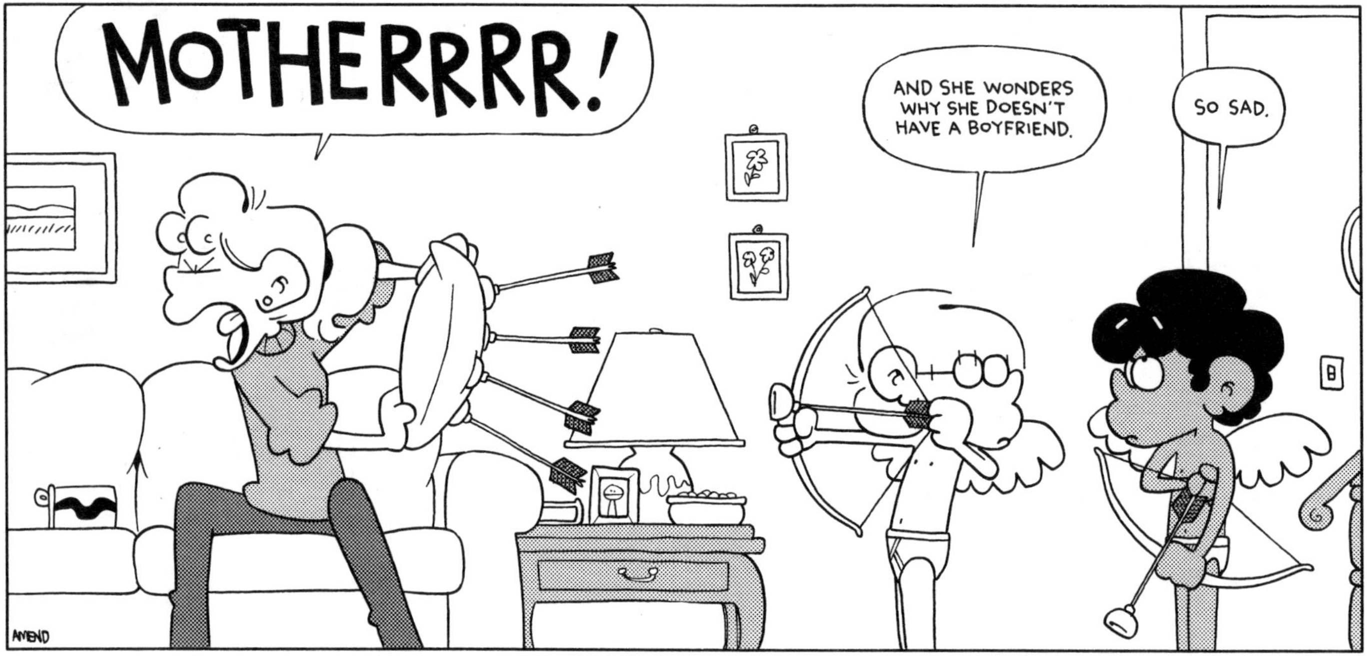
MOTHERRRR!
AND SHE WONDERS WHY SHE DOESN'T HAVE A BOYFRIEND.
SO SAD.
AMEND

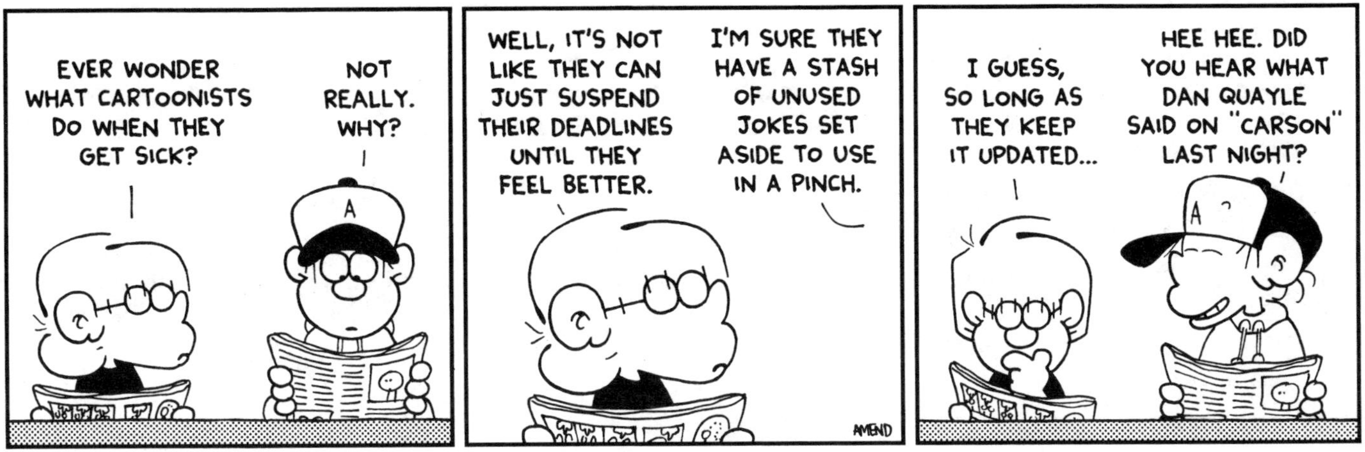
EVER WONDER WHAT CARTOONISTS DO WHEN THEY GET SICK?
NOT REALLY. WHY?
WELL, IT'S NOT LIKE THEY CAN JUST SUSPEND THEIR DEADLINES UNTIL THEY FEEL BETTER.
I'M SURE THEY HAVE A STASH OF UNUSED JOKES SET ASIDE TO USE IN A PINCH.
AMEND
I GUESS, SO LONG AS THEY KEEP IT UPDATED...
HEE HEE. DID YOU HEAR WHAT DAN QUAYLE SAID ON "CARSON" LAST NIGHT?

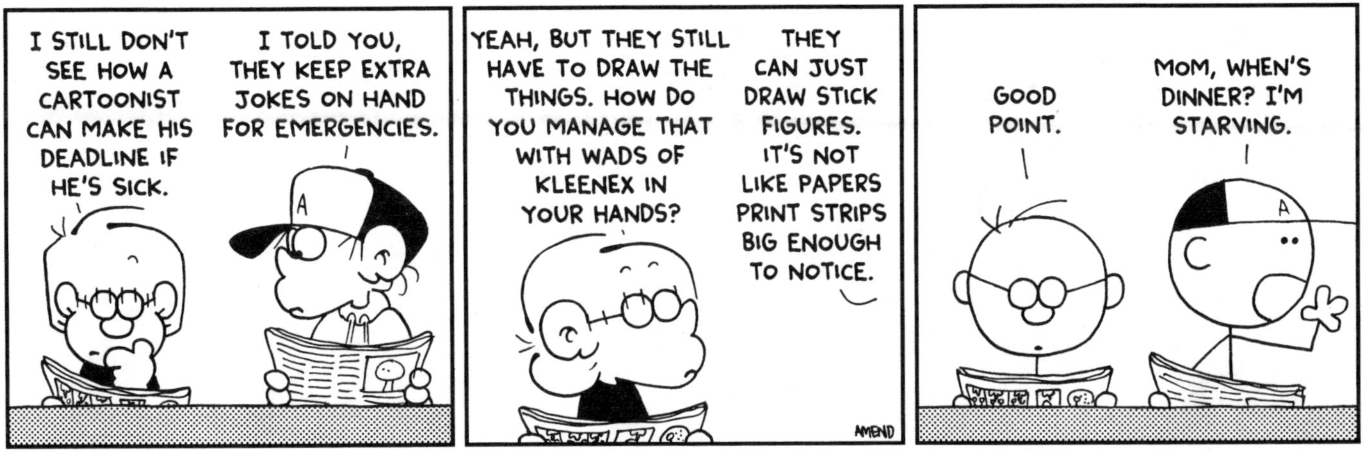
I STILL DON'T SEE HOW A CARTOONIST CAN MAKE HIS DEADLINE IF HE'S SICK.
I TOLD YOU, THEY KEEP EXTRA JOKES ON HAND FOR EMERGENCIES.
YEAH, BUT THEY STILL HAVE TO DRAW THE THINGS. HOW DO YOU MANAGE THAT WITH WADS OF KLEENEX IN YOUR HANDS?
THEY CAN JUST DRAW STICK FIGURES. IT'S NOT LIKE PAPERS PRINT STRIPS BIG ENOUGH TO NOTICE.
AMEND
GOOD POINT.
MOM, WHEN'S DINNER? I'M STARVING.

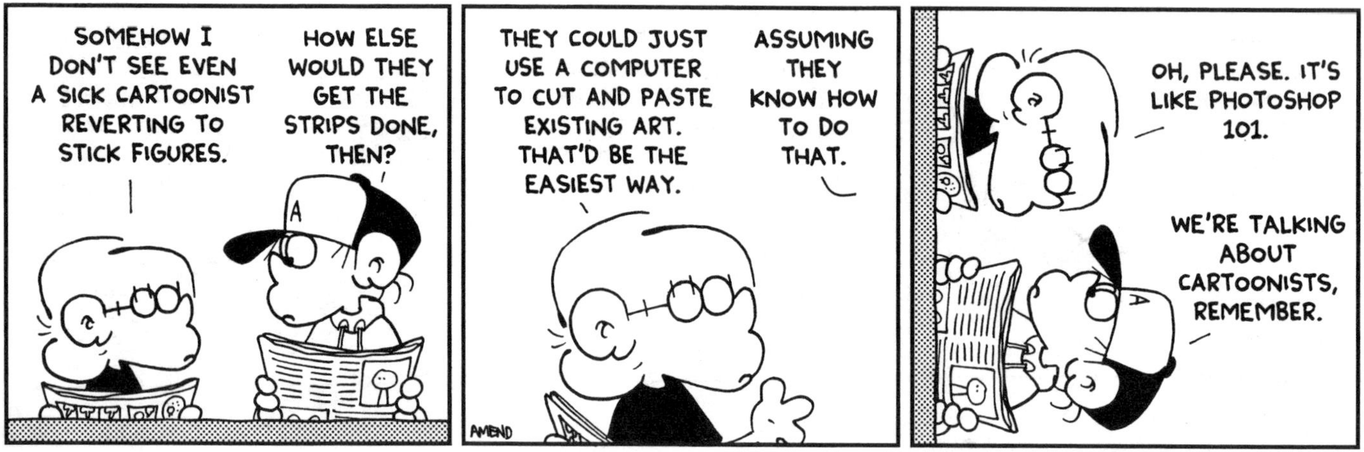
SOMEHOW I DON'T SEE EVEN A SICK CARTOONIST REVERTING TO STICK FIGURES.
HOW ELSE WOULD THEY GET THE STRIPS DONE, THEN?
THEY COULD JUST USE A COMPUTER TO CUT AND PASTE EXISTING ART. THAT'D BE THE EASIEST WAY.
ASSUMING THEY KNOW HOW TO DO THAT.
AMEND
OH, PLEASE. IT'S LIKE PHOTOSHOP 101.
WE'RE TALKING ABOUT CARTOONISTS, REMEMBER.

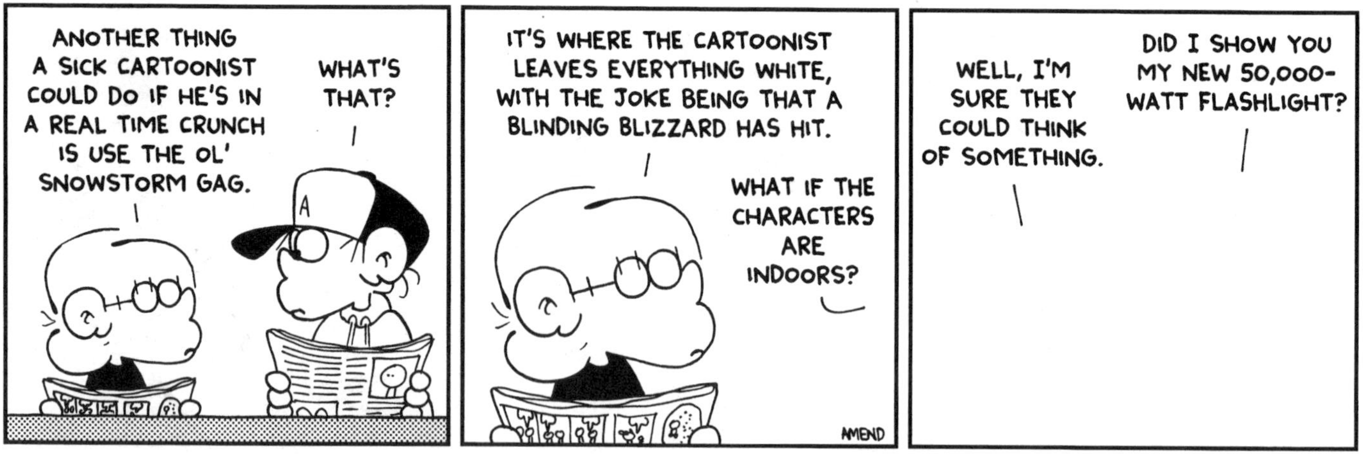
ANOTHER THING A SICK CARTOONIST COULD DO IF HE'S IN A REAL TIME CRUNCH IS USE THE OL' SNOWSTORM GAG.
WHAT'S THAT?
IT'S WHERE THE CARTOONIST LEAVES EVERYTHING WHITE, WITH THE JOKE BEING THAT A BLINDING BLIZZARD HAS HIT.
WHAT IF THE CHARACTERS ARE INDOORS?
AMEND
WELL, I'M SURE THEY COULD THINK OF SOMETHING.
DID I SHOW YOU MY NEW 50,000-WATT FLASHLIGHT?

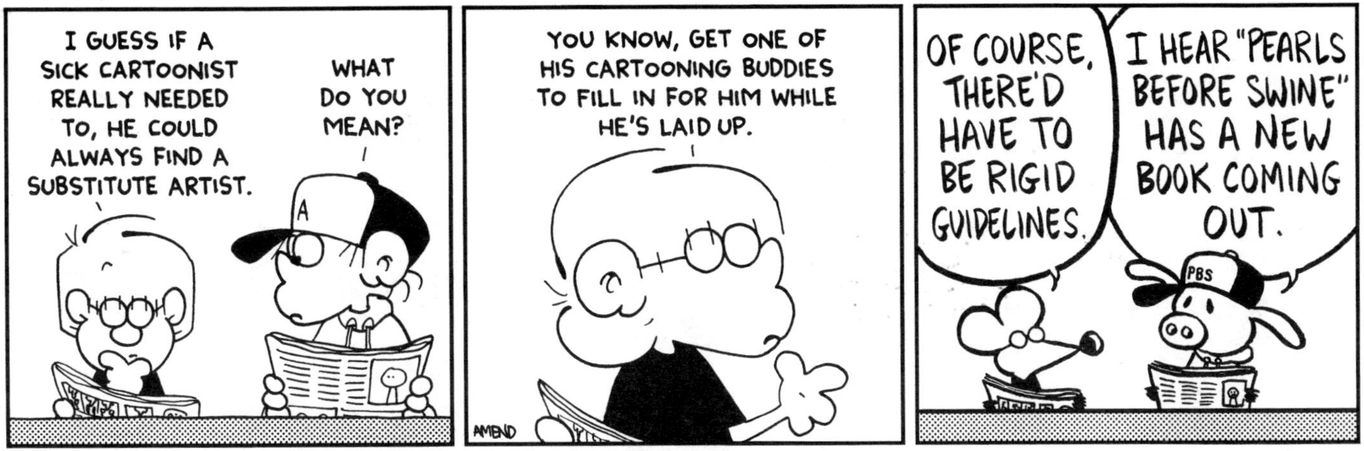
I GUESS IF A SICK CARTOONIST REALLY NEEDED TO, HE COULD ALWAYS FIND A SUBSTITUTE ARTIST.
WHAT DO YOU MEAN?
YOU KNOW, GET ONE OF HIS CARTOONING BUDDIES TO FILL IN FOR HIM WHILE HE'S LAID UP.
AMEND
OF COURSE, THERE'D HAVE TO BE RIGID GUIDELINES.
I HEAR "PEARLS BEFORE SWINE" HAS A NEW BOOK COMING OUT.
PBS

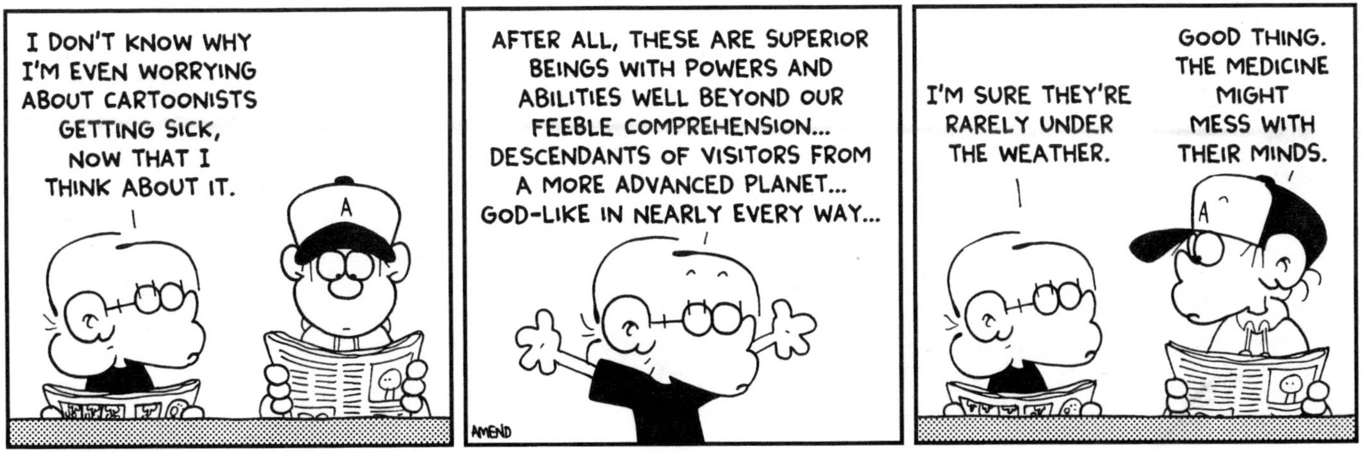
I DON'T KNOW WHY I'M EVEN WORRYING ABOUT CARTOONISTS GETTING SICK, NOW THAT I THINK ABOUT IT.
AFTER ALL, THESE ARE SUPERIOR BEINGS WITH POWERS AND ABILITIES WELL BEYOND OUR FEEBLE COMPREHENSION... DESCENDANTS OF VISITORS FROM A MORE ADVANCED PLANET... GOD-LIKE IN NEARLY EVERY WAY...
AMEND
I'M SURE THEY'RE RARELY UNDER THE WEATHER.
GOOD THING. THE MEDICINE MIGHT MESS WITH THEIR MINDS.

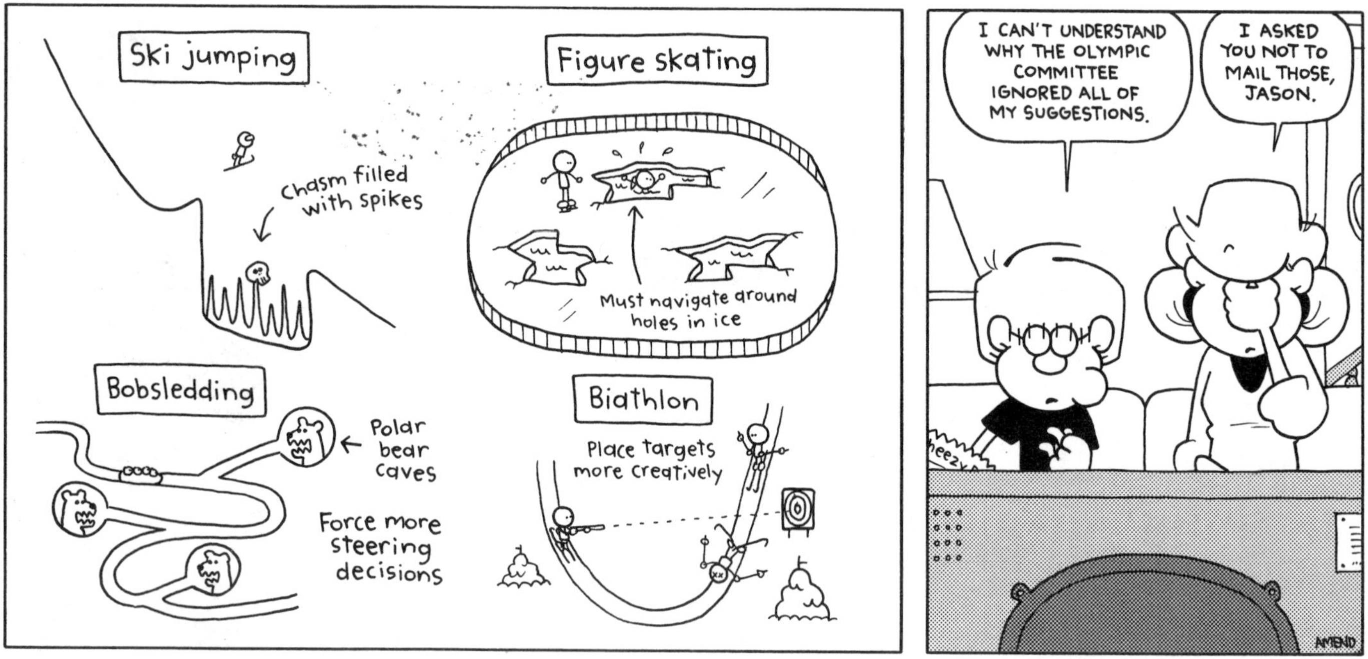
Ski jumping
Chasm filled with spikes
Figure skating
Must navigate around holes in ice
Bobsledding
Polar bear caves
Force more steering decisions
Biathlon
Place targets more creatively
I CAN'T UNDERSTAND WHY THE OLYMPIC COMMITTEE IGNORED ALL OF MY SUGGESTIONS.
I ASKED YOU NOT TO MAIL THOSE, JASON.
AMEND